NOAH'S CHOICE

CHARLES C. MANN
MARK L. PLUMMER

NOAH'S
CHOICE

The Future of Endangered Species

ALFRED A. KNOPF

New York 1995

THIS IS A BORZOI BOOK

PUBLISHED BY ALFRED A. KNOPF, INC.

Portions of this work were originally published in different form in *The Atlantic Monthly*, *Audubon Magazine*, and *Science*.

Library of Congress Cataloging-in-Publication Data

Mann, Charles C.
    Noah's choice : the future of endangered species / by Charles C. Mann and Mark L. Plummer. — 1st ed.
        p.   cm.
    Includes bibliographical references (p.   ) and index.
    ISBN 0-679-42002-9
    1. Endangered species—United States. 2. Nature conservation—United States. 3. Endangered species—Law and legislation—United States.   I. Plummer, Mark L.   II. Title.
QH76.M36   1995
574.5'29'0973—dc20   94-25807
                                                                          CIP

Manufactured in the United States of America
First Edition

To our children:

Sasha and Newell,
Robert and Elizabeth

What doth it profit, my brethren, though a man say he hath faith,
and have not works? Can faith save him?
If a brother or sister be naked, and destitute of daily food,
And one of you say unto them, Depart in peace, be ye warmed and
filled; notwithstanding ye give them not those things which are
needful to the body; what doth it profit?
Even so faith, if it hath not works, is dead, being alone.

—JAMES 2:14–17

Contents

NOAH'S CHOICE

Chapter One

SEVENTEEN BEETLES

Y EARS LATER, Karl Stephan would almost regret discovering the enormous insect. He unearthed it while pursuing what some people might describe as a hobby, and others as an obsession. Stephan himself prefers to use words like *avocation*. Whatever the term, he has spent the last seventeen years trying to collect every species of beetle that lives in the 768 square miles of Latimer County, Oklahoma. In that time, he has found more than four thousand species, many of them in his backyard, and pinned them into the special flat wooden boxes used by collectors and natural historians. Every year he finds, mounts, and identifies ten to twenty thousand insects—all from Latimer County. Stephan has had twenty-one species named in his honor, collected more than fifty holotypes (the specimen used as a standard for identifying the species), and become a principal benefactor of the Florida State Collection of Arthropods, one of the largest such repositories in the United States. In the world of beetles, he occupies a prominent place: he is the premier authority on the Colydiidae and Bothrideridae families. Stephan's neighbors were amused by his activities but for many years didn't think they were of much concern to the real world. All that changed when he found *Nicrophorus americanus*.

Latimer County is in the chunk of southeastern Oklahoma that locals refer to as "Little Dixie." Poor, remote, and not particularly welcoming to Yankee schemes of social betterment, Little Dixie consists mainly of three small mountain ranges that run across the county in parallel lines, east to west, like claw marks: the

Kiamichi, the Sans Bois, and the Winding Stair. In 1830, almost all of Little Dixie was awarded in perpetuity to the Choctaw Nation of Native Americans. Perpetuity lasted until 1907, when Oklahoma was admitted to the union. Today, Latimer County is a place devoted to mining, timber, natural gas, and cattle ranching. Not many people live there, and those who do tend to wear caps with the logos of farm-implement manufacturers on the brim.

Stephan's house sits about a mile south of U.S. 270, the main east–west route, which cuts across the middle of Latimer County. The nearest settlement is Panola, which has a church, a post office, a gas station, a defunct railroad crossing, and not much else. Five miles west is the county seat, Wilburton, population 3,092 in 1990, home to Eastern Oklahoma State College and its Mountaineers and headquarters of the Franklin Electric Company, the leading manufacturer of submersible motors. Except for the municipal airport, Wilburton doesn't throw out much light. On the night we visited, the stars in Stephan's backyard glowed as if the world were again empty of human beings.

The isolation was one reason Stephan picked this piece of Oklahoma for his home back in 1976. A big-featured man with graying hair, strong hands, and a soft tenor, he was working in Tucson as a machinist. His employer relocated, and Stephan decided to treat the change as an opportunity, rather than a disaster. Fascinated by insects since his childhood in Germany, he had spent countless happy weekends poking through fields with the collector's special mix of expectation and innocent greed. He had also developed strong feelings about conservation. Why not, he asked himself, put all these things together? "People in little city apartments are always crying, 'Conserve! Conserve! Conserve!' " he said to us. "But they won't put their money where their mouth is." Stephan did just that. Selling many of his dearest possessions, he bought eighty acres in Oklahoma for, he said, "the sole purpose of leaving it as I found it"—to create a small private nature reserve.

Life intervened. Good work was scarce in Latimer County. Scrambling along, Stephan did home repairs, fixed barbed-wire fences, spread grass seed, and set up an earthworm ranch; he kept cows, pigs, and chickens. His new house, a converted garage, was made from cinder block. Needing timber, he could turn only part of his land into a reserve. Still, he found solace in the natural world. The house had a small extra room where he kept his varnished wooden collecting trays—Schmitt boxes, as they are called. Against the far wall was a handmade table, painted yellow, with bottles of isopropyl alcohol, a battered desk lamp, and two microscopes. When Stephan worked outdoors, he always carried a thumb-sized vial of alcohol in his pocket. If something scuttled between his feet, he quickly knelt down and popped it inside.

Stephan saved his serious collecting for nighttime. He laid a sheet of white-painted plywood on the lawn next to his house. A few feet above, he set a glowing purplish blue wand: a fluorescent tube of ultraviolet light. The Day-Glo radiance drew in a buzzing mob of insects. Dazed with light, they bumped into the side of the house and fell. Some ran into the glass tube. They fell, too. A soft chitinous rain of stupefied bugs dropped to the plywood. Every hour, Stephan inspected the take. Little creatures by the score staggered beneath his fingers. He slipped the ones he found interesting into the vial. The uninteresting were released from their trance by turning off the light. That was what he was doing when he found the big fellow.

Reeling across the plywood was a lustrous mahogany-colored beetle with a bright orangy red spot blooming on its pronatum, the shieldlike plate behind a beetle's head. Smaller matching spots shone on its antennae tips and outer wings (beetles have two sets of wings, the outside ones serving as a cover). Although Stephan had never seen one before, he knew exactly what it was: *Nicrophorus americanus* Olivier, the American burying beetle.* It was almost an inch and a half long—enormous, as North American beetles go—and made curious chittering sounds. Dozens of tiny mites crawled over its underside. With the pleasure of an art maven spotting a Rembrandt at a garage sale, Stephan scooped up

---

*Every species has a scientific name with two parts: the genus name, which tells what group of species it belongs to, and the species name proper. Thus, *Nicrophorus americanus* Olivier belongs to the genus *Nicrophorus* and is the species *americanus*. Olivier, which is optionally appended, is the name of the man who collected the holotype.

his find and dropped it squeaking into the alcohol. A few hours later, he dumped the vial into a bowl, speared his new *Nicrophorus* with a clean number six pin, opened a Schmitt box, and sank the pin with its burden into the polyethylene foam on the bottom. When he had time, he typed up a label with the date of capture: June 5, 1979.

Stephan was unaware that the beetle he had just killed belonged to one of the most endangered species in the United States. Nor did he know that his discovery would entangle him in a web of biology and bureaucracy that ultimately included the U.S. Fish and Wildlife Service, the U.S. Forest Service, the U.S. Army, the Oklahoma State Department of Transportation, the Oklahoma National Guard, The Nature Conservancy, the Choctaw Nation, a startling number of local strip-mine and pipeline companies, and scientists from such remote outposts as Massachusetts and Washington, D.C. All these parties would be joined by the effort to save *Nicrophorus americanus*. That night, willy-nilly, Karl Stephan added himself to their ranks.

"HERE I AM," Curt Creighton said, "and I can't identify a beetle to save my life." In increasing order of generality, "here" was the cab of a four-wheel-drive vehicle; a badly rutted dirt road in Camp Gruber, a National Guard training facility; the border of Muskogee and Cherokee counties, in eastern Oklahoma. Creighton had kindly invited us to accompany him on a jaunt to learn about the imperiled American burying beetle and the measures necessary to protect it. It was late spring. With the truck windows shut against an inopportune rain, the cab filled with the scent of the tick repellent that each of us had sprayed on his clothes. Outside was a barely visible landscape of blackjack oak and thin knee-high grass: beetle habitat. A small red plastic flag on a stake was the signal to stop. "Beetle position number one," Creighton explained, pushing open the door.

Creighton was dark-haired, dark-eyed, solidly built; he wore a faded Hard Rock Cafe T-shirt, souvenir of a visit to San Francisco. Next to him, Joel Klumpp, Creighton's clipboard-toting assistant, wore another faded Hard Rock Cafe T-shirt, his from New York City. Creighton was a doctoral student in zoology at the University of Oklahoma, in Norman; Klumpp was an undergraduate biology major at the University of Tulsa. Hunched against the rain, they strode heavy-booted into the grass, jamming notes, writing materials, and jars of this and that into pockets.

A few days before, Creighton had placed six mouse carcasses in this glade, tying a length of blue dental floss to each. The hope now was, first, that American burying beetles had found the bodies; second, that the beetles had, true to their name, buried them; and third, that the beetles had not severed the floss in the process, but had left it protruding from the earth. "Watch out for snakes," Creighton warned. He bent over an ankle-high blue plastic flag on a thin wire staff. "Damn," he said. He patted the ground, muttering, "No mouse; no dental floss."

Mouse number two lay beneath its flag, flea-bitten, untouched by beetles but alive with ants. Mouse number three had vanished utterly. But a strand of dental floss emerged from the earth near the former location of mouse number four. "Eureka," Creighton said dryly. A small heap of loose earth marked a mouse-sized grave. Creighton's hand plunged inside, disinterring. In a moment, it emerged, gently clenching an orange-and-black beetle: *Nicrophorus americanus*. We had never seen one before.

Slowly Creighton opened his fingers. The beetle fluttered its antennae; walked to the ball of Creighton's thumb; tucked its head toward its chest in the crouch of a ski racer; abruptly thrust its rear end into the air; became motionless. "Playing dead," Creighton said.

We asked what the beetle hoped to accomplish by doing this. Creighton shrugged—who knew? "There are a lot of beetles," he said.

He was right. Latimer County alone is home to six species of burying beetles, examples of each being pinned in rows across one of Karl Stephan's Schmitt boxes. Another nine species live elsewhere in the United States. More than fifty others have been discovered in Europe, Asia, and Africa. And that's just burying beetles, which are but one of seven varieties—genera, to use the biological term—of carrion beetle in this country. All seven belong to the family Silphidae. As beetle families go, the Silphidae is unimpressive: worldwide, it has fewer than six hundred known members. Most beetle families are larger, and some are much larger, containing hundreds of thousands of species. About 140 families comprise the order of Coleoptera, or beetles. Together, these families may include as many as 12 million species.

Twelve million beetles! If each species was described on a sheet of notebook paper, the descriptions could be placed end to end in a white line stretching from New York City to the desert west of Salt Lake City. People couldn't do that even if they wanted to, though, because scientists believe that more than 80 percent of this vast cohort has not yet been discovered or named. If the unknown species could somehow be identified and recorded at a rate of one per day, researchers would have to work for more than 26,000 years. Little wonder that when the great evolutionist J. B. S. Haldane was asked what his years of research had taught him about God, he replied dismissively that the Creator had an "inordinate fondness for beetles."

Enormous as these numbers are, beetles form only one big part of the spectacular array of plants, animals, algae, fungi, and bacteria that biologists refer to as the "web of life" or "biodiversity." Scientists have named and identified fewer than 2 million species, but they guess that the total number of species on earth may be as high as 100 million. Each member of this horde has its own way of life, and each depends on the others around it. Predator and prey, host and parasite, producer and consumer: all compete and cooperate in a braid of interactions so intricately woven that scientists despair of ever charting it exactly, and so fundamental to human life that it is difficult to imagine how we could exist without it.

In its small way, the American burying beetle is a lovely example of the scope and variety of biodiversity. One of nature's sanitary engineers, *N. americanus* emerges from the earth every spring in its lustrous black-and-orange jacket. From the moment of its appearance, the beetle pursues its grail: a small piece of carrion. Dead field mice will do; so will fledgling birds that have fallen from the nest. Attracted by the smell, burying beetles cluster around the body, orange knobs at the ends of their antennae waggling like semaphore flags. If necessary, the insects fight over the prize, males against males, females against females, until the winning male and female drive all the others away. The victors, now a couple, dive under the corpse, almost swimming through the soil with their surprisingly powerful legs, and excavate beneath it. If they need to adjust the position of the body, they flip onto their backs, seize the fur or feathers with their feet, and shift it a fraction of an inch, repeating the action as often as necessary. Several hours pass as the carcass sinks into the soil, quivering eerily from the labor of the insects below. A minute, agile engineer, *N. americanus* is savvy about its task—it induces the body to go headfirst down a sloping tunnel, so the fur or feathers won't impede the job by being bent the wrong way.

Once the cadaver is entombed, the beetles crawl over it, exuding a strong chemical stew from their mouths and anuses that strips the body of hair and preserves the remains. The result is . . . well, after displaying the beetle to us, Creighton extracted from its burrow something that resembled a boned chicken thigh with a light dusting of flour. He encouraged us to stick our noses close and take deep breaths. We sniffed cautiously. There was a slight, not terribly unpleasant odor. We asked what we were smelling. Creighton smiled. "It's a week-old mouse carcass," he informed us.

The process by which beetles mummify the body is not yet understood. However it is accomplished, the female lays her eggs near the preserved remains. In a few days, the eggs hatch, after which the beetles feed their young from the carcass. The larvae rear up and stroke the jaws of their parents to get breakfast. "It's traditional family values," Creighton said. "You don't see that much with insects." In the short run, the result of this activity is more burying beetles; in the long run, the beetles help recycle the nutrients contained in the buried body.

Twenty-five thousand years ago, a prehistoric Audubon set down the earliest-known image of an insect: *Nicrophorus germanicus*, a Teutonic cousin to *americanus*, was the subject. The representation is surprisingly exact—or, perhaps, not so surprisingly, given the fascination that burying beetles have exerted on generations of naturalists. "This hoarder of dead bodies," marveled J. Henri Fabre, the great nineteenth-century natural historian, "with his stiff and almost heavy movements, is astonishingly quick at storing away wreckage. In a shift of a few hours, a comparatively enormous animal, a Mole, for instance, disappears, engulfed by the earth." How, he wondered, did the little wonders do it? In an attempt to discover whether the beetles were intelligent, he spent months watching them inter dead moles. Fabre's successors today are intrigued by the beetles' devotion to their young. At Boston University, a young scientist named Andrea Kozol has watched generations of burying beetles tend their grubs—behavior, she told us encomiastically, that is "practically mammalian."

Creighton himself was studying the darker side of beetle family life. Interested in behavioral ecology, he had written his master's thesis about brood reduction in cattle egrets. The term *brood reduction* is biologyspeak for the young birds' practice of killing their siblings in the nest. Evolutionarily speaking, it was not obvious why this is a good idea. The puzzle was interesting, Creighton thought, although the birds were hard to work with. He was mulling things over when he learned that burying beetles sometimes kill the young they have so carefully raised. Why? Deciphering the reason for infanticide, in Creighton's eyes, was not altogether dissimilar to researching siblicide. Burying beetles might make a pleasant side project: the insects had recently been discovered to be at risk of extinction, which made them, in the parlance, grantable. Newly funded, he found himself driving through backwoods Oklahoma in a four-by-four.

The remaining two traps were bait- and beetle-free. "Who knows what got them," Creighton said. "I once saw a stray dog running down the trail with a piece of dental floss hanging out of its mouth." Klumpp, the assistant, marked a notebook with slashed zeroes. "One out of six mice kind of sucks," he said. Raindrops plunked fat wet asterisks on the paper. By the vehicle, Klumpp amused himself by flicking half a dozen ticks from his pant leg.

Creighton bent over, inspecting. "Lone star tick," he informed us. "Male." Such expertise suggested that, contrary to his words, Creighton might be able to identify beetles if his life depended on it. We drove on, jolting through the ruts laid down by the National Guard. After a mile or so, we came to a meadow where Creighton had placed a few *N. americanus* as part of an experiment. The National Guard had ringed the site with signs full of stenciled lettering:

WARNING

ENDANGERED SPECIES
HABITAT
NO BIVOUACS
NO VEHICLE TRAFFIC
KEEP OUT

The beetle's needs are so simple—loose dirt, a supply of small dead animals—that it is hard to imagine how *N. americanus* could ever become extinct. At the turn of the century, it was common in thirty-five states and three provinces; then it began to slip away. No one knows why.* Collectors noticed in the 1960s that it was hard to come by. Still, it was not until 1980, a year after Stephan found his *N. americanus*, that an article in *The Coleopterists Bulletin*, a respected journal, raised a quiet alarm. Written by Lloyd R. Davis, Jr., a researcher in Florida, it stemmed from a question that had first puzzled Davis years before, while he was obtaining his master's degree at the University of Illinois. At the time, Davis, an eager beetle collector, had a part-time job as a weekend naturalist at a state park. In the mid-1970s, he met another student/park naturalist/beetle maven, who was writing his master's thesis on carrion beetles. The two men made collecting expeditions. Nei-

---

*Scientists once suspected that DDT was the culprit, but they now believe that the decline began before pesticides were widely used. Karl Stephan thinks the beetle, which is attracted to light, might have fallen victim to rural electrification. Farm porches glowed at night, he theorizes, and bats swooped down like so many avid insect collectors on the entranced beetles. Our favorite theory is that the insect's main food was once the passenger pigeon and that its decline was triggered by the bird's demise. This theory has the disadvantage of being almost certainly wrong. The most likely explanation, according to Andrea Kozol, is that the beetle was destroyed by its namesake: Americans. "In a hundred ways," she said, "we just moved in on it."

ther, it seemed, had ever caught an *N. americanus.* It developed
that the species had not been observed in Illinois since 1944. Intrigued, Davis wrote to everyone he could think of. Responses
trickled in. The last *N. americanus* found in Tennessee dated from
1952, when a scientist found twenty-nine. Surveys in the Midwest,
where the species was once abundant, had found none. Eight
months of trapping in New York had not produced a single specimen for one entomologist. (Entomologists are biologists who spe-
cialize in insects.) Another glum collector wrote that he had
"never met a live *N. americanus.*" Two more had not come across
one, either, including a researcher in Ontario who had specialized
in North American burying beetles for more than a decade. After
assembling the evidence, Davis concluded in his article that "this
species is actually disappearing from our fauna."

Davis's judgment did not make the front page of the *New York
Times* or warrant even a few column inches in the back.
Nicrophorus americanus is but one of thousands of endangered
species that call the United States home. The exact number is
unknown—probably unknowable—but few doubt that it is increasing. Worldwide, the problem is thought to be much worse;
scientists routinely describe what is happening as an "extinction
spasm," and many believe that millions of species will disappear in
the next few decades. "We are rapidly acquiring a new picture of
Earth," wrote Terry L. Erwin, curator of the department of entomology at the National Museum of Natural History, a branch of
the Smithsonian Institution in Washington, D.C. "Millions upon
millions of nature's species [are] on the verge of being replaced by
billions upon billions of hungry people, asphalt, brick, glass, and
useless eroded red clay baked by a harsh tropical sun."

After this awful prospect came to widespread public attention
in the early 1980s, it transformed the discussion of environmental
issues. Today, bookstore shelves groan beneath coffee-table books
about endangered species, Madonna campaigns to protect rainforest animals by headlining a rock benefit called "Don't Bungle
the Jungle," and the heroes of an animated cartoon called *Captain
Planet* save biodiversity every Saturday morning. A new scientific
discipline, conservation biology, complete with its own profes-

sional society and peer-reviewed journals, has been created expressly to combat extinction. The movement has even enlisted the power of American capitalism. Grocery stores feature Rainforest Crisp, a breakfast cereal with a package that asks, "How Will Buying This Cereal Save the Rain Forest?" (Eight percent of the contents are purchased from indigenous peoples in the Amazon, helping them resist economic pressure to cut their trees.) Enviro-Mints chocolates, made by the Enviromintal Candy Company of Seattle, Washington, come with baseball card–like pictures of endangered species; the wrappers claim that the company donates half its profits to "charitable wildlife causes." And so on.

For all the concern, the extinction spasm is surprisingly hard to quantify. Because most species remain undiscovered by humanity, no one can say with certainty how many face extinction. Moreover, extinction itself is hard to observe—one can never be sure that a few specimens somewhere have not been overlooked. Thought for decades to be gone, the Shoshone pupfish, found only in one hot spring in Inyo County, California, turned up in its native waters in 1988. The long-lost black-footed ferret was accidentally relocated when a ranch dog near Meeteetse, Wyoming, came home with a dead one in its mouth; excited conservationists then found a small colony of the weasel-like creatures. In 1983, the Los Angeles suburb of Rancho Palos Verdes bulldozed the last three known habitats of the Palos Verdes Blue butterfly. One site, in a park, became a softball field; the other two were cleared of brush to prevent fire, a custom in arid southern California. The insect vanished, and environmentalists could only mourn its extinction—until March 1994, when an entomologist came across a new population on a naval facility in San Pedro, the next suburb to the east. Scientific journals are full of such stories.

Still, no biologist doubts that extinction occurs, and most believe that it is now taking place at an accelerated rate. Their reasoning is simple: humans are altering the face of the planet faster and more furiously than ever, and these alterations change the areas where species live. This process—*habitat transformation*, one might call it—abruptly converts a place to which creatures have adapted over millennia into strange, hostile territory. It is as if the world's species are having the rug jerked out from under their collective feet; they will fall, fall hard, and never return. The irrevocability of extinction makes it different, and perhaps more alarming, than other environmental problems, such as pollution. To a great extent, lakes, rivers, airsheds, and even old-growth forests can restore themselves, though returning them to original condition may take centuries. But a species, once extinct, never comes back.

Species have come and gone for millions of years, of course. Indeed, today's biodiversity consists of but a small fraction of the number of plant and animal species that have ever existed; the rest are extinct. What worries scientists is the rate at which humanity is accelerating extinction. Absent a cataclysm, they say, perhaps one species out of a million should be expected to become extinct each year. If 10 million species exist (a low estimate), then 10 species should be expected to vanish this year—unless there is a cataclysm. And, in fact, there *is* a cataclysm: us. A conservative estimate of the current worldwide rate of extinction, according to Edward O. Wilson, a celebrated biologist at Harvard, is 27,000 species a year (using the same estimate of 10 million species). Somewhere on Earth, in other words, a species is doomed every twenty minutes. Figures for the United States alone are harder to come by, but Peter Hoch, of the Missouri Botanical Garden in St. Louis, has calculated what he calls a "rough but defensible" approximation: some 4,000 domestic species may become extinct within the next five to ten years.

Twenty-seven thousand species a year, 4,000 species in five or ten years—the predicted losses are so vast that they may seem hard to believe. And indeed, the figures are predictions that have not been verified. But it is demonstrably true that habitat transformation is proceeding apace, putting huge numbers of species at risk. The problem varies from place to place, ecosystem to ecosystem, and species to species, but it is almost always there.

Some 2,450 counties—almost 90 percent of the continental United States—are home to one or more species on the official endangered list, which most biologists believe is incomplete. Unlike Latimer County, those counties tend to contain large numbers of people. As a result, some 210 million Americans live close to at least one listed species, a number that will grow as the list grows. Indiana has the Indiana bat; Arizona, the Arizona hedgehog cactus; Florida, the Florida grasshopper sparrow; Oregon, the Oregon silverspot butterfly; Virginia, the Virginia round-leaf birch; Alabama, the Alabama cavefish. Each is on the list, and all are menaced by habitat transformation.

Their plight will not easily be resolved. Habitat transformation is not simply a matter of human greed and stupidity. People use land for many reasons—most unexceptionable, many praiseworthy. The homes we live in, the buildings we work in, the churches we worship in, the schools we learn in, the libraries, art museums, movie theaters, and concert halls we experience art in—all are built on land that once housed other creatures. As a consequence, conflicts between humans and other species are inescapable, because they stem from our deepest aspirations.

Traveling across the United States, we constantly encountered conflicts between human and ecological interests: the Karner Blue butterfly (menaced by stamping out forest fires), the Kanab ambersnail (threatened by bulldozing its home to make a recreational-vehicle park), the whooping crane (jeopardized by farming and hunting), the golden-cheeked warbler (imperiled by building new homes), the snail darter (troubled, famously, by building a dam). How can we find a balance between the butterfly and Smokey Bear? The snail and the RV park? The crane and the farms? The warbler and the houses? The darter and the dam? The list goes on and on. It includes the American burying beetle, at risk from a highway.

ABOUT FIFTEEN MILES southeast of Karl Stephan's land, near the town of Talihina, is the Choctaw Nation Indian Hospital. Built in 1938, it is a big castlelike structure made of stones hauled by oxcart from Buffalo Mountain, which rises just behind the hospital. The facility treats only Native Americans; more than twenty thousand—most Choctaw, but also Cherokee and Chickasaw—

come to it every year. Despite the efforts of its underpaid staff, the hospital can be a gloomy place; on the day we visited, its waiting room was thronged with silent, exhausted women. An overhead light flickered as a man with a clipboard slowly took down names. Rates of alcoholism, diabetes, infant mortality, cardiovascular disease, and premature death are high. The Choctaws are among the poorest people in the United States. A third have no phones. Almost the same number do not have a car, and the hospital cannot afford real ambulance service. Most have no other health care, which makes it especially hard if they are among the thousand or so Choctaws who live on the other side of the Sans Bois Mountains.

Starting just down the road from the hospital, State Highway 82 travels north to Red Oak, the next town to the east from Karl Stephan's house. Two miles from Red Oak, the official highway ends. Thirteen miles beyond, across the Sans Bois Mountains, 82 begins again, in the town of Lequire. A patchwork of narrow dirt roads and trails is the only way to traverse the gap. Four-wheel-drive vehicles can make it through; people without them must take a detour on twisting country roads that is at least forty-eight miles long. The Choctaws who live north of the gap must therefore drive a long way to see a doctor. "The delay is bad if we get patients in labor seventy-five or a hundred miles from us," chief hospital administrator Donald Crain told us. "Imagine those extra fifty miles through the mountains on a rainy winter night." For that reason, the Choctaw Nation road committee made completing Highway 82 its top priority for 1988. It promised to commit scarce tribal funds to the project.

The decision went over well with the Oklahoma Department of Transportation, which is universally called "oh-dot," after its acronym. ODOT had been trying for decades to join the two ends of Highway 82. Besides the hospital, the area's lumber, coal, and gas companies would profit from the reduced travel time the highway would afford; so would the students from adjacent counties who commute to Eastern Oklahoma State College. The Federal Highway Administration had agreed in principle to back the project, and the Oklahoma legislature finally budgeted its share of the cost in 1988. But the project still didn't get anywhere, because the Fish and Wildlife Service said the route would cause erosion. "That was probably a fair assessment," conceded Neal McCaleb, then the Oklahoma secretary of transportation. "So, trying to avoid the necessity of a full-blown, very expensive environmental-impact statement, we looked at an alternative alignment [for the roadway]—a lengthier, more circuitous, more expensive alignment. And *then* the Fish and Wildlife Service raised the issue of the highly vaunted, little-known *Nicrophorus americanus*, the American burying beetle."

If the highway had been built twenty years earlier, no one would have considered its impact on a beetle or any other creature. That changed in 1973, when Congress passed the Endangered Species Act at the end of the cascade of environmental laws that marked the Nixon administration. The law directs the Fish and Wildlife Service, a branch of the Department of the Interior, to maintain a list of species that are either endangered (in imminent peril of becoming extinct) or threatened (likely to become endangered in the near future). Once a species is listed, people are not allowed to "harass, harm, pursue, hunt, shoot, wound, kill, trap, capture, or collect" them. The service is required to list every species in trouble and save every species on the list. Mammal or plant, bird or bug, all shall be saved.

In the first five years after the law's passage, the Fish and Wildlife Service added ninety-six domestic species to the list, including twenty-one plants, twelve reptiles, ten fish, eight birds, six mammals, two amphibians, one crustacean, and twenty-nine mollusks.* Only seven insects, all butterflies, were added. Aware that most species are insects, the agency hired its first staff entomologist, Michael Bentzien, in 1979, telling him to list more creepy-crawlies. He asked for nominations through a notice in the *Federal Register*. Among the responses was a long letter from Lorus J. Milne, entomologist, conservationist, author (with his wife) of

*Why so many mollusks? One reason is that freshwater mollusks as a class are in trouble. Another is that one of the service's biologists during that time was a malacologist—a specialist in mollusks—who tried to use the new law to block water-development projects that would hurt these species.

dozens of popular books, and burying beetle fan since adolescence. Lloyd Davis, the Florida researcher, had written Milne about the difficulty he had in finding *N. americanus*. Milne, too, had been unable to find the creature. Now he urged Bentzien to look into its disappearance. The suggestion thrust the beetle into a newly created, peculiarly American ecobureaucracy.

Like the ecosystems it monitors, the ecobureaucracy has its own complex, interconnected, and poorly understood network of relationships. The beetle first fell into the hands of P. D. Perkins, an entomologist with the Smithsonian Institution. After poring through museum records, he reported no recent examples of *N. americanus*. It was as if the insect had vanished from the face of the earth. Based on Perkins's report, Bentzien awarded the beetle, in May 1984, what the government calls "Category 2" status: some evidence to suggest trouble, though not enough to support listing it as endangered or threatened. ("Category 1" species, by contrast, are those the service believes to be endangered or threatened but which it cannot list because it lacks the necessary money and staff to complete this laborious process.)

Bentzien delegated the quest for the necessary evidence to Paul Nickerson, head of the endangered species office in the service's northeast region, then in Newton Corner, Massachusetts, a suburb of Boston. In turn, Nickerson paid for a survey by biologists Dale F. Schweitzer and Lawrence L. Master, under the auspices of the Boston office of The Nature Conservancy, a private organization that buys land and sets it aside. Given the size of the beetle's original range, Schweitzer and Master realized it would be difficult to assess its present status over the whole area. Eventually, they dispatched entomologists, consultants, and beetle collectors to about half the beetle's known habitat. The surveys were thorough. Together with his students, one entomologist, Robert Allen of the University of Arkansas in Fayetteville, logged more than twenty thousand miles and set out five thousand pounds of carrion without finding a single specimen. (He missed Karl Stephan's yard, though.) Allen was not alone in his bad luck. None of the entomologists, consultants, and collectors turned up an *N. americanus*—showing, as Schweitzer put it recently, "a decline in its range by 99 percent. Probably more than that, 99.9 percent. Maybe you could use even more nines—it was virtually the entire range."

Virtually the entire range, because during the investigation Schweitzer contacted Charles L. Remington, a Yale University entomologist with whom he had once worked. For more than two decades, Remington had surveyed the insect life—the "entomofauna," as he called it—of Block Island, an island near the Rhode Island–Connecticut border. Unaware of their significance, he had caught American burying beetles there, on property owned, as it happens, by the same organization that had hired Schweitzer and Master, The Nature Conservancy.

Although Schweitzer and Master were delighted to find that the beetle still existed, the results of their national survey were dismaying. In two centuries, the American burying beetle had apparently diminished from a population of many millions across much of North America to a few hundred survivors on a remote New England island—the most precipitous decline ever recorded for any insect. Appalled, the two men sent a forceful recommendation in April 1987 to Nickerson and his colleagues at the Fish and Wildlife Service. "We told them," Schweitzer said to us, "that if they didn't want the species to vanish, they had to take quick action." Nickerson passed their recommendation to Anne Hecht, a staff biologist. Concluding that the Schweitzer-Master survey was unusually thorough, Hecht rapidly accepted its conclusions and wrote what is called, in the formal language required by the law, a "proposed rule," which suggested listing the beetle as an officially endangered species and asked for comments about the action.

At the same time, ODOT was assessing the environmental effects of the new highway route. As required by law, ODOT asked many agencies, state and federal, for information. Among them was the Fish and Wildlife Service. Dutifully consulting its list of endangered species in Oklahoma—two fish, three mammals, and nine birds—the service decided that the project would not affect any of them. In May 1988, the Tulsa office sent a form letter to ODOT affirming this conclusion. All looked well.

Just as the service was about to publish the proposed rule in the *Federal Register*, however, staffers in the Boston office came across the name Karl Stephan and learned that, peculiarly enough, there was a *second* population of beetles, in Oklahoma, thirteen hundred miles away from the one on Block Island. This chain of events owed everything to happenstance. That spring, Robert Allen, the Arkansas researcher, sent some of his students to learn beetle lore from Karl Stephan, whom he had befriended while collecting. Because, as Allen said, "beetle people talk beetles," the students told Stephan about their unsuccessful quest for the American burying beetle. "Oh, I've got some of those right here," Stephan said. The chagrined students took Stephan's specimens—he had turned up eight more in 1987 and 1988—to Allen. Allen phoned Master, who dropped a line to Patricia Mehlhop, a biologist at the Oklahoma Natural Heritage Inventory. (Natural Heritage Inventories are state programs that survey biodiversity; many have been established by The Nature Conservancy.) Mehlhop drove to Stephan's home in June. Never having worked with beetles, she was in the embarrassing position of supposedly vetting a discovery made by one of the world's experts on the subject. Stephan kindly showed her how to identify *N. americanus* and let her camp out on his property for several nights while she tried to catch some more.

Discovering the beetle's second home in Oklahoma meant that Fish and Wildlife had to revisit its sign-off on the highway. The agency sent ODOT a second letter in July, noting that *N. americanus* was about to be proposed for the endangered species list, that the highway was near the beetle's only known location in Oklahoma, and that the first letter was therefore inoperative. In December, after the *Federal Register* printed the proposed listing, Fish and Wildlife had to get tough. It told the Federal Highway Administration to survey the route for American burying beetles. The task of evaluating the results fell to Ken Frazier, a senior staff biologist at the agency's Tulsa office.

Self-effacing to the point of diffidence, Frazier is a thin, hardworking man who seems to fit naturally into the tan-and-gold park ranger–style uniform inflicted on Fish and Wildlife Service employees. Preparing to make wildlife management his lifework, he got a master's degree in wildlife biology and a second in wildlife and fisheries sciences. Neither, he told us recently, included courses of study in carrion beetles. Still, he didn't need a degree in entomology to see that the critter could mean trouble. Maps of Latimer County are chockablock with gas pipelines, coal mines, and logging zones, exactly the sort of habitat-transforming operations that run afoul of endangered species. Having been in Tulsa for nine years, Frazier knew that the locals would not want their plans disrupted by an insect.

In the spring of 1989, researchers drove around Little Dixie in pickup trucks with OKLAHOMA NATURAL HERITAGE INVENTORY painted on the doors. They dug holes in the woods and filled them with Mason jars that had themselves been filled with dead animals. The plan was simple: the beetles would sense the carrion, fall into the jar, and be unable to escape until morning. In this way, the researchers caught four *N. americanus*; two others were captured with a black-light trap. The beetle, it seemed, was there in numbers.

Nicrophorus americanus was formally placed on the endangered species list on July 13, 1989. ODOT, meanwhile, reviewed its options. The first route was out because it caused erosion. Now the second looked like it was going to have a beetle problem. So ODOT staffers tried to figure out a way to cram the highway onto the existing road-trail system, the notion being that by sticking to those roads the department would miss any beetles that might be in the area. Engineers surveyed that route—the third suggested for Highway 82—and found it expensive and impractical. Still, it was better than no road at all. In early 1990, Frazier told them they would have to look for beetles on both the old new route and the new new route. Mehlhop dispatched a team of three investigators to the proposed right-of-way that spring. They trapped four American burying beetles. More insect hunters went out in July and August. By that time, the team included Creighton, who had been lured from his more theoretical concerns with brood reduction by the promise of paid employment. It was strange work, he thought. When people in Little Dixie found out that he was taking so much trouble over an itty-bitty beetle-bug, they thought he was soft in the head. The team eventually found thirteen more beetles—eleven in one night. All seventeen turned up on a single two-mile stretch of land. Both of the new routes passed through it.

Seventeen beetles! To ODOT, the Federal Highway Administration, and the Choctaw Nation, that didn't sound like very many. Their representatives contemplated the bugs scuttling over the lumps of dead meat in the Inventory's Mason jars and were not impressed. To the Fish and Wildlife Service, however, those very insects were an appreciable fraction of the known world population of *Nicrophorus americanus*, an ancient species that humankind had driven to the brink of disaster. There was no question of ignoring them, especially because they were protected by the Endangered Species Act.

Alarmed ODOT staffers consulted with the Fish and Wildlife Service in September, trying to find a way to build the highway without harassing, harming, pursuing, hunting, shooting, wounding, killing, trapping, capturing, or collecting any beetles. Relocate the highway, Frazier suggested. Impossible, ODOT said. That piece of 82 had not been built in the first place because the roadway would have to twist through the Sans Bois Mountains. They had been trying to use the two easiest routes, which slipped through the valleys. All other routes would necessarily involve running the road through the peaks—impossibly expensive, and dangerous to boot. A round of frantic meetings failed to end the standoff, which, to Frazier's consternation, was drawing widespread community ridicule. The page-one headline on the October 7 edition of the Tulsa *World* was a public-relations nightmare: FLESH-EATING BEETLE BLOCKING HIGHWAY. Negotiations collapsed in December. On February 11, 1991, Michael Spear, regional director for the Fish and Wildlife Service, wrote his official opinion to the Federal Highway Administration:

> The proposed highway would permanently alter all the known occupied habitat of *N. americanus* north of Red Oak. Construction activities within the southern portion (2 miles) of the highway would destroy a significant number of the documented population and severely reduce reproductive capacity. . . . Given the large area

of North America which no longer has *Nicrophorus americanus*, and
the fact that the known wild population is less than 750 in two genetically isolated locations, the consensus among researchers is that
the species is precariously close to extinction. . . . Therefore, it is
my biological opinion that the proposed construction of SH82 between Red Oak and Lequire (and the related use, operation, maintenance, and cumulative effects) is likely to jeopardize the
continued existence of the American burying beetle.

The highway, in other words, was canceled.

Frazier was dismayed by the ruling, but understood its reasoning. He had no desire to stop the highway. But the law—and the
science—seemed clear. The beetle was known to live in just three
places: Block Island, Karl Stephan's property, and the planned
roadway. Completing 82 would be, in beetle terms, like paving
over a place where whooping cranes nested. You just couldn't do
that to a species so close to extinction. It was unfortunate about
the road, but surely something else could be done.

Oklahoma transportation secretary McCaleb was considerably
less sanguine. Even more than a year later, the mention of Highway 82 caused his face to cloud. "I perceive myself to be an environmentalist," he told us. "Although I admit that on a scale of
one to ten I probably err on the side of Billy Bulldozer rather
than a tree-hugger, I love trees. That's why I live here." Indeed,
his office was farther outside Oklahoma City than one would expect to find a powerful politician, even one in retirement from
public office. To emphasize his point, McCaleb waved a hand at
the flotilla of loblolly pines outside his office window. Latimer
County was impoverished, he said. McCaleb, a Native American,
felt particular sympathy for its Choctaw population. (He is a
Chickasaw.) In his view, they desperately needed a leg up. The
road, an investment in infrastructure, would provide jobs.
McCaleb found it hard to comprehend how Uncle Sam could reject a project that would benefit Native Americans—on environmental grounds. "Unbelievable," he said. Liking the sound of it,
he said it again: "Un-be-*liev*-a-ble."

A HIGHWAY that would improve access to a hospital serving the poor—can one imagine a more deserving public project? Yet through the enforcement of the Endangered Species Act, the interests of a beetle were, in effect, elevated above those of human beings. Confronted with this decision, many people, we suspect, would question whether any insect was worth it. Maybe if it was the magnificent bald eagle, they might say. Or a fierce grizzly bear. But this response would be mistaken, for in most practical respects the beetle is no less important, interesting, or valuable than the bald eagles, grizzly bears, and other beasts commonly labeled by the term *endangered species*. It is misguided to protect fuzzy-wuzzies (to use the conservationists' slang) while letting bulldozers run freely over creepy-crawlies. Once unwrapped, the genetic package of such "lower" forms of life, like any other form, may provide human beings with new types of food, fiber, and life-saving medicine. And all forms of life, large and small, help maintain the land, water, and air on which our lives depend; they generate soil, dispose of waste, control pests, regulate freshwater supplies, and stabilize the climate. Preventing extinction, then, is a matter of simple self-interest.

On a global level, these arguments are close to tautological. If we exterminate all the living things on which we depend, we will no longer be able to depend on them, and we will thereby exterminate ourselves. The need to avoid such a mass extinction is overwhelming. Applied to individual species, though, these reasons are less compelling. Is the beetle edible? Will it provide us with a cure for the common cold? If it becomes extinct, will Oklahoma be inundated with the carcasses of small mammals? On each count, *N. americanus* seems expendable.

"Expendable" is an arrogant conclusion, some scientists argue. Protecting genetic and ecological benefits to human beings, for all its importance, is not the "foremost argument for the preservation of all nonhuman species," according to Paul Ehrlich, a renowned biologist, and his advocate wife, Anne Ehrlich. (Both are based at Stanford University.) As they wrote in their book *Extinction*, the biodiversity crisis should be stopped principally because of the "religious" conviction "that our fellow passengers on Spaceship

Earth . . . *have a right to exist.*" True, *Homo sapiens* has behaved
for millennia as if other species existed at its pleasure; they were
used if valuable, ignored if benign, extirpated if bothersome. But
now, people like the Ehrlichs say, we recognize that it is an offense
against nature to eliminate a race of living beings from the Earth.
It is an offense even if species are proven to have no value to humans at all, in the view of David Ehrenfeld, an ecologist at
Rutgers University. They should be cherished anyway, simply "because they exist and have existed for a long time." This rule,
Ehrenfeld wrote, should be called the " 'Noah Principle,' after the
person who was one of the first to put it into practice."

To embrace the Noah Principle is to deny that we can legiti-
mately choose against nature. On moral, ethical, and spiritual
grounds, we must preserve biodiversity above all else—a position
that has been adopted, largely intact, in the Endangered Species
Act. Yet on the ground, in actual situations faced by real people,
this lofty principle seems to recede into the clouds. As the tale of
the beetle and the highway shows, we make most decisions about
biodiversity at a smaller, messier, more concrete level, and the
needs of either side are anything but overwhelming. The world
will not end if the beetle's habitat shrinks by another few counties;
nor will it end if Highway 82 remains unbuilt. Completing the
road would somewhat improve the lives of a thousand Choctaws.
Is the benefit enough to ignore the beetle? If not, what if *all* the
Choctaw Nation needed the highway? The planned route represents something like 10 percent of what was then the known habitat for the beetle. If the fraction were larger, would that compel
us to cancel the highway outright?

With so many species at peril in this country, these questions
will come up again and again. A bridge here; a housing development there; a golf course over there. There will be thousands of
beetles, thousands of highways, thousands of hospitals. One cannot
wish the choices away by, say, arguing that we should create a helicopter ambulance service to leap the Sans Bois Mountains or build
a second Native American hospital to the north of the gap (though
either plan might be preferable to the highway for other reasons).
Inevitably, the money for such measures would come from some

other deserving project, frustrating some other human aspiration. Always we will choose between aspirations, some more commendable than others, but nearly all worthy of consideration. Most of the time, the scale of these decisions will seem small, but their cumulative national impact, economic and ecological, will be enormous. And much of the time our best intentions will be forced to collide with themselves. What do we value more—a little bit of insurance for a struggling bit of our natural heritage (the beetle) or a slight easing of the pressure on some of our fellow citizens' lives (the highway)? To borrow from Freud, what do we humans *want*?

CURT CREIGHTON SPENT the spring and summer of 1991 trapping in Latimer, Sequoyah, Cherokee, and Muskogee counties. To the surprise of everyone, he captured 208 American burying beetles. The insect's range was evidently larger than had been thought. Frazier seized the opportunity to urge the service to reverse the biological opinion, which it did in February 1992. Completing Highway 82, it said, would not jeopardize the beetle.

The interests of the insect would still be respected, though. The service insisted that the department survey the entire route yet again for beetles, and trap and relocate any that it found. For almost a year, ODOT remained silent, the highway teetering on the brink of extinction. Finally, early in 1993, the state agency decided to put aside its collective annoyance and build. Because of the contretemps, the project had slipped from its perch atop the Choctaws' priority list, but they still wanted it. As a beginning, ODOT decided to try constructing the northernmost mile and a half of the road, which was farthest from the known beetle sites. It surveyed the right-of-way in the spring, when *N. americanus* is most active. No beetles showed up and the first segment of the project went ahead. In the spring of 1994, the department surveyed the rest of the route, turning up twelve beetles. These were duly relocated into a special burying beetle preserve, almost 300 acres in size, established by Eastern Oklahoma State College. ODOT let it be known that it hoped to begin construction on the rest of the project in January 1995, four years after Fish and Wildlife stopped the highway. Costs of the delay, human and economic, are difficult to ascertain.

Meanwhile, other beetle queries inundated Frazier's office. One company had already rerouted a pipeline at a cost that its local counsel estimated at many millions of dollars. Plans for seven more routes sat on Frazier's desk. All had to be surveyed for the beetle. Four coal companies operated in the area, one close to Highway 82. They, too, were paying the biologically knowledgeable to inspect their land for beetles. Creighton had been at Camp Gruber, the National Guard training site, partly because the Guard wanted to change its program to include mechanized infantry—tanks, in other words. Eventually, he found beetles, hundreds of them. Beetles, Frazier glumly suspected, would not get along well with tanks. "We may have to get into their business," he said. "The trainees there have been scraping off acres and acres of land." The beetle, he said, "had got their attention." Uniformed people kept summoning him to meetings. He was glad that his jurisdiction didn't extend to Arkansas, where burying beetles had been found at a landfill in Fort Smith, causing yet more furor when the city paid a consultant tens of thousands of dollars to survey them. In 1992, Frazier devoted more than three hundred hours to beetle consultations: eight forty-hour workweeks. The pace slowed in 1993. Frazier spent a little more than two full weeks on the beetle—a level of activity that continued in 1994, and seems likely to persist into the indefinite future.

"You know what?" he said. "The beetle is not even *the* endangered species of this office. The leopard darter and the least tern have had more controversy. Wait till I tell you about *them*."

Chapter Two

KINDS OF

ON THE NIGHT we met Karl Stephan, he invited us to meet some of the insects that shared his land. We left his living room and stepped outside. The night was warm and moonless. He had switched on a blacklight by his screen door; tiny bodies flitted about in its purplish glow. He plucked a few from their perches on the screen and let them explore his callused hand. Drunk with light, the insects staggered across his palm. Bringing his face close, Stephan glanced at each tiny assemblage of wings and legs and identified it by name. Then he gently shook his hand, returning the insects to the air, and caught and named some more.

It was wonderful to be in the presence of someone who had devoted so much loving regard to the natural world. At the same time, it made us feel foolish. We knew that the individual insects could, in principle, be labeled according to their species. But as our host proffered insect after insect for our inspection, a single word came blankly to mind: *beetle*. Stephan fared much better, of course. To him, the kinds of beetle number in the thousands.

"Kinds of" is a basic definition for *species*. Dogs, cats, and mice, for instance, are kinds of animals. Each is independent of the others, and the dividing line between them is plain to see. No half-dog/half-cat or one-third-cat/two-thirds-mouse has ever walked the Earth. But beyond such obvious differences, figuring out "kinds of" gets harder. If we were in charge of identifying species of beetle, we might come up with four or five, distinguishing them by the crudest of characteristics: big ones, little ones, black ones, brown ones. Karl Stephan, by contrast, classifies beetles according to such minute attributes as the roundness of the hip joint (globose procoxae, in the jargon) and the number of segments at the end of the beetle's foot (or tarsus, as Stephan would say). Details like those enable him to differentiate the row of *Nicrophorus americanus* in his collecting box from the adjacent row of *Nicrophorus orbicollis*, a slightly smaller but similar-looking cousin.

Yet visible differences alone are not enough. When the mutineers from the HMS *Bounty* and their Polynesian companions settled on empty Pitcairn Island, they numbered twenty-seven and had no communication with the outside world. Their descendants today are known for their distinctive appearance, the product of long isolation. No one believes that the inhabitants of Pitcairn Island are members of any species other than *Homo sapiens*. Why, then, do biologists think that they belong to the same species as Swedes and Nigerians, whereas *Nicrophorus americanus* and *Nicrophorus orbicollis* form two separate species? What makes a group of organisms one particular species and not another?

Answering the question has unexpected ramifications. Suppose *N. americanus* were not a separate species, but merely a collection of burying beetles that happen to have spots. Its disappearance then would not be regarded as an extinction, in the same way that the disappearance of all Swedes or Nigerians, though terrible, would not be an extinction. The possibility of extinction is conferred by an organism's status as a species. It happens when the last individual in a "kinds of" vanishes. We recognize the death of individuals as part of life; extinction, though, gives us pause. Why does it happen? How can species go along for millions of years and then disappear?

Species and extinction—any inquiry into biodiversity must begin with what a species is and how it becomes extinct. These are not simple matters; indeed, biologists grappled with them for centuries before achieving their present understanding, and in some aspects their questions have never been resolved.

FOR A LONG TIME the nature of species did not seem mysterious, at least to those in the Christian world. When the Supreme Deity fashioned the Earth, medieval thinkers reasoned, He placed in the Garden of Eden the prototype of each species: a pair if it reproduced sexually; a single individual if, like amoebas, it did not. They multiplied and spread across the globe. Then the Flood came, killing everything but the beasts that had filed two by two onto Noah's Ark. The world's creatures multiplied and spread for a second time, and all living things today are their unchanged descendants. The question of deciding what was a species thus boiled down to identifying and classifying the passengers on the Ark.

This comforting certainty broke down in the seventeenth century, when European vessels first sailed to the tropics and the voyagers returned with specimens representing hundreds of new species. The Bible spelled out the dimensions of the Ark: three hundred cubits long by fifty cubits wide by thirty cubits high. (A cubit is a measure of about eighteen inches, based on the distance between the fingertips and the elbow—*cubitum* is Latin for "elbow.") As they tried to cram the new discoveries into their existing zoos and herbaria, natural historians wondered how all the world's species could possibly have fit into a single boat. A German Jesuit priest, Athanasius Kircher, tried to make room in 1675 by designing an Ark that did not have the narrow V-shaped hull of a real ship; instead, his craft was shaped like a big brick, increasing its volume. Built to biblical dimensions, Kircher's vessel would take up 450,000 cubic cubits, a space equivalent to covering two-thirds of a football field with a two-story building. That was still not enough for all the newly discovered birds and beasts, not to mention their provisions for the journey. Other savants claimed that God's instructions did not use the ordinary cubit but, rather, the less common "geometrical" cubit, which is six times longer than the common cubit—a change that boosted the volume of the Ark by a factor of 216. Scholars fell to debating the proper cubit, but nothing helped. The onslaught of new species overwhelmed the Ark, and scientists quietly stopped believing in it.

The new species also overwhelmed the taxonomists. Taxonomy,

the science of classification, describes the relations among different groups of things. In biology, taxonomic systems identify the properties that one species shares with others, and then the properties that this group of species shares with another group, gradually increasing the inclusiveness of each grouping. The Greeks classified flora and fauna with logical dichotomies: animals and nonanimals (plants); animals with blood and animals without blood; animals with blood and with hair and animals with blood and without hair; and so forth. Later naturalists added their own permutations and revisions, but none could accommodate the new discoveries. Indeed, they threw biology into a taxonomic crisis.

Enter Carl Linnaeus, the great eighteenth-century botanist from Uppsala, Sweden. Having once studied for the ministry, Linnaeus remained a devout Lutheran, a piety that coexisted uneasily with an ego of biblical proportions. Describing himself as a "second Adam," he intended, like the first, to enumerate the kinds of things in the world. He believed this could best be accomplished by grouping organisms on the basis of common shapes, forms, and structures. Like most taxonomists before him, Linnaeus began with the two simplest, most inclusive categories into which species fit: plants and animals. (Today we know the picture is not so simple. Most modern biologists count five primary categories: plants, animals, bacteria, fungi, and protists—protozoa and other simple organisms.) Linnaeus broke down the animals into subcategories, such as insects, fish, birds, and mammals. All are animals, but the different subcategories share different characteristics: insects, he said, have wings, whereas fish have fins, birds have bills, and mammals have grinding teeth. Nested within the subcategories were sub-subcategories, each representing a finer level of distinction. In the case of mammals, these included primates, rodents, and cetaceans (whales and dolphins). These were then divided into still smaller, more closely similar collections of animals, which divided yet again to reach the final, finest category: species.*

*If a species' range is wide enough, apparent differences can crop up among distinct populations across that range. In this case, biologists often divide the species more finely into subspecies.

Linnaeus's system had five levels: kingdom, class, order, genus, and species. Today biologists use more, but their classification system is still known as the Linnaean hierarchy. It endows each species with a heraldry that identifies its place in the taxonomic universe. To the nonspecialist, the parade of Latinate terms can be overwhelming. Here, for example, is the complete taxonomic pedigree of the American burying beetle:

Kingdom: Animalia (animals)

Phylum: Arthropoda (invertebrate animals with jointed legs)

Class: Insecta (insects)

Order: Coleoptera (beetles)

Family: Silphidae (carrion beetles)

Genus: *Nicrophorus* (burying beetles)

Species: *americanus*

Every known species on the planet has a similarly ornate classification. Fortunately, the full list is not often used, partly because it is impossibly cumbersome and partly because Linnaeus at first thought that the only important category was the genus, which he thought of as the being's "essence." Different species of burying beetle, to his mind, were simply small modifications on the principle of what might be called "*Nicrophorus*-ness." Later, recognizing that differences were as important as similarities, he invented the now customary practice of referring to living things by both their generic and specific name: *Nicrophorus americanus*, theme and variation.

Like most scientists of the time, Linnaeus believed that the Earth's creatures had not changed in any important way since the creation. To think otherwise was tantamount to saying that the Lord had not gotten it right the first time around. Had Linneaus used burying beetles for an illustration, he might have pointed out that they live in forests, where small pieces of carrion frequently turn up on soil of excavation quality. That such species fit their habitat so well implied that any change in the former would render them less fit to survive. Species, therefore, were as fixed as the Earth itself; they could not change. *"Natura non facit saltus,"* Linnaeus wrote, famously, in 1750: Nature doesn't jump. A few years later, Linnaeus picked up his own copy of that work and crossed out the sentence. He had seen hybrids and mutations. (Hybrids are the offspring of two individuals from different species; mutations, organisms that are genetically unlike their parents.)

Linnaeus went to his grave in 1778 without being able to explain either phenomenon satisfactorily. Thirty-one years later came the birth of the man who would provide a solution: Charles Darwin. The story of Darwin and evolution—how the failed student from Shrewsbury ever so slowly pieced together his theory—is a staple of the high school classroom. Less well known is his struggle with the species question. Like Linnaeus, Darwin studied for the ministry; like Linnaeus, Darwin believed that all species had always existed in their present form. His ideas changed after an influential cousin wangled him a post as a staff naturalist on the HMS *Beagle*, a survey ship. Beset by seasickness, Darwin spent much of the five-year mission in bed; once ashore, though, he was an enthusiastic explorer, riding with gauchos, dodging bullets during armed insurrections, even rescuing expedition mates from a tidal wave.

The voyage let Darwin, a devoted hunter, amass a huge collection of specimens, which he gave to the Zoological Society of London in 1837, soon after his return. The collection included birds from the Galápagos Islands, a rocky archipelago six hundred miles west of Ecuador. Darwin was astonished to hear from the Zoological Society's staff ornithologist that what he had thought was a mishmash of warblers, grosbeaks, orioles, and finches was in fact a collection only of finches, all of which were new to science. Although Darwin had centered his attention on—and been misled by—the differences in their plumage and body size, scientists today regard the variation in their bills as most significant. Some species of Galápagos finch have the short, tough bills expected in finches, which use them to break open seeds; but others have longer, more slender bills, suitable for scooping up insects. Most islands have several types, short-, medium-, and long-billed—a "perfect gradation" that Darwin had already come to regard as a "most curious fact." Puzzling over this plethora of finches, he wondered whether all the birds had descended from a single species that colonized the archipelago. Now, separated on their different islands, the birds were somehow changing into different species—a process known today as evolution.

Scientists had previously concluded that species evolve, but Darwin first explained how it could occur. In basic form, his ideas were simple. (Indeed, the biologist T. H. Huxley is said to have reacted to them by muttering, "How extremely stupid not to have thought of that.") Imagine a pair of finches blown by a storm onto one of the Galápagos Islands. Few other birds are around, so the finches have the place to themselves. Without competition, their population rapidly increases. Eventually, they fill the island. It gets harder to find seeds to eat. By chance, some finches are born with stronger, thicker beaks, which allow them to crack bigger, tougher seeds. These finches fare better in the struggle for food and thus can leave more offspring. After many generations, the big-beaked population slowly displaces the others. In this way, the original bird eventually becomes a new species with a big beak. Meanwhile, another storm has blown some island finches to a second island, which has fewer big seeds and more insects. Again, chance operates; a few birds are born with longer, thinner beaks, better for scooping up insects. The finches on this island slowly evolve in a different direction, and eventually they, too, become a different species. From one species, two have been born.

Reality was even more complicated. One mainland species of finch ultimately led to no fewer than *thirteen* new species in the Galápagos, some of which are unlike any other birds. Two Galápagos finches are among the few denizens of the animal kingdom that use tools. After sticking twigs cigarette-style into their bills, they use these devices to scratch insects from crevices. If a twig is too long, they may break it in half and try again. Another species is the world's only avian vampire: it lands on the back of a big, slow-moving seabird called a boobie, pecks at the wing and tail of its unwilling host, and laps up the blood. Mysteriously, the hypothetical mainland species has never been found. Its absence is one reason that the ever-meticulous Darwin got nervous and at the last minute pulled the section on Galápagos finches from *The Origin of Species*, his treatise on evolution.

Implicit in Darwin's work is an astonishing thought: species in the Linnaean sense do not exist. What Linnaeus had imagined as a set of immutable clones, Darwin revealed to be a seething mass of competing individuals, each somewhat different from its fellows. Nature selected among them, changing the very characteristics scientists like Linnaeus used to divide the world's masses into species. From this perspective, the concept of species was an arbitrary device by which taxonomists imagined that they had kept tabs on nature. This insight, Darwin was convinced, closed the door on the issue. "The endless disputes whether or not some fifty species of British brambles are good species will cease"—a prospect, Darwin imagined, that taxonomists would greet with "no slight relief."

Taxonomists experienced no relief, slight or otherwise. A walk through the park sufficed to make it clear that dogs, cats, and mice were not purely subjective categories. If Darwin thought the nature of species was "undiscovered and undiscoverable," his critics asked, why write a book called *The Origin of Species*? How can species evolve if they don't exist? If individuals are the only real biological entities, how could the differences among them show that species change? Darwin dismissed the objections, but they were cogent and did not go away.

The argument eventually broke biologists into two camps, geneticists and naturalists. Geneticists, like Darwin, repudiated the existence of species. They based their arguments, though, less on evolution than on the laws of genetics, which burst on the scientific scene at the beginning of this century. The breakthrough was soon followed by the realization that chemical units called genes control the physical characteristics of living things. Each member of a species has a different set of genes from every other member, as shown by the variations in their appearance. At the same time, the ability of plants and animals to form hybrids shows that each species shares some genes with other species. To early geneticists, the difference between one creature and another thus seemed to boil down to the percentage of genes they have in common. Were they members of the same species if they shared 75 percent of their genes? Ninety percent? Maybe that's enough—but then chimpanzees and humans, which share about 95 percent of their genes, would be members of the same species. Ninety-nine percent, then? Any choice would be arbitrary, the geneticists said, and so species themselves were arbitrary.

Naturalists, by contrast, clung to the concept of species. They focused on the broader question of how, when, and where today's diversity of life originated. To measure diversity, they needed a unit of measurement, and the species fit this role. Typical of this approach was ichthyologist David Starr Jordan, founding president of Stanford University and president of the American Association for the Advancement of Science, who argued in 1905 that biology "begins with the searching out of the units which with Linnaeus we call species." (Jordan was true to his word—in a lifetime of taxonomy, he named and described more than 2,500 species of fish.)

Balderdash, the geneticists in effect replied. Dividing nature into artificially distinct units like species is a waste of time, proclaimed botanist Charles E. Bessey, another president of the American Association for the Advancement of Science, in 1908. Species, he said, "have no actual existence in nature. They are mental constructs, and nothing more." But living things nonetheless *act* as if they belong to different species, the naturalists countered. Dogs mate with dogs, not with cats; mice mate with mice, not with dogs. How can anyone say that these are not real categories?

Eventually, this concept—species are special groups of organisms that breed together—resolved the dispute. If two groups of mice avoid each other's intimate company, they probably belong to different species, no matter how similar their physical appearance, no matter how different their genetic endowments. Ernst Mayr, the doyen of twentieth-century evolutionary biology, expressed the concept in its conclusive, jaw-breaking form: *"A species is a reproductive community of populations, reproductively isolated from other populations, that occupies a specific niche in nature."*

"It's not the most beautifully phrased scientific truth there is," Mayr said to us not long ago. "Nor is it the most perfectly applicable in all situations. But I don't think anybody has come up with a better formulation." Mayr's definition, generally accepted as the best of an imperfect lot, has three parts, each with its admitted caveats and exceptions.

First, a species is a *reproductive community of populations*, which is to say that it consists of more or less cohesive groups of organisms that can reproduce freely one with another. The caveats here are twofold. To define a species in terms of a reproductive community implicitly restricts the term to sexually reproducing organisms. Asexual entities like amoebas, which reproduce by splitting in two, do not fit into this scheme. For this reason, some taxonomists believe amoebas and their ilk should be classified as "quasispecies" and identified by sets of distinctive genetic sequences. In any case, the picture is unsettled.

The other caveat is more subtle: a population is easier to define in the abstract than to observe in nature. One exception is the Owens pupfish, which was long confined to a pond near Bishop, California. Visitors could see a complete population—indeed, the entire species—swimming at their feet. In August 1969, the pond almost dried up, and Edwin Philip Pister, a biologist for the California Department of Fish and Game, transferred the entire species in two buckets to another, wetter location. If they had stayed in their buckets, the species would have had two populations. But Pister emptied the buckets into a new pond, and it had one. Most other populations are not so easily demarcated. Few would disagree that the Block Island and Oklahoma American burying beetles are separate populations, but should one further break down the beetles in Oklahoma? Do the beetles on Stephan's land and those a few miles away on Highway 82 belong to separate populations? What about the beetles outside Latimer County? Without tracking individual beetles as they disperse in search of mates, there is no obvious way to tell.

Second, a species is *reproductively isolated from other populations*, which means that under natural conditions members of the species will reproduce *only* with one another. Technically, this means that the species has a common pool of genes that in most circumstances is closed to outsiders. Lions and tigers are an example. The two big cats have been induced to mate in zoos, producing ligers and tiglons. In nature, however, they do not associate. Lions hunt in groups in grasslands, whereas tigers are solitary, like house cats, and live in tropical forests. To the best of our knowledge, they are prevented by their habits from mating—unless the two cats are set up by a matchmaking zookeeper. Therefore, they are distinct species: *Panthera leo* (the lion) and *Panthera tigris* (the tiger).

The weakness here is that hybrids do occur in nature, especially when the ranges of two similar species overlap. The process can benefit both species by increasing the size of the gene pool, which provides greater potential to adapt and change. At the same time, too much hybridization can be harmful. If a tiger and a lion were to reproduce in the wild, the offspring might be ill-suited for either a solitary life in the trees or a communal existence in the plains. Generally speaking, though, reproductive isolation is the rule.

Third, a species *occupies a specific niche in nature*. *Niche*, like *population*, is a fuzzy but valuable term; it refers not only to where a species lives but also to what it feeds on, when it becomes active, where it forages, and so forth. An ecological niche is a role within an ecosystem—a notion that was once summed up by Charles Elton of Cambridge University, one of this century's most important ecologists, as a species' *occupation*. Note that the job descriptions for these occupations are dauntingly specific. Scavenging for small carrion in woodlands, for instance, would seem to be a natural occupation. It is held by ants, carrion flies, and many species of burying beetle. Do they occupy the same niche? No. The description is incomplete. Both *Nicrophorus orbicollis* and *Nicrophorus tomentosus* are burying beetles, but the former becomes active in April and reproduces before early September, whereas the latter becomes active in mid-June and doesn't reproduce until September or later. Like workers on a split-shift schedule, they avoid interfering with each other. Another species, *N. defodiens*, ducks the niches of the other two members of its genus by hunting just before sunset—*N. orbicollis* and *N. tomentosus* are nocturnal. Once a niche is specified in detail, two species rarely occupy it.

Nature is endlessly inventive about niches. When the *N. americanus* played dead on Curt Creighton's hand, it revealed a belly aswarm with dozens of cream-colored mites. The mites, which accompany almost all American burying beetles, are phoretic—hitchhikers, to put it plainly. When the beetle finds a piece of carrion, the mites leap onto the surface of the carcass and lay their eggs. The mites repay the beetle for the ride by killing the eggs of carrion flies, which often get to the corpse first. The relation between the two species is known as "mutualism." The mite reduces competition for the carcass, helping the beetle, and the beetle transports the mite to more places to feed and reproduce than it could reach on its own.

No one knows how many populations of organisms fit Mayr's definition of a species. Counting every one would require enumerating every ecological niche, which would mean scrutinizing every square foot of the planet, not to mention the surfaces and interiors of every living thing. Paul Ehrlich, the biologist and advocate of the Noah Principle, described the task as "impossible" in 1964 and questioned whether it was worth the bother. "Should a large group of biologists continue to look for, find, briefly describe, and name new organisms, or would much of the energy now expended on this activity be better spent in deepening our knowledge of organisms already known? . . . What is the justification of [the] random collection and description of new mite species?" Twenty-seven years later, Ehrlich had changed his mind. In 1991, he and Edward O. Wilson, the Harvard biologist, called for a crash program of "national biological inventories" to assay life forms in every nation. An essential first step in dealing with the extinction crisis, they said, is to know how many species the Earth has to lose.

Unfortunately, Ehrlich was partly right the first time: mounting a census of the world's store of biodiversity is impossible. Nobody is sure how many species we have already located, let alone the number that remain to be found. Estimates of discovered species range as high as 1.8 million, but one cannot be sure. Many creatures—tens or hundreds of thousands—are known only from descriptions in spidery handwriting on three-by-five index cards in huge wooden file cabinets at institutions like the American Museum of Natural History, in New York City. Charles Remington, the entomologist who turned up American burying beetles on Block Island, works in one such repository, the Peabody Museum of Yale University. When we asked whether anyone was computerizing the Peabody's vast holdings, Remington chuckled at our naïveté. "Do you know how many data processors Yale would have to hire?" he asked.

Such considerations led biologists to a simple method for estimating the global roster of species: guessing. They estimated the number of discovered species and speculated that the number of undiscovered species might be something between half a million and a million and a half. Adding the two together led various investigators to totals between 2 and 4 million. As the extinction crisis highlighted the inadequacies of this procedure, somewhat less haphazard methods came into play. These involved extrapolating from a subset of well-known species, usually birds, beetles, or butterflies, which hobbyists have tracked extensively. Peter Hammond of the Natural History Museum in London employed this approach to appraise the number of insect species worldwide. He observed that Britain, home of many insect collectors, is thought to host some 22,000 species of insect. Sixty-seven of these are butterflies. Because butterflies are targeted by legions of amateur lepidopterists—"leppers," as the writer Vladimir Nabokov, himself an ardent butterfly man, called them—Hammond assumed that the 17,500 recorded species of butterfly form an almost complete global inventory. The final tally of butterfly species should be, he guessed, no more than 20,000. He then asked a question reminiscent of the word problems that bedevil children in elementary-school mathematics: if the ratio of Britain's 67 butterflies to Britain's 22,000 insects is the same as the ratio of the world's 20,000 butterflies to the world's complete number of insects, how big is the global roster of insect species? Answer: 6 million.

Hammond based his estimate on the assumption (shaky, as he acknowledged) that the composition of the insect species throughout the world resembles that of the insect species on a fair-sized island off the coast of northern Europe. It doesn't. Unlike their northern counterparts, tropical forests contain a fabulous potpourri of insects, which is why Terry L. Erwin, curator of the department of entomology at the National Museum of Natural History, a branch of the Smithsonian Institution, used a forest in Panama to make a now-notorious estimate of insect diversity. In the late 1970s, he placed a grid of wide-mouthed funnels under nineteen Panamanian trees, then pumped insecticide into the leafy canopy above. Dead insects rained into the funnels, which fed into giant versions of the alcohol vials that Karl Stephan carries in his pocket. Erwin counted and labeled, counted and labeled. Even though he restricted his attention to beetles, the task took years. About 1,200 species of beetle reside in and around the top of the single species of linden tree that Erwin examined most closely.

Erwin found this thought-provoking. As a heuristic exercise, he made, in 1982, a chain of assumptions. Entomologists often say that beetles comprise about 40 percent of the insect world. If that figure held true in the canopy (a guess, but why not?), the 1,200 species of beetles would represent 40 percent of the insects there, which would imply that the canopy contained a total of about 3,000 insect species. Moreover, if the lower parts of the tree, known to be less rich than the canopy, contained half as many species as the top (another guess, but it seemed reasonable), a full inventory of the insects in the linden tree would have yielded 4,500 species. Of these, Erwin knew that some reside *only* on the linden tree. He put the proportion at 13.5 percent (yet another guess), which meant that about 600 insect species were exclusively associated with the linden. Assume every other species of tropical tree has a similar number of associated insect species (one more guess). The Earth is believed to contain 50,000 species of tropical tree. Multiplication problem: 600 insect species per tree times 50,000 tree species yields . . . 30 million species of insect.

Nor are insects the only creatures present in such staggering numbers. Fungi have been said to number 1.6 million or so. Add another million wormlike nematodes to the tally. Ten million more creatures may live on the ocean floor. And scientists have barely dipped into the protists and bacteria, which comprise two of the world's five kingdoms. As the estimates continue to appear, some wonder how much credence should be given to them. When other scientists inspected Erwin's estimate, they pointed out that he had strung so many assumptions together that the data could plausibly support figures from 7 million to 80 million insects. His figures, we were reminded by Edward F. Connor of the Department of Environmental Sciences at the University of Virginia, in Charlottesville, "were based on one set of samples from one site at one time. From that he got the whole world!" The biggest trouble, in Connor's view, is that the extrapolations are untestable. Biologists are far too few to perform the ecological observations and breeding experiments necessary to find out whether all those postulated beetles and fungi and nematodes actually exist.

Nobody, though, disputes the general picture painted by these estimates: our planet is stuffed to bursting with life. Millions of reproductively isolated gene pools throng the Earth, each wending its separate evolutionary way, each with its uniquely shifting pattern of heritability. No two are exactly alike, though the distinctions among them may seem trivial to outsiders. The extent of life is vast, unfathomable. The British Museum's collection of half a million insects occupies a six-story building; a complete collection, if Erwin is right, would require a building a hundred times as large. In another heuristic exercise, Wilson calculated that the total genetic base of the world's species represents about 1 quintillion bits of information. A quintillion—one followed by eighteen zeroes—is a fantastically large number. If each bit of information was represented by a one-inch-square postage stamp, the collection of genetic information would cover the combined surfaces of the Earth and Mars. Wilson calls this incredible figure "still an underestimate."

Maybe so, but it provides something to think about. Recall that the carpet of postage stamps represents only the genetic information in the world's species. Not included are their physiological, behavioral, ecological, and taxonomic characteristics. Incorporating these would add many more layers of paper to the surface. This thick stratum of information is something like what biologists mean when they define biodiversity as "the variety of organisms considered at all levels." Now imagine that pockets of fire suddenly appear and spread. Trillions of bits of paper turn to flame, ashes whirling upward in the fiery draft. The information goes up in smoke. Big stretches of the planet are burned clear. *That* is something akin to what biologists mean when they speak of the extinction crisis.

IN THE FALL of 1780, an Anglican minister named Robert Annan decided to drain a wetland on his farm in upstate New York, near the present-day town of New Paltz. He hired a man to cut a ditch between the swamp and the Walkill River; the swamp water would pour into the river, leaving arable land. Inspecting the work site one day, Annan discovered that his employee had dug up the teeth of an enormous animal. He took them home, had them washed, and arranged them on a table as if they were still embedded in the jaw of their owner. The result astonished him, because the animal must have been huge. He called over a neighbor who knew the area better than he did. The neighbor, too, was amazed—he had never seen the like. "What could this animal be?" the minister wondered.

The two men returned to the ditch, Annan later reported, "and fell eagerly to digging." They found many bones—huge, rotting, broken things, bigger than those of the biggest elephant. A joint was more than twelve inches across; the teeth, four inches high; the vertebrae stretched far into the ditch. To contemporary eyes the scene is irresistible: the men in Colonial garb shoveling wide-eyed through the mire, exclaiming as each incredible find came to light. It was irresistible to Annan's contemporaries, too. As word of the discovery spread, he was visited by scientists and curiosity seekers, including General George Washington, taking a break from the Revolutionary War. Washington told Annan that he also owned a gigantic tooth, his from the banks of the Ohio River. He, too, had never seen anything resembling the monstrosity from which it must have come.

"Shall we, sir, suppose the species to be extinct over the face of the globe?" Annan asked the president of the American Academy of Arts and Sciences in a letter. "If so, what could be the cause? It is next to incredible that the remains of this animal could have lain there since the flood"—the Flood, that is, of Noah. But it was also incredible that these huge beasts could still walk the Earth. It was all very confusing, Annan reported. "Some gentlemen, with whom I have conversed, have supposed that [the animal's] extinction (as it is probable that they are extinct) is owing to some amazing convulsion, concussion, or catastrophe, endured by the globe. But I know of none that could produce such an effect, except the flood." Yet how could a benevolent Deity have denied this species the sanctuary of the Ark? Why wasn't it saved? "Great and marvelous are Thy works, Lord God Almighty!" Annan concluded.

Like many of his contemporaries, Annan was unable to credit that extinction could occur, except possibly if humans hunted down a species. His disbelief in extinction may seem surprising, given that people had encountered fossils of huge, strange creatures since the days of ancient Greece. But for centuries, they regarded fossils as little more than curious patterns in stone—the rocky equivalent of cloud formations that look like birds. Not until Annan's time did scientists take a closer look and realize that fossils of identical creatures had turned up in widely scattered places. One might expect to see a strange-looking cloud in any particular part of the sky, but it would be alarming to see identical clouds in several directions. On the other hand, admitting that fossils were the remnants of animals that no longer existed was hard to swallow, theologically speaking. Finding fossils of a lion or eagle would not be surprising; finding those of the dinosaurs implied that the planet had lost some kinds of animals. According to the then-current view, God in His majesty stood guard over the Great Chain of Being. Extinction implied the heretical notion that He sometimes fell asleep on the job.

The fossil remains of seemingly extinct organisms thus had to be explained, or explained away. But the explanations were far from satisfactory: fossils were distorted early versions of currently existing species (but too many oddities turned up that resembled nothing known); they were the remains of the creatures killed by the Flood (but too many were obviously aquatic and would have survived); they were preserved specimens of organisms that now lived only in places Europeans hadn't visited (but voyages like that of the HMS *Beagle* failed to find the lands that could house such species).

Darwin had different ideas. Implicit in his theory of evolution was a concomitant theory of extinction (although he hedged a bit because he wasn't sure). He imagined one species "seiz[ing] on the place" of another, taking its food, usurping its nest sites, driving it away. Eventually, the original species would thin out and die, its niche filled by the newcomer. If that happened in enough places to the first species, the new species would, Darwin wrote, "have caused its extermination."

Despite the intuitive clarity of this notion, Darwin failed to resolve the extinction question. The extraordinary prowess of evolution—the butterfly wing that mimics a leaf in every detail, including the spreading veins and the little holes bored by grubs—makes it seem that living creatures can adapt to *anything*. The struggle for existence is, in great part, a struggle to avoid competition, not to embrace it and risk losing. As a result, Darwinian-style extinction has rarely been observed. Unless one species is uniformly superior to another in every habitat, it will not eradicate the other. But if Darwinian extinction is rare, what happened to the dinosaurs?

The increasingly plausible theory is that historically most extinctions have occurred when disaster struck so fast and hard and wide that species didn't have a chance to run away or adapt. A renowned example is the asteroid—or, perhaps, comet—that hit the north edge of the Yucatán Peninsula 65 million years ago, causing, some scientists believe, a globe-spanning dust storm, an ecological collapse, and the elimination of the dinosaurs. Other paleontologists are skeptical, proposing instead that the impact was the coup de grâce for some other process. Whatever the cause of their demise, a few dinosaurs survived and evolved into birds (or maybe not: paleontologists fight over that point, too). Mammals, always in the wings, grabbed center stage. Much later, the curtain parted on *Homo sapiens.* Seemingly, we owe our present eminence to the Earth's chance interception of a big rock.

Darwinian extinctions may take thousands of generations, while species duke it out for dominance. Catastrophic extinctions may take place in a period of hours or days, when a volcano erupts or an earthquake rips open the land and species with limited distributions are destroyed. Somewhere between is what people have done—the phenomenon one might call "polar bear" extinctions, after a parable by Charles Lyell, the great nineteenth-century geologist.

An influence on Darwin, Lyell once mulled over the consequences of moving a species from place to place. Sometimes little would occur; sometimes, though, a migration by a single species could upset the entire ecological applecart. To illustrate his point, Lyell described what might have happened when the first polar bears reached Iceland. If they had floated across the Denmark Strait aboard an iceberg, he wrote, "a great number of these quadrupeds might effect a landing at the same time, and the havoc which they would make among the species previously settled in the island would be terrific. The deer, foxes, seals, and even birds, on which these animals sometimes prey, would be soon thinned down." On the other hand, he noted, some species would prosper. If polar bears killed most of the deer, the plants the deer ate would enjoy a growth spurt; so would the insects that depend upon those plants, and the birds that depend on those insects. Meanwhile, of course, the polar bears might eat so much that they would run out of food. The exact impact would be hard to predict, except that much would change.

Since the days of the Ice Age, human beings have been the world's biggest, baddest polar bears. Indeed, it sometimes seems that the whole of human history reprises Lyell's tale of polar bears and Iceland. The metaphor is surprisingly exact: twelve thousand years ago, a band of humans—"paleo-Indians," they are sometimes called—came to North America across the arrow of land that then connected Siberia and Alaska. They arrived in what to modern eyes would have seemed a fantastic continent-sized bestiary, achurn with camels, rhinos, cheetahs, lions, even elephants. There were beavers the size of bears, bisons with horns six feet across, and ground sloths able to stretch the height of a two-story building. Vulturelike teratorns, their wings sixteen feet across, filled the sky; below the treetops plodded a four-foot turtle that weighed a ton.

None of the creatures in this new land had seen people before. The paleo-Indians took advantage of this circumstance. They swept through the continent. It was an orgy of slaughter. Flint-headed spears, flung in coordinated onslaughts, made short work of deer, dromedaries, and *Dasypus*, the nine-banded armadillo. For a while, it didn't matter because there weren't enough paleo-Indians. Then the population hit a critical density, and in no time at all species vanished by the score: mammoths, sloths, horses, eagles, camels, tapirs, giant wolves, saber-toothed tigers. Almost every New World mammal of significant size disappeared. In all, some paleontologists calculate, thirty-three genera were expunged, perhaps within two hundred years, certainly within two thousand; in contrast, the previous million years had seen the loss of just thirteen genera. The result was, in the words of naturalist Alfred Wallace, "a zoologically impoverished world, from which all of the hugest, and fiercest, and strangest forms have suddenly disappeared."

The extinctions at the end of the Ice Age remain subject to scientific quarrel. Some researchers believe the drastic changes in climate at the end of the Ice Age were the principal cause. But an increasing number assign responsibility to the paleo-Indians, and the evidence to back the polar bear effect is impressive. Climate changed across the globe, but the extinctions occurred solely in the Americas, which suggests that weather alone cannot have been responsible. Moreover, the only big mammals that avoided extinction were, by and large, those that crossed the Bering Sea with the paleo-Indians. Today's moose and grizzly bear, for instance, were native to Asia, where they had adapted to human hunters; their hick relatives in the Americas had no experience with us and were overwhelmed. But perhaps the strongest evidence is that exactly the same thing happened when humans first arrived on islands like Madagascar, Australia, and, especially, New Zealand.

Isolated New Zealand had wildlife like no other place in the world. It had no mammals except bats, which somehow flew over from Australia, 1,300 miles away. Instead, the niches normally occupied by mammals were filled by flightless birds: twelve species of moa, ranging in size from two to nine feet tall; three kiwis, about the size of a hen; and dozens of other species. The rest of the fauna was equally strange: the weta, a sort of flightless giant cricket, which scurried about at night on the forest floor like a mouse; several frogs that had no webs between their toes and were not born as tadpoles; and the tuataras, two reptiles that resembled small dinosaurs, had unique bony arches on their heads, and possessed a sort of third eye of unknown function. People, in the form of Polynesian islanders, arrived in the eighth century A.D. In the next few hundred years, they burned down much of the forest and ate every species of moa into extinction.

Such destruction was no accident. The Polynesians did exactly the same thing throughout the Pacific islands, which they settled in waves that rippled from Samoa to Hawaii. David Steadman, a paleo-ornithologist (a specialist in prehistoric birds) at the New York State Museum in Albany, has spent years excavating early Polynesian campsites. Often the islanders set up shop in caves, which means that the fire beds and garbage dumps were protected from the elements and preserved more or less intact. Steadman has excavated thousands of bird bones from them. The majority belong to species that no longer exist. He has suggested that in a few centuries the Polynesians may have extinguished up to *three thousand* species of bird—a fantastic number, given that fewer than ten thousand exist in the world today.

These catastrophes were not always caused by human hunters; indeed, hunting is a comparatively minor part of the polar bear effect. Another part is due to *H. sapiens*'s own collection of phoretic species—creatures that piggyback on our predilection for them. One of them accompanied the Polynesians throughout the Pacific: *Rattus exulans*, the Pacific rat, imported because it was a favorite at the dinner table. Landing in places with no mammals, *R. exulans* cut a wide swath. In New Zealand, it wiped out six of the smallest birds and many reptiles. When the Europeans arrived there, they, too, were accompanied by rats—*Rattus rattus*, a different species. Unlike the Polynesians, the Europeans detested their rats. To keep them down, they carried a second phoretic species: *Felis domestica*, the house cat. Rat and cat continued the tradition of devastation. When Captain James Cook sailed into the southern island's Dusky Bay on his second expedition, the happiest member of the crew was the ship's cat. This animal, noted one chronicler of the voyage, "had no sooner perceived so excellent an opportunity of obtaining delicious meals, than she regularly took a walk in the woods every morning and made great havoc among the little birds, that were not aware of such an insidious enemy."

Many species, unable to survive on the main islands of New Zealand, fled to tiny islets offshore. Among them was *Xenicus lyalli*, the Stephens Island wren. Small, steep, and rocky, Stephens Island sits in the passage that cuts between the north and south islands of New Zealand. A local landmark, it consists of a forest atop a ring of cliffs that face the ocean. A lighthouse beams at passing traffic. The first lighthouse keeper, one D. Lyall, arrived in 1894. He was accompanied by several cats. Wandering through the woods atop the island's rocky cliffs, the cats amused themselves in feline fashion by hunting birds and presenting the limp corpses to their master. One of the bodies drew Lyall's attention. He was a bird-watcher and had never seen its like.

Lyall conveyed the carcass to Walter Buller, an itinerant judge in the Native Land Court, who was then New Zealand's leading bird expert. Buller was intrigued. Lyall's bird was obviously a passerine, or songbird, the order to which more than half of all birds belong. But this songbird had such stubby, useless-looking wings that it seemed unlikely to be capable of flight. A flightless passerine was a find; none had ever been seen before. Buller shipped the specimen, now preserved, to the British scientific journal *Ibis*, with an article proclaiming his discovery of a remarkable new species. Hearing of the bird, collectors descended on the island, its only home. The cats meanwhile kept depositing wren cadavers on Lyall's doorstep. Lyall himself was busy clearing the forest to create a pasture for his cows. The combination of cats, clearing, and collectors was fatal; *X. lyalli* disappeared by the end of 1895, a year after its discovery. Today the bird is known only from twelve specimens in museums—small, silent presences that seem to exemplify the biodiversity crisis in miniature.

Such tales are legion across the world, but nobody knows the exact tally. Biologists, unsure of the number of species, are also unsure of the number of victims claimed by the polar bear effect. The most careful efforts to ascertain the worldwide toll of extinction come from the fifty scientists and support staff at the World Conservation Monitoring Centre in Cambridge, England. The WCMC is jointly sponsored by the United Nations Environmental Programme; the International Union for the Conservation of Nature and Natural Resources, a consortium of private agencies based in Gland, Switzerland; and the World Wide Fund for Nature, a group best recognized in this country under its former name, the World Wildlife Fund. Every few years, the WCMC publishes what are called "red books" or "red lists" of endangered species. "It's an enormous task," said Jo Taylor, an information officer at the WCMC. "By the time you finish the back of the book, the front is out of date."

In October 1994, when Taylor last spoke to us, the red list contained 26,333 species and subspecies of plant, 2,754 invertebrates, 979 fishes, 970 birds, 741 mammals, 316 reptiles, and 169 amphibians. Between one-tenth and one-third of the species in each group are classified as "endangered" ("Immediate danger of extinction—that's endangered," said Taylor). Most of the rest qualify as "vulnerable" ("Looks like it could become endangered if what goes on carries on," she explained). The rest are "indeterminate" ("Insufficiently known to be sure—you can't count or measure them, but you're pretty sure they're in trouble"), "rare" ("Species like the panda . . . their numbers are low"), or "commercially threatened" ("That's obvious, isn't it?").

Accompanying the red list of endangered species is a list of extinct species. Inevitably dubbed the "black list," it records the creatures known to have vanished since 1600. As of October 1994, it included 654 species and subspecies of plant, 364 invertebrates, 103 birds, 63 mammals, 33 fishes, and 20 reptiles and amphibians—1,237 creatures in all. Inevitably, the reckoning is incomplete: the cautious WCMC refuses to declare any species extinct until it has not been seen in the wild for fifty years. The list also has its arbitrary side. The Stephens Island wren is on it, but not ten of the twelve species of moa, let alone the thousands of Pacific birds, all of which perished a few centuries before 1600. Despite the lacunae, though, it is clear that extinction climbed in the late eighteenth century, jumped higher a century later, and continues to rise. The number of extinct birds has grown by almost 20 species since 1981; the number of birds at risk, by almost 600.

Although these extinction rates are terribly fast from an evolutionary point of view, they are nothing like those estimated by such scientists as Wilson, who projected in 1992 that one species is doomed every twenty minutes. The WCMC has registered 1,237 extinctions since 1600; if Wilson is right, the Earth is losing that many species every *seventeen days*. Between 1900 and 1992, according to the WCMC, 161 plants vanished. At that rate, a quarter of the world's plants will vanish by about the year 3500. The prospect is uncomfortable, but it is far short of the frightening claim by Peter Raven that those plants will be gone by 2010, before today's toddlers graduate from high school. Observation and prediction differ by several orders of magnitude. Why, then, do Wilson, Raven, and many other biologists cling to their predictions? Don't the WCMC figures contradict them?

Unlike the dispute over the number of species, which is intriguing but abstract, the discrepancy between predicted and observed extinction rates is of obvious practical importance. If the WCMC figures are taken at face value, extinction today is a slowly accumulating problem that will not reach a critical level for centuries to come—a few puffs of smoke on a planet carpeted by millions of species. Humanity will have centuries to ponder its response. But if Wilson, Raven, and their colleagues are right, a significant proportion of the planet is already on fire, much of the rest is beginning to smolder, and people must act immediately, lest they perish in the conflagration.

Puffs of smoke or global conflagration—which vision is accurate? It is hard to think of a question more imperative to our crowded planet. The cautious approach taken by the WCMC—

relying on the lack of observations for fifty years—cannot account for the loss of species that have yet to be named, or even discovered. If only a small fraction of the planet's species has been cataloged, the WCMC cannot tally more than a similarly small fraction of the planet's extinctions—*if*, that is, those extinctions are actually taking place. But if we have never seen most of the species we think are being lost, how can biologists give such precise figures for the number that are becoming extinct? In other words: Why do scientists believe there is an extinction crisis?

Chapter Three

THE CRISIS

ONE DAY in 1945, a remarkable man named Frank W. Preston took a train ride. By the time his trip was over, he had sown the seeds of the extinction crisis. Preston was an engineer by training, a consultant to the glass industry by profession, and a bird-watcher by inclination. He was also an amateur biologist—one of the vanishingly small number who have made important contributions to science in this century. Born in Leicester, England, in 1896, he was granted a scholarship to Oxford but decided that its classical education was not for him. He apprenticed himself instead to a civil engineer. In his spare time, he taught himself enough chemistry and physics to earn a degree from the University of London in 1916. After working nine years for a British optics company, he returned to the university, submitted several previously published papers in lieu of a Ph.D. thesis, took the oral examination, and got his doctorate—all in the space of a few months. Elated, he spent much of his savings on a round-the-world bird-watching binge. The last of his money went to found an engineering firm, Preston Laboratories, near Butler, Pennsylvania, where he had earlier met people in the glass business. He became a giant in the industry, writing more than sixty papers for solid-state physics journals and obtaining some twenty industrial patents. He died in March 1989 at the age of ninety-three.

On weekends, Preston explored the hundred-acre campus of his business with binoculars, counting birds and plants. Numbers of living things—it was a subject he wondered about. Some bird species on his grounds were represented by dozens of nesting pairs, whereas others had only one or two. Why were some species so much more abundant than others? If he surveyed a similar hundred-acre spread in the neighboring county, would he find the same number and pattern of species? And if he surveyed a thousand acres, or ten thousand, how would the number or pattern change? On the train home one evening in 1945, he pored through *The Ecology of the Birds of Quaker Run Valley*, a detailed census of all the breeding birds in a valley in western New York State. Preston ran through the list in his mind and was struck by the way the numbers seemed to fit together. It was, as scientists say, a Eureka! moment. He scribbled frantically in the margins of his newspaper.

Preston's flash of insight was more than a step toward grasping the extinction crisis. In an intellectual sense, it generated the crisis. Considering the distribution of birds in a single valley eventually led Preston to what he regarded as a law that held true everywhere on Earth. The law, now called the "species-area curve," describes in mathematical terms the relation between the size of a particular area and the number of species that can inhabit it. By implication, it tells how many species will be lost when human activity cuts into a wilderness. The species-area curve is not able to foretell everything, like a crystal ball; indeed, some scientists regard it as hopelessly imprecise and even misleading. Nonetheless, the species-area curve—fruit of an amateur ecologist's inspired mathematical doodling—is the basis for all the current predictions of mass extinction.

PICTURE TWO TERRITORIES, one of which is ten times the size of the other. Now imagine counting every living thing on both. Will there be more species in the bigger one, or more individuals from the same species? Biologists have long known the answer: bigger tracts almost always have more species. One reason is that no two places on Earth are identical, and bigger areas have more habitats for species to fill. But imagine that the two territories were identical, except for size. Would the larger one still have more species? In other words, would area *by itself* play a role? If so, scientists could survey a small part of, say, Quaker Run Valley and then use the relationship between area and species number to project the tally of species in the entire valley. To make that estimate accurately, they would need a precise mathematical statement of the relationship between area and number of species. On the train ride, Preston began an intellectual quest that led him, seventeen years later, to that mathematical statement—or, at any rate, what he thought was that statement. When finally published in the journal *Ecology* in 1962, his work was a wild, almost unintelligible salad of algebraic manipulation. Nonetheless, it set off an explosion in theoretical ecology.

To explain why requires examining Preston's work with some care—a procedure for which we ask the forbearance of the mathematically disinclined. Underlying his species-area curve is the equation $S = cA^z$. The equation says that the number of species in a place, S, is equal to the area of that place, A, raised to some power, z, and multiplied by some other number, c. It is used to project the number of species in areas of different size.

In this equation, the value of z is all-important, because it determines how much the number of species changes when the area grows or shrinks. Reading *The Ecology of the Birds of Quaker Run Valley*, Preston learned that 79 species of bird regularly bred in the 17,000-acre valley. In a species-area curve with a value of z equal to 1, a similar valley that is twice as large (in other words, a valley of 34,000 acres) would contain twice as many species of breeding birds (158 species); a valley half as large (8,500 acres) would be home to half as many (about 40 species); and so forth. For a value of z between 0 and 1, the change in the number of species lags behind the change in area. In this case, a valley that is twice as large would contain fewer than twice as many bird species; a valley that is half as large would contain more than half as many species. The exact numbers would depend, of course, on the exact value of z. No one thinks that in nature z is equal to 0 (because that would be mathematically equivalent to saying that all areas have the same number of species, which they don't) or more than 1 (because that would mean that the change in the number of species occurs faster than the change in area—implying that a valley only slightly smaller than Quaker Run Valley couldn't house nearly as many species, which biologists know to be untrue).

Using complex algebraic arguments, Preston showed that under certain assumptions the value of *z* should come out to a "canonical" or standard value of 0.262, about the number that he derived when he combined data from *The Ecology of the Birds of Quaker Run Valley* with dozens of other measurements. Biologists today believe it ranges between 0.15 and 0.35, depending on the type of organism and the relationship of the area under consideration to other areas, but they use 0.3 as a rule of thumb. Applying that value gives the species-area curve depicted in the graph below. A valley 10 percent bigger than Quaker Run Valley would hold 81 species (an increase of 3 percent); a valley twice as big would have 97 species (23 percent more); ten times as big, 158 species (100 percent more). The relationship works the other way, too. A valley

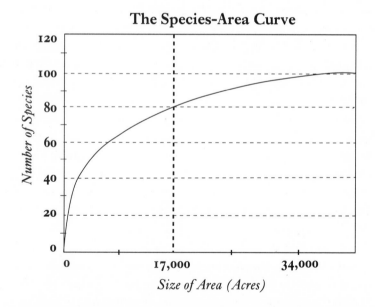

The Species-Area Curve

Quaker Run Valley (the vertical dashed line) covers 17,000 acres and has 79 species of breeding bird. A typical species-area curve with a *z*-value of 0.3 shows how the number of species should rise or fall in similar valleys that are larger or smaller. A valley that is twice that size, for example, would have 97 species—an increase of nearly one-quarter. One that is only half as big would have 64 species, a decrease of almost one-fifth.

half the size of Quaker Run Valley would have 64 species (a decrease of 19 percent); one that is only one-tenth its size would have about 40 (a decrease of 50 percent).

Biologists before Preston had noticed the relation between species and area, and some had written it down in exactly this form. They saw it, however, as a useful empirical regularity, like the dog owner's observation that mutts are more likely to have pleasant temperaments than purebreds. Preston instead regarded it as a law of nature, fully the equal of the physical and chemical laws used in engineering. This way of treating ecological problems was a startling innovation; he treated organisms in much the same way that physicists treat falling bodies and inclined planes.

Consider a marble at the bottom of a goblet, Preston might have said. Physicists say the forces on the marble (gravity, pushing down; the glass goblet, resisting up) are in equilibrium, and the marble will stay where the theory predicts it will stay. Imagine holding the marble in place, tilting the goblet a bit, then letting go of the marble. The marble, now out of equilibrium, rolls down the side, stops, then rolls a bit the other way. After a few cycles back and forth, the marble finds a new equilibrium point between the bottom and the lip. Just as the marble inside the goblet must obey the laws of physics, Preston in effect argued, species inside a territory must obey the law of $S = cA^z$.

Consider an island, Preston told his readers. It will have a number of species given by the species-area curve—an equilibrium number, a number that represents a balance of natural forces. Now picture the result, as he put it, if "some strange accident divides [that] island into identical halves with an impassable barrier between them." Immediately after the accident, each new island will be half the size of the original but will contain the same number of species as before. (He assumed that all species were spread evenly through the original island.) Because each half-island would no longer have the "right" number of species for its size, the new islands would be out of equilibrium. Pushing them back into equilibrium, Preston believed, was the heightened danger of extinction created by the reduction in population each species would suffer. Eventually, species would vanish from the islands, continuing to disappear until their number hit the new level predicted by the species-area curve.

Preston's reasoning runs in reverse, too. Go back to the original island. Instead of cutting it in half, imagine leaving it the same size but removing some species. The island is out of equilibrium again. The number of species is too low. An "impulse toward extensive subspeciation," as Preston put it, would be created, and new species would eventually appear. Ultimately, the number will once again return to its original level, as it must. All of this, he believed, was every jot as inevitable as the marble rolling to its new equilibrium in accordance with the laws of physics.

Preston's ideas astounded Daniel S. Simberloff, an ecologist at Florida State University, in Tallahassee, who first encountered them as a graduate student in the mid-1960s. "I'd never seen anything like them," he told us. "Here was this man saying that this one [equation] could in essence solve all these terribly difficult problems that ecologists had labored over for so many years." In hindsight, the task Preston had set for himself—uncovering one of the fundamental laws of biodiversity—was preposterously ambitious, overweening in a mad-scientist sense. Much of Preston's elaborate theoretical framework seems today, in Simberloff's words, like "numerology." The papers were, Simberloff said, "*full* of ideas, but also terribly misleading ones, and people got into all sorts of sidetracks because of it."

Equally astonished was Simberloff's thesis adviser, Edward Wilson. Independently, Wilson and Robert H. MacArthur, a mathematically inclined ecologist at the University of Pennsylvania, had developed similar ideas. MacArthur, who died in 1972, knew Preston well. Nonetheless, MacArthur hadn't known what his friend in the glass trade was up to. He was stunned to discover that Preston had arrived first, planting his flag down with a thump in the pages of *Ecology*. "It was completely out of the blue," Wilson told us. "But I was also heartened, because it meant that we might be on the right track." The Wilson-MacArthur paper appeared in another journal, *Evolution*, eighteen months later.

Although Wilson and MacArthur fully acknowledged Preston's work, they ended up with most of the scientific credit. Unlike

Preston's recondite exegeses, their article was sharply focused; it was easy for biologists to understand. Wilson and MacArthur also provided a clear picture of the forces that generated the species-area curve. Islands, they said, are in a state of dynamic equilibrium. On the one hand, new species are always drifting in, like the finches that settled in the Galápagos Islands. On the other, old species are always disappearing, snuffed out by predation, disease, and, especially, what is now called "demographic stochasticity"— the chance mishaps that plague small populations, such as having too many offspring of one sex, or too many parents that fail to reproduce, or too many unlucky combinations of genes. As a result, islands experience a constant turnover of species, but the total number of species on each island stays approximately the same.

After the two men expanded on their ideas in a monograph, *The Theory of Island Biogeography*, they asked Simberloff to criticize the manuscript. Simberloff, known today as a sharp critic, was unsparing even in his student days. The idea of looking at the number of species on an island as a balance of immigration and extinction was clever, Simberloff said, but it was just an idea. No experimental data supported it. Wilson had been thinking about experimentally testing it for two years. "Well," he said, "then why don't you help me test it?"

Fair enough, Simberloff thought. He adopted the project as his doctoral thesis. The obvious way to test these ideas, Wilson said, would be to kill every living creature on some island and then see whether its fauna would be returned to the same level of abundance, as the theory predicted. Of course, Simberloff and Wilson would not be allowed to do that on the sort of big island on which mammals and birds live—they could hardly wipe out, say, Nantucket. But even very, very small islands have large collections of insect species. Poring over maps of North America, Wilson narrowed the choice down to the thousands of tiny islets off the southern coast of Florida. Little more than clumps of mangrove trees protruding from the warm shallows of the Gulf of Mexico, they are often no larger than a suburban living room. Many suitable candidates lay in the protected waters of the Everglades National Park and the Great White Heron National Wildlife Refuge. Aha, Wilson said.

After obtaining permission for their murderous work from the park and refuge managers, Simberloff and Wilson spent much of 1965 and 1966 island-hopping in a fourteen-foot boat. The mangroves were silent and unpeopled, each island a miniature lost world only a few miles by dory from traffic-choked U.S. 1, with its ranks of motels, motor homes, and McDonald's restaurants. Jumping into the surf that crashed against the mangroves, the two researchers crawled across every square inch of these small muddy places, counting the insects, spiders, and other arthropods. Annoyed by the sticky mud he had to wade through, Simberloff built snowshoelike plywood pads for his feet. He sank in the goo up to his knees the first time he tried to use them, and had to be hauled free by Wilson. Accepting the impasto of mud on their clothing as inevitable, they kept counting bugs. When they finished, Wilson called pest-control firms in Miami with a novel request. Would they zap an island?

"The first three or four said, '*Whaaat?*'" Simberloff recalled. "Then we reached this one guy at a company called National Exterminators who said, 'Wow, that's very interesting.'" National Exterminators sprayed two islands with pesticides until they were dripping. Simberloff and Wilson inspected the results. Not good enough—ants and beetles had survived, mostly in hollow twigs. Good-humoredly, the company agreed to cover the islands in nylon shrouds and drop fancy bug bombs inside. This involved surrounding the islands with scaffolding, draping the shrouds over the framework, and pumping in methyl bromide (an insecticide) and chloropicrin (tear gas, which annoys insects, driving them from hiding places to where they can be eliminated by the methyl bromide). A few hours later, they opened the tents, revealing six insect-free islands—perhaps the only ones in the world. (They also had two untouched control islands.) Within days, tiny six- and eight-legged creatures reappeared on the zapped mangroves, survivors of voyages as heroic as those of Magellan. Before a year was over, the six islands were back where they had started, with almost the same numbers of species.

The experiment demonstrated that empty islands fill up to an equilibrium level. It did not prove another part of the theory of island biogeography: that changing the size of an island will change the number of species on it. To test this, Simberloff again selected mangrove islands—nine of them this time. He surveyed the islands in the summer of 1969, again going through the tedious business of censusing invertebrates. After the survey, he hired several people with chain saws. They hacked up eight islands (one island was left intact as a control), reducing them in size by one-third to one-half. Then the crew loaded the cut-up chunks of each island onto barges and dumped them in the ocean. During the next two years, Simberloff visited the islands; on each visit, he performed another census. Just as the theory predicted, the number of species declined on the islands he had cut down in size; on the island he'd left alone, the number of species rose a little, ruling out the possibility that the whole system had been hit by some mysterious species-eliminating force. Simberloff published the results in 1976. "Species number," he wrote, "increases with island size alone, independent of habitat diversity."

The experiments galvanized ecologists, who were used to groping their way through thickets of natural observations, hoping to come across something that would provide some insight. Wilson and Simberloff had confirmed a theory by experiment, just like physicists. And the idea of manipulating entire small ecosystems was fascinating. Scores of papers covering some aspect of island biogeography poured forth in the 1970s. Ants on islands, land snails on islands, flies on islands, flies on dead snails, mice on islands, mites on mice, mussels in rivers, fish in lakes, insects in caves—almost anything resembling a species on an island was fair game. Island biogeography had extended the frontiers of science. In fact, biologists were only beginning to learn where it would take them.

AS SIMBERLOFF SAID, Preston was *full* of ideas. Toward the end of his presentation, almost hidden, one of those ideas outlined an intellectual path that led to today's fears of an extinction spasm. The species-area curve could be used, Preston pointed out, to assess the limitations of wildlife preserves. If the number of species always shrinks when area is reduced, he wrote, then "it is not possible to preserve in a State or National Park, a complete replica on a small scale of the fauna and flora of a much larger area." An ardent conservationist, Preston was dismayed to find his theory predicting the inevitable failure of nature reserves to protect the species inside them. One way out, he hoped, might be to "prevent the area from becoming [isolated] by keeping open a continuous corridor with other preserved areas." Even so, he came to the unpleasant conclusion that the number of species would eventually fall as "natural conditions are replaced by unnatural ones."

"Unnatural" areas replacing "natural" ones—Preston had extended the species-area curve from islands to terrestrial ecosystems hit by deforestation and other types of human disturbance. Cutting half of a forest, he was suggesting, was much like cutting an island in half, and the same natural forces governed both situations. His notion was taken up by John Terborgh, a primate and bird specialist then at Princeton, and Jared M. Diamond, a physiologist turned ecologist at the University of California at Los Angeles. In articles written independently in the late 1960s and early 1970s, the two men looked at islands—Terborgh's in Panama; Diamond's in New Guinea—much bigger than the tiny dots of land in the Wilson-Simberloff experiments. Terborgh examined a forested hill that had been transformed into an island by the rising waters behind a dam. Diamond surveyed peninsulas that had become islands thousands of years ago when sea levels rose. Despite the dissimilarity of their subjects, their results were strikingly similar. Terborgh's hilltop, once part of a tropical forest, seemed to have lost many of its birds; Diamond's islands, erstwhile pieces of New Guinea, seemed to have lost many of their birds, too. This demonstrated that the species-area curve applies to almost any area, both men said. And they sounded the Prestonian warning that present-day nature reserves are too small to support the full roster of their flora and fauna.

Fatefully, Diamond extended the argument one crucial step further. Because "many rain forest species cannot persist in other habitats," he noted in 1972, logging those forests "would destroy many of the earth's species." Until then, biologists had thought of island biogeography in terms of *local* extinction, in which a species is extirpated from a given area but does not vanish everywhere else. In Simberloff's chain-saw experiments, for example, extinction was described in terms of a species' absence from a given islet, not from the world. Diamond suggested instead that cutting into a unique habitat like the rain forest would lead to *global* extinctions. Some species would disappear for good.

Diamond derived this conclusion from the hypothetical relation between area and species rather than from empirical data on the prospects of extinction for individual species. This change was revolutionary. In the 1950s and 1960s, ecologists had become aware that many species were getting hard to find, which led them to worry that extinction was on the rise. The plight of some species, like the African elephant and the sperm whale, could be documented. But the state of most biodiversity could not, because most species were unnamed and undiscovered. Scientists who relied on information from known species were thus unable to ascertain most of the effects of a problem that they believed to be real and important. The species-area equation seemed to provide a way to quantify the loss; it was a godsend. Wherever an area A of habitat was reduced or disrupted, the theory said, the number of species S in that area was bound to fall by a predictable amount, even if nobody knew exactly which species would be lost.

The first place that scientists applied this insight was the rain forest, especially that of the Amazon delta. The Amazon, the biggest river on the planet, has the biggest delta—its 2.7 million square miles account for almost 5 percent of the world's land area and about half of its remaining tropical forest. Unlike equatorial areas in Asia and Africa, Amazonia was for the most part untouched by colonial farmers, loggers, builders, and scientists. Only in the 1960s did the Brazilian government actively proclaim its intention to settle the hinterlands. Much as North American governments in the nineteenth century promoted their western frontiers, the military rulers of Brazil subsidized logging, farming, and building in Amazonia. The result was the deforestation of large areas, especially in the savannas. Scientists cried in dismay. Amazonia had represented, in the phrase of historian Ronald A. Foresta, "a nearly clean slate of conservation opportunities." Yet farmers and loggers were being encouraged to plow and axe it out of existence.

In 1974, biologists at a conference sponsored jointly by the Smithsonian Institution and the World Wildlife Fund guessed that clearing the Amazon would wipe out a million species. Five years later, Norman Myers, an ecologist in Oxford and Nairobi, published *The Sinking Ark*, the book that kindled popular awareness of today's biodiversity crisis. He, too, focused on logging in tropical forests, which Myers warned would expunge one species every hour. In 1980, the U.S. Council on Environmental Quality published the *Global 2000 Report to the President*, a catalog of environmental disaster that included an analysis of extinction by Thomas E. Lovejoy, then of the World Wildlife Fund. The Earth, Lovejoy concluded, was likely to lose between 15 and 20 percent of its species by the end of the century. Paul and Anne Ehrlich argued a year later in their book *Extinction* that the exponential increase in world population implied an equally swift rise in deforestation, which in turn meant that almost all species in the tropics would be obliterated by the year 2025. "Someone had better get on with the job [of preventing this awful scenario]," the Ehrlichs admonished, "for *Homo sapiens* is no more immune to the effects of habitat destruction than are the Chimpanzee, Bengal Tiger, Bald Eagle, Snail Darter, or Golden Gladiolus."

Journalists, activists, and even scientists seemed to compete with one another to shout out the newest claim. Twenty percent of all species will vanish by 2011. Extinction will soon claim forty thousand species a year. One million species will be doomed by the end of the century. Or half a million. Or maybe 3 million. In any case, it will soon reach several hundred species a day. It is increasing exponentially. By 2041, 25 percent of the Earth's species will be gone. As many as 20 percent will disappear by 2000. Five species a day. One an hour. Six an hour. Between half a species an hour and twelve. And so on.

The tidal wave of extinction predictions troubled some cautious ecologists, including Simberloff. The claims—strident, inconsistent, often data-free—could not all be true. Indeed, many of them seemed to have been plucked from thin air. Norman Myers was typical. "Let us suppose," he wrote in 1983, "that as a consequence of this manhandling of the environment, the final quarter of this century witnesses the elimination of one million species." Why, one could ask, should people suppose this? Why shouldn't they instead suppose the loss of 100,000 species? Or 1,000? What's to stop them? Lovejoy and Ehrlich had been only slightly more scientific. In *Global 2000*, Lovejoy sketched out a species-area curve that "underestimate[d] the impacts of the projected deforestation." But his curve was no underestimate—a 50 percent decrease in area produced a 33 percent drop in species numbers, not 19 percent as in the usual species-area curve (with a z of 0.3). No explanation was provided for this unusual choice of parameters. Still more tenuous was the Ehrlichs' calculation in *Extinction*. Thick with such words as *assume* and *guess*, it was based on the claim that in deforestation "the diversity of species will be lost more rapidly than the forest itself"—an assumption hard to find elsewhere in the scientific literature, because it is equivalent to saying that z can be greater than 1, which biologists know to be next to impossible. Little wonder Simberloff feared that a serious question would be reduced to slogans and sound bites!

In 1984, he combined a careful assessment of tropical deforestation with a conservative species-area curve, producing the first rigorous projection of the extinction rate in Amazonia. If current deforestation rates continue, Simberloff calculated, almost half the tropical forests in the Americas will be gone by 2000. Applying a conservative species-area curve to this calculation led him to predict the loss of about 12 percent of Amazonian birds and 15 percent of the higher plants within the next hundred years. (He looked at birds and plants because their prevalence is comparatively well known.) These numbers are much smaller than those of Myers, Lovejoy, and the Ehrlichs. Nonetheless, they suggest that conservationists have good cause to worry. Because the Amazon is incredibly diverse, these small percentages add up to a lot of species: 86 birds, 13,819 plants. Since then, others have repeated Simberloff's calculations many times, for many types of organisms, with similarly unpleasant results. Fair enough, Simberloff in effect said. Carefully used, the species-area curve might not actually claim that a full one-quarter of the planet is ablaze, but the loss of biodiversity it predicts is still deeply dismaying.

That didn't mean that biologists like Simberloff were quite ready to endorse the alarmists. Predictions are only as good as the theories used to make them. Carefully applied, astrology can forecast a person's entire life history from a single datum—date of birth—but few scientists pay heed to such prognostications, no matter how carefully they are calculated. As the extinction predictions piled up, some biologists plodded behind, trying to make sure the foundation for these predictions—the species-area curve—was solid. Among them was, unsurprisingly, Simberloff himself.

SIMBERLOFF'S DOUBTS began when he revisited the data from his own chain-saw experiments and concluded that some of the local "extinctions" he had observed were probably the disappearance of a species that had been on the islet only temporarily. This was like seeing robins land on a branch in an apple tree and fly away and then describing the event with the assertion that robins had become extinct in that tree. Simberloff concluded that some real extirpations *had* taken place, and he wasn't entirely wrong. But the whole business was shaky. When he looked back at the dozens of experiments that "tested" the species-area curve, he found that most had merely counted the number of species in areas of different sizes and shown that the results fit it. But these tests had not demonstrated Diamond's claim that shrinking a single area would predictably produce extinctions—a crucial step, if one is going to make claims about extinction on the basis of species-area curves. The results, he told us, "just didn't say what [the researchers] thought they said."

Such concerns prompted Simberloff to ask two graduate students—Edward Connor, now an environmental scientist at the

University of Virginia, in Charlottesville, and Earl D. McCoy, now at the University of South Florida, in Tampa—to pore through the literature on the species-area curve. Their investigation, published in 1979, sprawled across forty-two pages in *The American Naturalist*, an ecological journal. It caused a stir. After sifting through scores of species-area studies, the two men concluded that almost all of them were riddled with faulty assumptions, logical disjunctions, and mathematical errors. "I was a Simberloff student," McCoy told us. "So I had expected to find some problems. What I didn't expect was just how bad so many published, peer-reviewed papers could be."

Central to their appraisal was the way biologists had statistically analyzed their results. Because measurements are always a little inaccurate, they produce a shotgun-scatter of data points, rather than the sort of smooth line found in theories. Researchers use the tools of statistics to compare the imperfect observed data with the perfect theoretical line. When the statistical analysis showed a good fit between the data and the theory, the articles' authors invariably concluded that the species-area equation held true.

Wrong, Connor and McCoy said. The vaunted $S = cA^z$ was merely one of innumerable mathematical formulas capable of expressing a relation between species number and island area. In the dozens of articles they examined, Connor and McCoy found three other formulas, each a different version of the species-area equation, although not many researchers had used them. The two men then asked the statistical question: Of the four equations, which produces the *best* fit between the data and the theoretical line? Extracting the data from the many species-area experiments they had collected, they found that $S = cA^z$ was the statistical winner less than half the time. The other three equations did no better. Predicting extinctions was therefore problematic. For the same loss of area, the four equations would produce different predictions, and an extinction prognosticator would have no way of knowing which, if any, was right. Although these conclusions in no way contradicted the warning that shrinking habitats would produce some extinctions, they cast grave doubt on the practice of casually transforming that warning into an exact prediction.

The complaints did not stop there. A still sharper critique appeared in 1984, this time from the pens of William J. Boecklen, now at New Mexico State University, in Las Cruces, and Nicholas J. Gotelli, now at the University of Vermont, in Burlington. At the time, both were students of Simberloff at Florida State University—one reason they have been called members of a "Tallahassee Mafia." Like Connor and McCoy, Boecklen and Gotelli worried about how their colleagues had handled the inevitable uncertainties in their analysis. These uncertainties introduce an inescapable margin of error. Yet ecologists using the species-area curve rarely reported the extent of this margin—an unfortunate omission, to say the least.

Boecklen and Gotelli demonstrated exactly how unfortunate when they examined a study of nature reserves in East Africa that had alarmed environmentalists when it appeared in 1979. The authors of the study concluded that Nairobi National Park, a forty-five-square-mile reserve just south of Nairobi, the capital of Kenya, would lose almost nine-tenths of its resident species in the next five thousand years, meaning that in the long run all its lions, gazelles, rhinoceroses, giraffes, antelopes, and zebras are doomed, as are most of its hundreds of bird species. Boecklen and Gotelli calculated the margin of error for this scary prediction. It was huge: statistical analysis showed that the scientists could argue only that in the next five thousand years the park would lose between 0.5 and 95.5 percent of its species. Anything at all could happen, in other words. With the restrained language customary in science, Boecklen and Gotelli described this conclusion as "not impressive."

The bigger the extrapolation, they noted, the bigger the margin of error. The extrapolation is enormous when scientists try to use species-area data from tiny mangrove islands in Florida to predict extinction rates in the Amazon rain forest, which is two-thirds the size of the continental United States. "The errors pile up and pile up until they swamp whatever it is you're trying to look at," Boecklen told us. "As a result, you have to be extremely cautious, because you just *don't know* what is going to happen." This lesson, he grumbled, "has yet to sink in."

Worse, these statistical complaints do not even address the question of whether, size notwithstanding, the species-area equation can justifiably be extended from islands to patches of habitat that are not islands. When islands are chopped in half, McCoy pointed out to us, part of the habitat turns into water. Landlubber insects have nowhere to go. Clearing a forest is different. Unless it is paved over, the disturbed area is still full of life. Many species can survive in the cleared zone; some even thrive in it. Those that can't make their way have a chance to escape, because the forest is bounded not by an ocean but by more land, perhaps more forest. The species-area curve, developed with islands in mind, takes no account of this.

All of these shortcomings left Simberloff in two minds about the species-area curve. The man who had claimed in 1974 that "area is usually the best single predictor of species number" was reminding his colleagues in 1986 that "area is a very crude predictor of diversity." Both statements are true, he told us recently. He believed that some credence should be placed in $S = cA^z$ but that nobody could know how much. And until that question is ironed out, he said, "people should be extremely cautious about these predictions, which they sometimes aren't."

The level of caution necessary was underlined in a study by Keith S. Brown, Jr., a biologist at the Universidade Estadual de Campinas, in São Paulo, and his son George, an agronomist at the University of Wisconsin in Madison. They examined the populous Brazilian state of São Paulo, where forests have shrunk to almost one-tenth of their original extent. These forests, they wrote in 1992, "should represent an ideal test to measure the effects of deforestation on species extinction. Island biogeographical theory would predict a loss of about 50% of the species." The Browns compared this prediction with a list of extinct animals recently compiled by the Brazilian Society of Zoology, whose members had long experience in the region. It consisted of six species—two birds and four butterflies. As the Browns noted, one of the birds had been spotted recently by a bird-watcher, and the other could easily have been overlooked because its song is not known; the four butterflies had not been observed for decades, but neither had they been searched for carefully. "Thus," the two scientists wrote,

> the group of zoologists could not find a single known animal spe-
> cies which could be properly declared as extinct, in spite of the
> massive reduction in area and fragmentation of their habitats in the
> past decades and centuries of human activity. . . . Examination of
> the existing data . . . supports the affirmation that little or no spe-
> cies extinction has yet occurred (though some may be in very frag-
> ile persistence) in the Atlantic forests. Indeed, an appreciable
> number of species considered extinct twenty years ago, including
> several birds and six butterflies, have been rediscovered more
> recently.

These results could represent ignorance or a lack of data, the
Browns conceded. But as Brazilian zoologists worked harder to
catalog biodiversity in São Paulo, the trend was *away* from extinction. Scientists turned up species they had thought vanished, reducing the tally of losses.

That same year, Vernon H. Heywood and Simon N. Stuart
tried to check whether the overall extinction spasm predicted for
the world's tropical forests was in progress. Heywood is the
former director of the scientific team that produced the *Flora
Europea*, the definitive taxonomic compilation of European plants,
and the plant officer of the International Union for the Conservation of Nature and Natural Resources (IUCN), a sponsor of the
WCMC; Stuart is the executive officer of the Species Survival
Commission at the IUCN. The two men contacted taxonomists
throughout the world, believing that these researchers, who spe-
cialize in compiling lists of species, would be the most likely to
know about recent extinctions. Despite what Heywood and Stuart
described as "extensive inquiries," they were "unable to obtain
conclusive evidence to support the suggestion that massive extinctions have taken place in recent times."

Taxonomic lists of species are always incomplete, which creates
the possibility that the extinctions are among species yet to be described. But defending the species-area curve by arguing that huge
numbers of mystery species might have slipped away unnoticed
exasperates conservative ecologists like Patrick Kangas of the

University of Maryland, in College Park. Such a defense, Kangas told us, puts scientists in the epistemologically awkward position of postulating the demise of creatures that nobody has ever seen. "You have to ask, how can we go into a deforested area and claim that we know that X number of unknown species were wiped out there?" he said. "Is the proof that those X species aren't there now? But that's absurd. It's like me looking at my emptied bank account and concluding that once millions of dollars were in it."

A second confounding factor is that the extinction effect is not instantaneous, a phenomenon known to biologists as "relaxation." When the São Paulo forests were cut back, according to this notion, few species would have vanished immediately. Instead, the clearing would have knocked the forest out of equilibrium, which set forces into motion that (in theory) commit species to extinction. Eventually, the number of species should "relax" to a new equilibrium level.

How much time do we have before the extinctions kick in? A hint of the answer comes from the work of Jared Diamond, who surveyed islands off tropical New Guinea. These islands had once been peninsulas. Thousands of years ago, the sea rose, cutting off the peninsulas at the base. The new islands had too many bird species. Diamond tried to estimate how long the islands took to reestablish equilibrium—that is, how much time elapsed before the number of birds fell to the level predicted by the species-area curve. For almost all of the islands he studied, the relaxation time was in the realm of ten thousand years; for even the smallest, which he argued should lose species the fastest, it was centuries long. Taken literally, these measurements of relaxation time mean that destroying huge tropical forests will lead to an extinction crisis—one that will reach full flower in many hundreds, perhaps thousands, of years.

Is the extinction crisis, then, a chimera, the figment of some biologists' imagination? The answer is more complex than a simple yes or no. Extinction rates are surely on the rise, but the number of verified disappearances is a tiny fraction of the multitude of species thought to exist. The belief that thousands or millions of extinctions are taking place comes from an equation loosely tied to a theory that is itself controversial. Even if this theory is sound—which it may well be—the species-area curve does not tell us whether the extinctions it predicts will happen immediately after habitat loss, or soon after, or in millennia to come. ("The real mystery is the relaxation rate," Wilson told us.) The available evidence, such as that from the São Paulo forests, suggests that the consequences of habitat transformation may not be felt for a long time. We need much more evidence to believe that the world is in the midst of an immediate extinction crisis.

Is this absence of evidence, then, evidence for the absence of any problem? Is there nothing to worry about? Simberloff doesn't think so; neither do Connor and McCoy, or Heywood and Stuart; nor do any of the other critics of the species-area curve that we contacted. They argue that the threats to biodiversity are real, but that they are not usefully or accurately described by the shrieking predictions derived from $S = cA^z$. Something rather different is taking place, these ecologists suggest, something more subtle, less regular, perhaps equally pernicious, certainly more complex. Understanding the real biodiversity crisis, however, does not require trips to the Amazon or other tropical forests. Important clues can be found in our own backyard.

IN THE MID-1980s, the U.S. Fish and Wildlife Service asked ornithologist Jerome Jackson a momentous question: Is the ivory-billed woodpecker extinct? The biggest woodpecker in North America, it lived in and around big, dying trees in the forests of Cuba and the southeastern United States. Making chunks of wood fly, the bird drove its awl-like bill into these trees, emerging triumphant with a squirming beetle grub. The grubs are large; during a trip to Cuba in 1988 Jackson saw an ivory-bill happily swallowing one at least four inches long. That was the last time he or anyone else is known for certain to have seen an ivory-bill.

Many factors contributed to the bird's decline. To obtain enough food, Jackson estimates, each pair of ivory-bills needed old trees from about four square miles of unlogged forest. Unfortunately, farmers regarded those same big trees as obstacles to this country's agricultural expansion. Forests throughout the South shrank in size until the Second World War; in Florida, the decrease, fueled by the state's perpetual real-estate boom, has yet to stop. Woodpecker habitat vanished. Hunting, too, aided the bird's decline. "They are shot for food," wrote one observer in 1893, "and the people . . . consider them better than ducks!" By 1942 the ivory-bill was so rare that the Audubon Society hired an ornithologist, James T. Tanner, to hunt for it. He spent much of the next three years searching the swamps and forests of eight southern states, eventually traveling more than forty-five thousand miles by car, train, boat, horse, and foot. In the thick, fetid swamps of Louisiana, Tanner sighted a few of the birds; he guessed that still more might be found in Florida swamps. Other than that, nothing. The woodpecker, he said, was making its last stand.

The ivory-bill was one of the first members of the endangered species list. With hopes dimming that the bird still survived, the Fish and Wildlife Service asked Jackson to retrace Tanner's steps in a last-ditch attempt to find the bird. Jackson spent weeks stumbling through the bogs with a tape recording of woodpecker calls. On one expedition, Jackson's assistant thought he heard an ivory-bill respond, but Jackson, who is a little hard of hearing, could not make out the sound; neither ever saw the bird. A cautious scientist, Jackson would not tell Fish and Wildlife to prepare the paperwork for declaring the ivory-bill extinct. "Maybe it was on one side of the swamp while I was on the other side," he told us. "I can't rule that possibility out. But it's functionally extinct, that's for sure."

Fully extinct or only functionally extinct, the ivory-billed woodpecker was a casualty of one of the greatest ecological convulsions in recent history—the clearing of the eastern forest of the United States. When the *Mayflower* landed at Plymouth in 1620, the Puritans disembarked at the edge of a forest of staggering size. It stretched, almost without interruption, from Massachusetts to

Missouri, and from Maine to Florida, an area of almost 600 million acres. The newcomers found it horrible. Accustomed to life in pastoral Britain, the Puritans were repulsed by the vast sweep of American forest—"a hideous and desolate wilderness," in the words of William Bradford, a longtime leader of the Plymouth colony. By godly effort, they intended to transform this tree-choked wasteland into productive farms. Axes aswing, the pioneers set to, marching toward the Mississippi.

They were prodigiously successful. Except for Maine, New England was almost half stripped by 1850; Rhode Island, with almost two-thirds of its trees gone, was the hardest hit. The deforestation was a tide that swept violently across the continent, east to west, Massachusetts to Michigan and beyond. At its height in the 1870s, a greater proportion of the eastern forest disappeared than the world's tropical forests lost during the 1980s. By 1920, almost half the original eastern forest had been logged, put to the plow, or "improved" in some way.

This figure may understate the true impact. Clearing, often carelessly accomplished, led to erosion, pollution, and, especially, forest fires. In the 1880s and 1890s, for example, fire raged uncontrollably through New York, Pennsylvania, Michigan, and Wisconsin, blackening the sky with smoke and leaving hundreds of miles of ruin in its wake. Such disturbances should properly be included in evaluations of the eastern forest, as they are included in discussions of the Amazon delta. So should the edge effect. When people cut forests, the unsettling impacts are not limited to the cut-over area, but reach for hundreds of yards into the remaining forest. Predators from cowbirds to hunters gain entrance. Exotic species of plant infiltrate the border. Trees at the newly cut edge are suddenly exposed to different levels of wind, sun, and precipitation, changing the composition of the forest. All can have malign consequences. Worries about the edge effect led biologists in 1993 to more than double their assessments of the present impact of deforestation in the Amazon. No one can make similar calculations today for the past clearing of the eastern forest, but James C. Greenway, Jr., curator of birds at Harvard's Museum of Comparative Zoology, made the oft-cited claim that during the three centuries after the *Mayflower* Americans disturbed *99 percent* of the land east of the Mississippi.

How should we think about the consequences of this devastation? The standard approach is to use the species-area curve, a task of some effort in the case of the eastern forest. On the right-hand side of the equation, $S = cA^z$, is "area." Before the Europeans arrived, the extent of the eastern forest was about 600 million acres; the high point of eastern deforestation came in the second quarter of this century, when the forest stood at about half its original size. On the left-hand side is the number of "species." Naturalists have inventoried the fauna of North America since 1634, when William Wood celebrated its munificence in his *New England's Prospect*. Birds in particular are well known. At the time the *Mayflower* landed, according to Stuart Pimm, an ecologist at the University of Tennessee, about 160 species of bird lived in the eastern forest.

Using all of these data—amount of original forest, amount of deforestation, number of original bird species—it is possible to predict the number of bird extinctions that should have taken place. But unlike the species-area predictions of extinction in Amazonia, a prediction of extinction in the eastern forest could be tested against reality. The number of bird extinctions there during the past 300 years is well known. The ivory-billed woodpecker is one; here is the rest of the "black list" of eastern forest birds:

- *The passenger pigeon.* That this species could become extinct seems incredible. According to some ornithologists, at the time the Pilgrims landed one out of every four birds in North America was a passenger pigeon. After hunters' indiscriminate slaughter split the big colonies into fragments, this intensely social species produced fewer eggs each year. It rapidly declined; the last bird, Martha, named after Martha Washington, died in the Cincinnati Zoo on September 1, 1914.

- *The Carolina parakeet.* Like the ivory-billed woodpecker, this bird nested in the cypress swamps and other forested wetlands that lined southeastern rivers. Suffering from the loss of those forests, it was also a victim of the nineteenth-century craze for putting colorful feathers on women's hats. The last of these elegant fowl known with certainty to exist was named Incas. Like Martha the pigeon, Incas the parakeet lived in the Cincinnati Zoo, where he died on February 21, 1918.

- *The heath hen.* The heath hen, a subspecies of the prairie chicken, preferred grasslands within the forest. Colonists preferred the same territory, because transforming it into farmland did not involve cutting down and removing a lot of big trees. They also liked the heath hen, which was both tasty and stupid about guns. By the 1870s, it survived only on Martha's Vineyard; after 1929, only a single male remained. It was last seen on March 11, 1932.

- *Bachman's warbler.* Small, yellow-breasted, and olive-backed, Bachman's warbler was probably the most sparsely distributed bird in all of North America. Like the Carolina parakeet, it nested in southeastern river swamps, migrating to Cuba every winter. Forest clearing in both the Southeast and Cuba hastened its demise. Bachman's warbler was last observed by human beings in 1962.

All the elements are in place for testing the species-area equation for the eastern forest. The data are far from perfect, of course. No one knows the exact extent of the original forest or the amount of deforestation. Making more than a rough estimate would require accounting for areas already cleared by Native Americans, natural openings in the middle of otherwise forested land, and other parts of the forest that were long devoid of trees. The tally of original bird species includes some that ranged far across North America, putting them outside the boundaries of the eastern forest "island." Even the black list could be disputed. If extinction predictions are based on habitat loss, as Preston envisioned, why count the passenger pigeon? And why not count other birds that are barely hanging on? It is entirely possible to examine each issue thoroughly—but the entire exercise would be of no value whatsoever for understanding America's biodiversity crisis.

Returning to Preston's original work shows us why. Recall his island-cutting example: Cut an island in half and each species' population will be cut in half, increasing the chances of extinction and eventually driving down the number of species. Note the symmetry, however: half an island, half a population. Preston assumed that species are spread uniformly throughout an area. This assumption, the type often made in mathematical exercises, underlies his species-area curve. Indeed, it is the equation's theoretical keystone. If one takes that assumption away, the mathematics does not come out right. For example, suppose the individuals of one species are not spread uniformly around an island but live, say, on just the southern half. Then dropping the northern half of the island into the ocean will have no effect on that species. Alternatively, if the individuals of a second species live *only* on the northern half, dropping that half into the ocean will produce an instantaneous relaxation effect—drowned across its entire range, the species will vanish immediately. In general, the effect of reducing the area of an island cannot be predicted without detailed knowledge of the habits of each species.

Quibbling in this way with Preston's assumption is not mere pedantry. Members of species are *not* uniformly distributed. Consider the black list of eastern forest birds. Three of its five members—the ivory-billed woodpecker, Carolina parakeet, and Bachman's warbler—lived exclusively south of Pennsylvania. They occupied only one portion of the eastern forest island, as it were. Yet it was another portion—New England and the northern Great Lake states—that was hit hardest by settlers in the eighteenth and nineteenth centuries. Dropping the northern portion of the eastern forest into the ocean, so to speak, had as little effect on these species as wiping out forests in China. (The passenger pigeon was much more widely distributed, but most biologists agree it was lost mainly to hunting, not deforestation; the heath hen, which was also widely distributed, suffered both from hunting and from fire suppression, which turned the openings it preferred back into forest.)

Looking even more carefully, the woodpecker, parakeet, and warbler were distributed throughout only a small fraction of the grand eastern forest, living almost exclusively in bottomland forests and swamps. Suppose Europeans had cleared *only* those bottomlands—the most valuable agricultural land—and presciently replaced them, acre for acre, with new plantings elsewhere. In other words, as they cut down the oak-gum-cypress forest along the banks of rivers such as the Mississippi, Apalachicola, and San-

tee, they planted saplings at the edge of the spruce-fir forest of
Maine, the maple-beech-birch forest of Pennsylvania, and the
aspen-birch forest of Wisconsin. In a Prestonian world, denizens
of the bottomlands would simply follow the forest to new homes
in Maine, Pennsylvania, and Wisconsin; in the long run, the birds
would adjust and be no worse for the journey. But in the real
world, the woodpecker, parakeet, and warbler could not have survived in Maine, Pennsylvania, or Wisconsin. They would still have
died out. Which is to argue the obvious—that these birds were
imperiled by farms and lumber mills in the South, not settlers' activities in Maine, Pennsylvania, or Wisconsin.

The fate of these birds suggests why it makes little sense to
clump geographically and ecologically disparate areas into one
grand "eastern" forest. It makes even less sense in the Amazon
forest, an area that is three times larger and composed of at least
seven major regions with distinct plant associations. Because these
areas are not unitary "islands"—their species marching in lockstep
toward extinction as the habitat shrinks beneath them—the
species–area curve is almost useless as a tool to understand the
plight of biodiversity in such places. And even within any one of
the areas, the amount of knowledge needed to apply the curve
wisely is staggering to contemplate. Species–area practitioners are
thus caught in a Catch-22: the whole purpose of the species–area
curve is to make predictions about places where scientists do not
have detailed knowledge, but the species–area curve is likely to be
of little value in understanding the process of extinction in those
same areas. One is left with the original general relation between
area and species: less area usually means fewer species. The possibility of large-scale extinction is real and important, but at present all we can say is that it may happen sometime if circumstances
don't change.

Worse, extolling these sweeping predictions may impede understanding of the nature of our difficulties with biodiversity as well
as their real solution. The minute we closely examine satellite
maps of Amazonia, we see that people are not nibbling away at the
forest evenly, like a tide, but are scattered in random-looking

clumps throughout the interior (as they are in North America, for that matter, or anywhere else). Some places are being turned into homes, some into farms, some into cities, and some back into forest—it's a jumble in the jungle. As a result, its species face problems more complex than simple extinction. Populations, races, and strains are declining, as well as the connections among them. The losses nibble away at the pool of shared genes that is a species' greatest resource. These multiple small-scale declines—none of which are expressed in the species-area curve—vary widely in scope, form, and place. Their solutions will vary greatly, too, both in their means and their impact on the local human population.

What is true for the tropical forest systems applies with equal force to this country. In the crowded, relentlessly growing strip of California between Los Angeles and San Diego, for instance, housing projects menace at least thirty-five species of animals and fifty-nine plants. But the onslaught of red-tiled roofs, suburban cul-de-sacs, and swimming pools there has little to do with the problems in unpopulous southern Utah, full of national parks and forests, where different threats face the desert tortoise, the Colorado squawfish, the Mexican spotted owl, and the Kanab ambersnail. And neither one of these places has much implication for the west coast of Hawaii, where cattle ranches surround the last flock of 'alala, a crowlike bird found only on the island. Nor do they provide much assistance in fathoming the situation on the Gulf Coast of Florida, where residences for the elderly fill the burrows of gopher tortoises, imperiling both the tortoise and the dozens of invertebrate species that exist only in its tunnels. None of these tell us what to do about the scores of dams and projects associated with the Tennessee Valley Authority, which have pushed more than thirty species and subspecies of mollusks to the edge of nonexistence. Indeed, almost three-quarters of the nation's freshwater mussels are losing out to dams, dredging, pollution, pesticides, and introduced competitors. And on and on.

We face, in sum, not the onrushing, all-destroying wave of extinction described by $S = cA^z$, but an immense aggregation of small, individual situations that is not reducible to a simple equation. These situations are nudging a large (though exactly how large is unknowable) fraction of North American biodiversity down the path toward extinction. Predicting the exact time of arrival is less important than recognizing our direction of travel and that we are picking up speed *now*. In other words, our biodiversity problem is better thought of in terms of endangerment today than extinction tomorrow. Although the latter will surely occur if the former is not controlled, we have time for considered action, not panicky reaction.

This shift of emphasis from extinction to endangerment is "as it should be, in a sense," according to Norman Myers (though he is not a critic of the species-area curve). "Extinction refers to the last one disappearing from Earth," he told us in the course of a long conversation. "That's not what is important, because by the time there's only one or two left, all the damage has already been done. The argument over whether this or that extinction prediction is right bypasses the more complex but more vital observation that major, verifiable destruction of biodiversity is occurring *this minute*. When I knock out a particular part of a tropical forest, I may not be causing any global extinctions—though I would wager that I am—but I am incontestably harming biodiversity. The extinction is dreadful, but the damage to biodiversity is what matters in the end."

Preston's train ride was not in vain. His search for a natural law of species and area helped to produce a generation of ecologists justly alarmed by the encroachment of humankind on the natural world. Nonetheless, his species-area curve—however elegant in theory, however simple in application—cannot help us assess the harm wreaked by that encroachment, nor tell us what we should do in response. These birds here; those lupine flowers over there, and the butterflies that depend on them; the frogs in both places, and the housing developments that threaten them; a mass of separate, unpredictable problems, each case with its own history, causes, possible remedies. A gas station knocks out a population of ants here, an apartment building takes out a group of rare ferns there, a day-care center destroys some bird habitat over here, as does the industrial park next door. . . . Although we scarcely notice these events as they occur, the losses add up, accumulating imperceptibly into a decline in the ecological equality of life.

Over the next century or so, humanity will face a staggering number of small choices, few of them alike, between accomplishing some goal (building a highway to a hospital) and protecting some part of nature (one population of a beetle). Not many will involve anything so dramatic as a certain extinction; most will weigh a tiny bit of harm to a few species against a tiny bit of benefit to a few people. Extinction, if it occurs, will be far off, almost irrelevant, merely putting an official seal on what at some point became inevitable. Yet summed together these Lilliputian choices will represent a fateful decision about how much of the natural world accompanies us on our journey to the future. We may wish to fly over whole continents and make grand claims about global extinction, but we will not truly encompass our predicament until we touch down on individual points in the landscape, the places where butterflies bask and people change their lives in myriad ways as they try to save them.

Chapter Four

UNCOOKING THE FROG

I N MAY 1831, the first steam-powered locomotive in the United States took its inaugural run, chuffing from the city of Albany, on the Hudson River in upstate New York, to the town of Schenectady, sixteen miles to the northwest. The three coaches glowed with celebrities, including Enos T. Throops, governor of New York State; Erastus Corning, one of the railroad's owners and a promoter of industry who was soon to have the city of Corning named after him, along with its famous glassworks; and Stephen Van Rensselaer, member of Congress, founder of the Rensselaer Polytechnic Institute (the nation's first engineering school), and eighth and last Patroon of Rensselaerswyck, a great estate, twenty-four miles long by forty-eight miles broad, that had completely surrounded the site of Albany when it was purchased by his family two centuries before. All three were enthusiastic supporters of the new railroad, which they hoped would bring prosperity to the area in which they lived.

The train left from an improvised station at the intersection of Madison and Western avenues, which at the time stood at the farthest outskirts of Albany. A mile west, the train passed through a long stretch of choppy sand dunes that had been covered by a heavy forest of pine until settlers used the trees for firewood and housing. The open slopes were now carpeted with the splayed and spatulate flowers of the wild eastern blue lupine. The day was bright, and if Throops, Corning, and Van Rensselaer had looked up from their champagne, they might have seen thousands of

Karner Blue butterflies, each not much bigger than a thumbprint, rising from the lupine in a celestial cloud.

Taxonomically, the Karner Blue is a subspecies, *Lycaeides melissa samuelis*. The first part of its common name comes from a now-unused whistle-stop, Karner, near Albany, where the holotype was collected. It is called a Blue not so much because of its color, but because it belongs to a worldwide group of butterflies known as "Blues." Like most Blues, though, *L. m. samuelis* is, in fact, blue; its wings are cobalt, almost violet, on the upper side, and a foggy blue, almost silver, on the underside, with tiny peacock spots running along the bottom edges—the butterfly is a tiny, elegant cobalt-and-silver flash as it dances above the lupine. The fate of the insect is tied to the lupine, for Karner Blue larvae will eat nothing else. For decades, that lupine-covered expanse of sand just west of Albany contained what was apparently one of the world's biggest colonies of Karner Blue butterflies. They *swarmed*, one butterfly-collector claimed, like cicadas.

The fortunes of the west Albany colony began to change in 1888, when two enterprising real-estate speculators announced a plan to convert some abandoned farms near the train station into quarter-acre lots, each with a single home, in which families could escape from the clamor, stench, crime, and disease of the teeming city center three miles away. Advertising in the local newspapers, they claimed that children would not fall sick in these healthful surroundings. The idea of living so far away was slow to catch on, and the speculators went bankrupt in the crash of 1893, their creditors picking up the real estate for a song. When the economy recovered, moving to the outskirts was fashionable. The lots sold briskly, and the newcomers created the neighborhood of Pine Hills. Each home nibbled away at the lupine.

In 1895, another venturesome developer converted a mile-long strip of Washington Avenue, the road just north of Western Avenue, into a racetrack for sulky horses. Albanigensians flocked to the races, and the trolley lines followed. The city extended Washington Avenue through the middle of the lupine patch, and the excited new residents of Pine Hills flooded to the just-opened

Albany Country Club at its end. New streets branched out from Washington Avenue like the ribs of a fish and new houses went up beside them; much of the remaining lupine—and, with it, the butterfly—disappeared beneath the lawns and sidewalks on which a generation of Albany children played. Still, enough survived that in the 1930s Albert C. Frederick, a local butterfly collector, could pluck thirty from the air with a single sweep of his net.

New Yorkers elected crime-busting prosecutor Thomas E. Dewey as governor on a reform ticket in 1942. Operating in a swirl of activity, Dewey announced that he was transferring many state employees to a radiant new state office complex, half a mile on a side, which would eventually contain twelve large buildings arranged about an oval drive—flattening much of the remaining butterfly colony. While the complex was being finished, still more lupine vanished beneath new construction to the north: a Niagara Mohawk power substation and the four blacktop lanes of Interstate Highway 90. When the complex, the highway, and the power substation were finished, the west Albany colony, which once covered some 1,200 acres, was reduced to a few scattered clumps of lupine on the grounds of the Albany Country Club.

Even these did not escape Nelson Rockefeller, who became governor in 1959 and set about transforming sleepy Albany into a metropolis. The country club became the nucleus for the new campus of the State University of New York at Albany. Rockefeller threw up buildings with reckless abandon until he had created a facility for 16,000 students. When he was finished, there was almost no lupine left and only a few Karner Blue butterflies.

By the summer of 1993, when we traveled through this area, we found Karner Blues in towns like Wilton, several miles to the north, and talked with people who had seen them in what is called the Pine Bush, an area several miles to the west—but the west Albany colony was gone. On the university campus, students ran to classes, decorated the grass with their lounging torsos, peered out windows to call friends, put up posters for multicultural events. Next door, police trainees marched about in crinkly new uniforms as state office workers raced to their cars, apparently vying for the privilege of being first in line at the nearby fast-food emporia. Farther down Washington Avenue, we saw churches, schools, houses, apartments, gas stations, convenience stores, video outfits, laundromats, and pizza palaces. We also saw the people who owned and used them: teenagers shooting hoops; retirees sunning themselves on porches; parents negotiating sidewalks with baby carriages; students driving cars with bumper stickers urging Americans to save the rain forest. All had replaced butterflies.

No single monstrous activity eliminated this colony of Karner Blues. Instead, its disappearance was caused by thousands of individual actions, few of them blameworthy regarded in isolation. Bit by bit, average men, women, and children overwhelmed this population of butterflies, slowly burying it beneath the ordinary business of their lives. The process has been repeated throughout the Northeast and Midwest. Karner Blues once inhabited a string of grassy openings that stretched from New Hampshire to Minnesota. Almost everywhere along that string, people moved into those openings, replacing butterflies. In the process, they slowly, almost invisibly, squeezed a grand entomological empire down to a few struggling duchies that are themselves continuing to shrink. Without concerted human effort, the butterfly will almost surely flicker out of existence.

The slide of the Karner Blue is evoked in a parable well known to biologists: the Cooked Frog Problem. Drop a frog in a pot of boiling water, they say, and it will immediately leap free. But put that same frog in a pot of cool water and gradually turn up the heat, and the frog will happily sit and be cooked to death. Each action that we take to threaten biodiversity is equivalent to turning up the heat another notch. A gas station here, an apartment building there, a day-care center over here, an industrial park next door—we scarcely notice them. This one may not pose much of a problem; nor will that one over there, or the one beyond it. But such small losses add up, cooking this part of the species here, then that piece over there, then . . .

No one action can halt the slide of the Karner Blue—can, so to speak, uncook the frog. Instead, its restoration will require hundreds of individual actions, few of them noteworthy regarded in isolation. The next church, or the next day-care center, or the next housing development, or the next gas station—to avoid further harm to the butterfly, each will have to be built in a different place, or in a different way, or not at all. Any one of these projects could be altered or eliminated with relative ease. The necessary human adjustments would range from trivial to serious, but in no individual case would sensibilities be so offended that people might revolt.

But stopping further deterioration might not be satisfactory. Although such measures would probably save *L. m. samuelis* from extinction in the foreseeable future, the butterfly would still be scrabbling for existence in a diminished landscape. In many places, it would survive only in enclosed tracts—butterfly parks. To return the Karner Blue to something like its original status, human beings must actually *improve* its condition, not just avoid further loss. In other words, people would not merely have to alter their future plans, but actually give back some of what they have already taken. Think now about removing some of the parking lots in the state office campus and returning that land to the butterfly. Then do the same thing with some of the homes in Pine Hills, and the Niagara Mohawk power substation, and one or two of the four cloverleaf interchanges along I-90.

Again, each action, taken alone, would not be out of the question. Although the state office workers, deprived of parking, would cry out (as would the owners of the houses, the utility company ratepayers, and the students who commute to the university), the decision to remove these things would not destroy Albany. Yet the losses would slowly add up, just as they added up against the butterfly. Some people would find daily life less convenient and enjoyable; others would have to put off aspirations; still others would lose their jobs, even their homes. If we waved a magic wand and transmuted the university, the office campus, the roads, and the entire neighborhood back into lupine and butterflies, the human disruption would be considerable. Indeed, considering first the efforts to save the Karner Blue in New York, then the efforts to restore the insect's former empire, and then those necessary to do the same for every species endangered today and likely to be endangered in the future, the task of resolving the problem swells to enormous proportions.

It is impossible to enumerate all the changes necessary to reverse the damage we have done to biodiversity, but some indication of their range can be seen in the Karner Blue butterfly. The Karner Blue is not a "typical" organism, but then no organism is typical; it is just one of many imperiled beings, some with greater import to humankind, some with lesser. We had never heard of *L. m. samuelis* before we came across the few pages in the *Federal Register* that granted the butterfly a place on the endangered species list in December 1992. The notice made us wonder why it was in trouble (surely nobody would deliberately harm a pretty blue butterfly) and what saving it might mean for the people nearby (surely most of them had never heard of it). We set out to learn more about the Karner Blue and the measures under way to save it.

EVERY APRIL, Karner Blue caterpillars hatch from reticulated eggs barely larger than grains of sand. Bristly, leaf green, and half an inch long when fully grown, the caterpillars pass the next few weeks munching the leaves of the wild eastern blue lupine (*Lupinus perennis*), a sweet-smelling perennial that is one of about two hundred in its genus. Actually, Karner Blues don't eat lupine so much as *mine* it—they eat out the juicy interior of the leaf, leaving behind the translucent outer cuticle. The result is a thin "windowpane." While eating, the larvae protect themselves from predators with a coterie of bodyguards—a dozen or so species of ant. The ants are attracted to sweet secretions emitted from glands on larval abdomens; gathering to grab a snack, the ants deter attack from other insects. Thus guarded, more Karner Blue caterpillars survive long enough to metamorphose into smooth green chrysalides that resemble exotic nuts.

In late May, the adult butterflies crack open their caskets like miniature Draculas and unfold their blue-violet wings. For ten to fifteen days, they feed on nectar from the flowers of shadbush, blueberry, wild strawberry, and, of course, lupine. Male Karner Blues often flock to draw moisture and minerals from damp sand, the throng forming tremulous azure pools that scientists sometimes call "mud-puddle clubs." After mating, females lay eggs on or near flowering lupine. The eggs hatch in about a week. Like the previous brood, this second brood feeds, pupates, emerges, and mates in the space of a few weeks. Once again, eggs are laid on or near lupine plants, which by this time have finished flowering and are drying up for the year. This second generation of eggs remains dormant until the following spring, when the entire cycle is repeated.

In 1861, when William Saunders of Ontario caught the first example of *L. m. samuelis*, the butterfly had scores of thriving populations from southern Minnesota all the way to New Hampshire and possibly Maine.* In the Midwest, these populations mainly inhabited what are known as oak savannas; farther east, they lived in pine barrens. Both are halfway between open prairie and closed forest: shrubs and trees sprinkled through clearer, grassy patches,

---

L. m. samuelis acquired its name in a roundabout way. Saunders sent his specimen to William Henry Edwards of Philadelphia, who assigned it to the species *Lycaena scudderii*. Succeeding lepidopterists (butterfly specialists) assigned Saunders's specimen and others like it to several genera, though most picked the genus *Lycaeides*. There the matter remained until it was taken up by writer Vladimir Nabokov, an amateur lepidopterist of considerable attainment. In 1941, one of Nabokov's admirers at Harvard University managed to win him a nonpaying curatorial position, unusual for an amateur, at the Harvard Museum of Comparative Zoology. He decided to sort out the North American members of *Lycaeides*, which had been classified in several mutually contradictory schemes. After exhaustive inspection of such minutiae as the shape of male genitalia and the arrangement of wing scales, Nabokov concluded that the many proposed species and subspecies in the genus were really an agglomeration of two species, each with several subspecies. Butterflies like the Karner Blue, he concluded, were not a separate species, *Lycaeides scudderii*. They were really another species, *Lycaeides melissa*, although different enough to be classed as a subspecies, which was later named the Karner Blue, because the holotype came from Karner. The proper scientific name was hard to choose. The butterfly's former name, *scudderii*, honored Samuel H. Scudder, a nineteenth-century entomologist whose many accomplishments included helping to found the Museum of Comparative Zoology. Nabokov, in fact, worked with his collection. To take the butterfly away from him—"my namesake," Scudder had called it—was the height of rudeness. Yet Nabokov was prohibited by the rules of biological nomenclature from reusing an incorrect name. He substituted Scudder's first name instead—hence, *L. m. samuelis*. Although Nabokov was intimately familiar with mounted specimens of *L. m. samuelis*, he had never seen one in flight. Only in 1950 was he able to set out for Karner to rectify that omission. After seeing the butterfly in the wild, he changed his mind, deciding that it was a full species: *L. samuelis*. Many of those who work on the butterfly share this belief, but the name has not been changed officially. Indeed, some lepidopterists have tried to classify it as another genus, *Plebejus*.

a rolling, jumbled landscape that resembles a city park gone to seed. The comparison is unjust, in that these places have beauties of their own, but it is not entirely off the mark, for both ecosystems are in constant ecological upheaval—one reason that Karner Blue colonies always flirt with extinction.

The butterfly's fortunes are tied to lupine, the sole food of the caterpillar. When the eggs hatch, the first thing the tiny grublike larvae do is look for lupine. They die if they cannot find it in a few hours. Without the lupine, in other words, *L. m. samuelis* cannot exist. Thus, wherever the butterfly is found, so, too, is lupine. But lupine itself lives only in certain places: areas recently cleared by fire or some other form of disturbance. Too much shade is its nemesis, as is too much sun; lupine can survive neither the dimness of a deep forest nor the intense heat of the open prairie. Oak savannas and pine barrens, clear of undergrowth but partially shaded by trees, are the perfect compromise. This poses a problem. Except in extreme conditions, open areas do not remain so for long—shrubs and trees rush to fill them in the more or less well-defined sequence called "ecological succession." Because lupine grows at an early stage of succession, it is always being overwhelmed by trees like cherry and dwarf oak, which arrive afterward, during later stages. And because the butterfly depends on this early-stage plant, it, too, is overwhelmed. Day in and day out, ecological succession tries to destroy Karner Blue habitat.

L. m. samuelis would have become extinct long ago if nature marched through the successional stages in lockstep. Indeed, the continents would be covered only by the ultimate or "climax" stages of succession, usually tall forest, which is not Karner-friendly. Fortunately for the butterfly, detours and setbacks from succession are also part of nature. Tornadoes, windstorms, blizzards, landslides—all turn forestland back into open country, or prevent open country from turning into forestland. On the level of the landscape, the result is a rough overall balance, as some areas move up the successional ladder while others are knocked down. On the level of an individual piece of land, though, the rule is perpetual change. A few years or decades of tranquillity may see grasses replaced by a stand of shrubs and trees that in turn may be flattened by a violent thunderstorm, permitting the grass to thrive again. After a while, the shrubs and trees come back—only to be wiped out by a flood. And so on. Different ecosystems are characterized by different types of disturbance: floods in the Mississippi, landslides on the steep pitches of the Andes. Oak savannas and pine barrens are dominated by fire.

In the myth of Prometheus, the gift of fire forever severs humanity from nature. But fire has always played a role in nature, and only recently have humans tried to drive it from the stage. "The earth," wrote the early fire ecologist E. V. Komarek, "born in fire, baptized by lightning, since before life's beginning has been and is, a fire planet." Ignited by lightning, wildfires shuffle the ecological deck, changing the array of plants and animals on the terrain. Because tender new growth rises in its aftermath, fire calls elk, moose, and deer into recently burned areas; because berry plants also expand into those places, fire encourages bears. On the other hand, burning off lichen discourages the caribou that feed on it. Fire benefits some types of insects while hindering others; in turn, bird populations rise and fall. And all of these changes beget still more in the carnivores and raptors that feed on the elk and caribou, the swifts and sparrows. In this way, fire helps regulate ecological character.

Frequent low-intensity blazes keep the ground clear of brush while allowing a sparse overstory of oak or pine to remain—just the conditions needed by lupine. The flames inflict surprisingly little long-term damage on the lupine itself. The plant consists mainly of an extravagant subterranean network of rootlike structures known as "rhizomes," which may penetrate six feet into the soil—astonishing, given that the stalks and leaves above ground are hardly more than ankle height. When fire comes through, the aboveground vegetation is burned off, along with young sprouts and seeds. But the rhizomes of mature plants survive and send up new leaves.

The Karner Blue is another story. Although it depends on fire for its habitat, the butterfly itself cannot survive immolation. Eggs, caterpillars, pupae, and adults, all go up in smoke. The species avoids fiery extinction by existing as a metapopulation—a set of loosely connected subpopulations, or demes, as ecologists call them. The west Albany colony was one deme in a metapopulation that stretched west and north of the city. Fire or succession may snuff out individual demes, but others spring up as lupine sends up new shoots on the disturbed land. The whole business resembles a benign form of musical chairs: one patch of habitat is taken away, but most of the time another patch is added nearby.

For millennia, Native Americans contributed to the ecological game by augmenting the natural supply of fire. To be sure, they had little interest in propagating the butterfly, which has no known food or medicinal value; instead, they used fire for a host of other reasons, which incidentally benefited the Karner Blue. The most important was for hunting. Deer in the Northeast, alligators in the Everglades, bison on the prairies, grasshoppers in the Great Basin, rabbits in California, moose in Alaska—all were pursued by fire. Native Americans made big rings of flame, Thomas Jefferson wrote, "by firing the leaves fallen on the ground, which, gradually forcing animals to the center, they there slaughter them with arrows, darts, and other missiles." Not that they always used fire for strictly utilitarian purposes. At nightfall, tribes in the Rocky Mountains entertained the explorers Meriwether Lewis and William Clark by taking torches to sap-dripping fir trees, which then exploded like Roman candles.

More than a weapon or mode of entertainment, fire allowed Native Americans to shape the environment for their comfort and convenience. Constant burning of undergrowth kept the landscape in the lower stages of succession that produced fodder for the elk, deer, grouse, quail, and other wildlife whose huge numbers so impressed the first Europeans. Annual burning in the dry autumn was common. "Such a fire is a splendid sight when one sails on the [Hudson and Mohawk] rivers at night while the forest is ablaze on both banks," enthused the Dutch colonist Adriaen Van der Donck in 1656. "Fire and flames are seen everywhere and on all sides . . . a delightful scene to look on from afar." But Van der Donck understood what he was seeing. By controlled burning,

Native Americans turned much of the grasslands and open forest of this continent into a vast and exceedingly well managed game farm.

This way of life had enormous ecological impact. To modern eyes, the "hideous and desolate wilderness" that so terrified the Puritans would have looked open and parklike—in many places, carriages could race through the trees unimpeded. Indeed, it was so full of glades and grasslands that creatures of the prairie flourished in its depths, imported eastward along a path of indigenous fire. In Van der Donck's day, bison roamed as far afield as Georgia and New York; the heath hen, actually a type of prairie chicken, bubbled in every pot in the Massachusetts Bay Colony. Two thousand miles to the west, Native Americans had burned the Great Plains so much and so often that they increased its extent; in all probability, a substantial portion of the vast grassland celebrated by cowboys was established and maintained by its first inhabitants.

Did the Karner Blue flourish because of Native American pyrophilia? No conclusive evidence exists, but one can readily believe that thousands of years of human fire helped spread *L. m. samuelis*, one fire zone to the next, all the way from the oak savannas of the Midwest to the Adirondacks and beyond. And there the situation might have remained for millennia if the balance among its metapopulations had not been disrupted by the influx of Europeans.

The butterfly was affected indirectly, its changing fortunes a small by-product of the swift, terrible decline of Native Americans. In addition to the families, animals, and religious customs Europeans deliberately brought to North America, they inadvertently imported measles, cholera, hepatitis, chicken pox, and smallpox. Native Americans had no natural defenses against them and so died in droves. Smallpox was the worst. Its first documented epidemic in North America broke out in the Northeast in 1633–1634. The results were horrifying; in some villages, the fatality rate was 95 percent. During the next few decades, the disease ricocheted back and forth among the tribes of the Northeast and the Great Lakes, killing half the Huron and Iroquois.

Eighteenth-century outbreaks wiped out huge numbers of Chero-
kees in eastern Tennessee and Catawbas in the Carolinas; later,
equally horrific epidemics followed the European push westward.
The devastation transformed North America into an ossuary, allowing the newcomers to conquer a continent with little resistance.
Indeed, many New England settlements arose on the sites of indigenous villages emptied by disease.

Because humans were a major ecological factor in North America, their removal did not create a wilderness, in the sense of a
place untrammeled by the presence of humanity. Wilderness has
not existed in North America for at least ten thousand years; the
idea that people are not part of the ecological picture, fire historian Stephen Pyne told us, "is itself a human artifact"—a cultural
myth. The loss of the Native Americans created the same kind of
environmental upheaval that would be created by the removal of
any other vital ecological component. In areas previously kept
open by human fire, the open, parklike character of the forest disappeared within several decades; eighteenth- and nineteenth-
century settlers pushed into an eastern forest that was increasingly
choked and impassable. Indeed, the junglelike "forest primeval"
celebrated by Romantic poets and painted by members of the
Hudson River school was created by their grandfathers' largely ac-
cidental genocide of Native Americans. An unnoticed detail in this
vast eco-convulsion was the probable decline of many Karner Blue
demes, casualties of the loss of open space brought about by the
disappearance of the indigenous peoples.

As European numbers grew, abandoned native villages became
too small for the colonists' needs, and the new stands of the eastern forest began to fall. In these days of chain saws, hydroaxes,
and bulldozers, it is difficult to appreciate how hard it was for
newly arrived European immigrants to clear the land with saws,
axes, and shovels. A typical farm family could strip perhaps fifteen
acres in a year of unremitting labor. That only began the work.
The wood had to be disposed of and the stumps removed before
the land was fully arable, tasks that soaked up labor and time. And
still the trees surrounded them. Each colonist's home in the Midwest, recalled a nineteenth-century pioneer in Bloomfield, Ohio,

was "in the center of a small opening or clearing like an island in the midst of a vast ocean of dark forest."

In slow bits and pieces, the clearing accumulated, until perhaps half the forest was gone. The ecological effects of this change were complex and hard to measure. Some forest species were certainly hurt, and a few became extinct. Others, like the Karner Blue, may have benefited. Deforestation offered additional open space to wild lupine, thus creating additional habitat for *L. m. samuelis*. Like the Native Americans whose places they usurped, many early settlers kept these spaces open with fire.

That didn't last. As more and more land turned into real estate, people stopped viewing fire as a tool for land management and instead regarded it as a danger that had to be strictly controlled. New York passed its first fire code as early as 1743, empowering the inhabitants of certain counties to compel their neighbors to help stamp out fires. As the twentieth century dawned, the frontier disappeared, pseudopods of suburbia extended from cities, and the U.S. Forest Service took the offensive against forest fires. Hit both by permanent conversion to human use and the suppression of fire, oak savannas and pine barrens as a whole became two of the most threatened ecosystems in the United States. Oak savanna once covered 45,000 square miles of the Midwest, according to one frequently cited study; today, it has shrunk to less than 10 square miles—a loss of 99.98 percent. About half the pine barrens have disappeared for similar reasons, although the losses have never been measured precisely.

After the near-total loss of its ecosystem, the Karner Blue was left with scattered patches of lupine that cropped up after some form of disturbance. A developer would bulldoze a small lot, or a work crew would clear a railroad right-of-way, or farmers would burn their trash and, inadvertently, a few neighboring acres: in places like these, lupine could persist for a few years, and with it, small groups of butterflies. But the dynamics of its far-flung metapopulations were broken. Without a constant source of disturbance, anathema to modern civilization, a deme would wink out and not be replaced. The metapopulations shrank, disappearing completely in some areas, barely hanging on in others.

Today, the cumulative effect of cooking the butterfly for the past seventy-five years is clearly visible. Not many Karner Blues survive in Minnesota. Wisconsin and Michigan are home to dozens of small, fragmented populations, most with fewer than a hundred butterflies. Indiana has but a single strong population left; Illinois may still have a straggler or two; Ohio lost the last of its Karner Blues by 1990 at the latest. The butterfly still hangs on in New Hampshire. New York contains several scattered populations, one of them fairly sizable, all actively monitored. Because New York is probably the leader in Karner Blue protection, it was the first place we visited to learn about how its human neighbors are now trying to save it, and the impact on them of their effort.

FOR THE TOWN of Wilton, New York, the spring of 1993 was one of the wettest on record. As a consequence, the mosquito crop that summer was one of the biggest on record. Wilton, in the upper Hudson River Valley, is one freeway exit north of its famous neighbor, Saratoga Springs, a high-society playground for almost two centuries. Full of parks, mineral springs, and Greek Revival mansions, site of a celebrated racetrack, summer home of the New York City Ballet and the Saratoga Music Festival, Saratoga Springs attracted so many urban refugees in the 1960s and 1970s that it spun off several minisuburbs, Wilton among them. What had once been a collection of farms was revamped into a place with addresses like Hopeful Road, Nonchalant Drive, and Ho Hum Lane. Fresh from urban life, the newcomers were thrilled by the prospect of such country-based activities as barbecuing in their spacious yards. One pictures a family buying a home in October, enduring the cold winter of upstate New York, doffing their parkas on the first sunny days of spring, and stepping outside into—a cloud of mosquitoes. Wilton is home base for a world-class squadron of midges, blackflies, mosquitoes, and other noxious insects. By 1979, the outcry was loud enough that the town supervisors hired airplanes to spray every square inch of inhabited land with pesticides.

That was the plan for 1993, too, until the town planning board received a letter and a set of maps from the New York State Department of Environmental Conservation. The maps marked off more than two dozen Treatment Exclusion Zones, ranging in size from less than an acre to more than 194. Each zone contained patches of wild eastern blue lupine—and Karner Blue butterflies. Under the authority of the state endangered species act, the department banned spraying in these areas between April 1 and August 15. April to August being insect season, Wilton town supervisor Roy J. McDonald was apoplectic. "They should start thinking about people for a change," he told the Schenectady *Gazette*. The sites were in places ranging from the back edge of an automobile-compacting facility in the northeast corner of town to a vacant yard in a half-complete housing tract in the southwest corner. Protecting the Karner Blue, McDonald protested, would mean abandoning a large part of Wilton to blackflies and mosquitoes.

The Department of Environmental Conservation held fast. Wilton used an all-purpose insecticide named Scourge; its chief active ingredient, resmethrin, is used to control gypsy moths. Because Karner Blues belong to the same order (Lepidoptera), they could be vulnerable to Scourge. Widespread spraying, the agency said, was not acceptable.

Wilton had sprayed for years and not managed to kill off the butterfly, McDonald argued. Now the town was being ordered to stop during the worst bug outbreak in decades. Find another way, the agency said.

Tempers frayed. Town councilmember John Cannone received angry calls at his deli from constituents who had the misfortune to live near patches of lupine. "I'm going to take my lawn mower to the stuff," they said. Or: "I'm going to spray those plants with Agent Orange and end this once and for all." Rumors flew that developers were pulling back on projects needed for the town tax base, that the local Boy Scout camp had canceled plans to sell its property to raise money for charity, that the tidal wave of blood-drinking insects would drown Wilton in awful diseases like equine encephalitis and even AIDS. To calm the citizenry, McDonald asked the agency to attend a town meeting about Scourge on the evening of June 2, 1993. This turned out to be a mistake.

More than two hundred Wiltonites showed up, few in a conciliatory mood. The room was too small for the meeting and the temperature rose high enough that doors and windows had to be opened. Mosquitoes poured in. The walls echoed with the wet smack of hands slapping skin. Laura Sommers, a biologist at the Department of Environmental Conservation, had thought she was there to explain the spraying ban. Instead, she found herself functioning as a target of abuse, her answers drowned by shouts and heckles. Sommers, a shy woman, responded stiffly, leading audience members to conclude that she was condescending to them. Laughter erupted each time she swatted at a mosquito. But their derision did no good. Although the state compromised on the method of spraying, it remained adamant on the central point: No Scourge in the Treatment Exclusion Zones.

For Wilton, living with mosquitoes is part of the effort to save the Karner Blue. In an attempt to stop the butterfly's slide toward extinction, Wilton and other communities in Albany, Saratoga, and Warren counties are changing the way they live. Most of the changes are small, inexpensive, and voluntary; sometimes, though, they are big and expensive and have been compelled by lawsuits and government edicts. These communities are engaged in an experiment of sorts. They are learning firsthand how they can, as it were, uncook a small part of the butterfly.

The three counties are located at the northern edge of the Hudson Valley. Thousands of years ago, this land was covered by a prehistoric lake. It disappeared, leaving behind the collection of beaches and sandy bottomland known as the Hudson Valley Sand Belt. Atop the sand rose a pine barrens: sand dunes thick with grasses and lupine, dotted with pitch pines and scrub oaks; between the dunes, bogs filled with cranberries, larches—and mosquitoes, the bane of the pine barrens. Relics of twenty-two such areas exist in the Northeast. The Hudson Valley Sand Belt contains three: the Glens Falls Sand Plain, the northernmost; the Saratoga Sand Belt to its south, which contains Wilton; and the

Albany Pine Bush, south and west of the other two, stretched between Albany and Schenectady.

Covering forty square miles, the Pine Bush was the biggest continuous stretch of inland pine barrens in North America. It holds a special place in Karner Blue lore, for within it was Karner, the type locality for *L. m. samuelis*. Before white settlers arrived, the Pine Bush was regularly burned by the local Mohawks. As a result, the first European colonists—Dutch farmers, who set up Fort Orange, the ancestor of today's Albany, in 1624—thought that the Pine Bush resembled a European public garden, with meadows interspersed by shrubbery and a few trees. Because this was an ideal environment for lupine, one imagines that in the late spring the Dutch walked through a Pine Bush that held a thriving metapopulation of Karner Blues. (No butterfly-collecting records exist, but the idea seems plausible.) Smallpox destroyed the Mohawks in 1633. Within a century, the Pine Bush was thickly treed. Again, no records exist, but it seems likely that the butterfly went into severe decline—lupine cannot survive in a closed forest. Fortunately for the local Karner Blues, they were rescued by the inhabitants of Albany, who needed fuel and timber. Colonists stripped bare the forest at the edge of town, re-creating Karner-friendly conditions and thereby almost certainly engendering the hordes of butterflies in the west Albany deme.

The rest of the Pine Bush followed a similar path, although a little more slowly. A glass factory appeared near Karner in 1786 and gulped down sand and wood. By the turn of the century, Albany had become the state capital and the remaining Pine Bush forest had been logged over and abandoned. The butterfly handily survived the logging, which reopened the forest. In the early nineteenth century, naturalists reported huge swathes of lupine in the cleared areas; by the 1860s, the Pine Bush had become the most famous insect-collecting ground in the northern United States. Entomologists discovered more than seventy species there, including the Karner Blue. In 1869, Joseph A. Lintner, later to become the official New York State entomologist, observed that the butterfly "abounded in flocks" in the barrens west of Albany.

Humans in the twentieth century have not been as kind to the

Karner Blue. Since the 1920s, when Albert C. Frederick caught thirty with a single sweep of his net, people have besieged the Pine Bush. They hit the west Albany deme of the Karner Blue first and hardest, but the rest of the metapopulation did not fare much better. Close to the freeway between two major towns, its sandy soil easy and cheap to build upon, the Pine Bush was readily converted to suburban homes. By the 1960s, its forty square miles had shrunk to about four. Most of the remainder was in an irregular three-thousand-acre parcel that was, by coincidence, just beyond the west Albany deme, northwest of the university campus. A few hundred acres of this land had been set aside as a preserve. It contained the remaining bits of the Pine Bush metapopulation of *L. m. samuelis*, which was rapidly dwindling in size.

Just when things looked darkest, the metapopulation acquired several champions. The first was James Cane, an energetic high school senior who was the secretary of an insect club run by the curator of entomology at the New York State Museum in Albany. Learning at his club of the butterfly's decline, Cane wrote in 1973 to the Xerces Society, a new organization dedicated to the conservation of invertebrates. (The name comes from the Xerces Blue, the first butterfly known to have become extinct in North America.) One of its early members was Robert Dirig, then working at Cornell. Jo Brewer, co-founder of the Xerces Society, asked Dirig to write a memorandum about *L. m. samuelis* and talk to Cane's insect club. Dirig had never seen a live member of the species he was supposedly describing. One month before his lecture, he visited the Pine Bush for the first time. It was an amazing sight, Dirig told us. About one-third of the area was afire. The rest was overwhelmed by dirt bikers, snarling over the dunes in giddy sprays of sand. Dirig didn't find any butterflies, though. The season was still early, he learned afterward. He also didn't know where to look. But part of the reason for his failure to observe the Karner Blue was that the butterfly was almost gone.

In 1975, the Albany City Council announced plans to rezone the eastern half of the remaining Pine Bush for immediate development. Dirig enlisted the Xerces Society for a fight. Five lepidopterists were among the thirty-nine witnesses who testified against rezoning at a public meeting. More important, Dirig joined forces with Don Rittner, the city archaeologist, who was friendly with Erastus Corning, Albany's powerful mayor and a descendant of the Erastus Corning who rode on the first steam train. After listening to Rittner's pleas, Corning informally awarded most of the southern half of the contested land to an industrial park and promised to set aside much of the northern half, where most of the butterflies lived. "He did the Solomon thing," explained Dirig's friend and Pine Bush coworker John Cryan, then an undergraduate at Cornell. "He cut the baby in half. But that didn't stop it. The development pressures kept coming."

Plans emerged the next year to build a shopping mall in a 165-acre tract in the southeast corner of the Pine Bush, a small area that Corning supposedly had not awarded to developers. The shopping-mall builders pledged to set aside a few acres for the butterfly, along with a trust fund to manage it. *"Great,"* Cryan said to us, sardonically summing up his reaction to this offer. "What you really need is thousands of acres for this shifting population, and they promise to put a fence around part of a dune and destroy a hundred and fifty acres of land that could be recovered." Despite his opposition, the Crossgates Mall went in anyway, burying two small butterfly demes beneath a twelveplex movie theater, more than a hundred stores, and acres of asphalt. The mall created a butterfly reserve on three and a half acres of potential parking space.

More developers filed more plans, many in the northern half of the Pine Bush, which Cryan, Rittner, and the other activists had thought Corning's informal arrangement would protect. They went to court in 1985. The suit sought to void the zoning scheme for the area because it did not consider the cumulative impact of all the proposed development, as required by law. In Cryan's view, plans had to take into account what he called "the minimum-area question": What is the minimum acreage—and the configuration and location of that acreage—required to preserve the Pine Bush ecosystem and the Karner Blue butterfly? To provide an answer, Cryan turned to the species-area curve, which he had studied at

Cornell. The Pine Bush had lost about 90 percent of its original area. Using his version of a species-area curve, Cryan predicted that the reduction in area would induce the loss of about half of the species in that area. Although no strong evidence showed that this had yet occurred, Cryan believed that the message was clear: any further loss would push the Pine Bush over the edge. Development had to stop. Immediately.

The city council did not agree. The Pine Bush was the last large undeveloped parcel of Albany. Closing it to builders would eliminate a sizable chunk of tax revenues, a big concern to a small city scrambling to pay for schools, libraries, hospitals, and roads. As important to the city was the need to extend its landfill—right into the east side of the Pine Bush. The subsequent clash involved a skein of trials that the city lost at every turn, appealing and losing, appealing and losing, well into the 1990s.

To disentangle itself from some of the lawsuits and save its landfill, the city government agreed to come up with a plan that would address the minimum-area question, thereby perhaps saving the butterfly and the Pine Bush. It handed the task to a team of three biologists experienced in such matters. Although they attacked Cryan's use of the species-area curve, their conclusions were similar. To preserve the species in the Pine Bush, they said, at least two thousand acres would have to be set aside. Because the existing park and reserve was considerably smaller than that, the city was going to have to start buying land. Mere acquisition would not do the job, though. The undeveloped part of the Pine Bush was now so thick with brush and trees that it would have to be burned repeatedly. But setting big fires at the edge of a crowded city is no easy task, legally or politically.

Accepting the biologists' recommendations, the state legislature established the Albany Pine Bush Commission in 1988 to create and manage a new Albany Pine Bush Preserve, financed through a combination of city, county, state, and private funds. The law also gave the commission special permission to burn the Pine Bush. By the fall of 1994, the preserve had grown to more than 2,100 acres, three-quarters of which was potential pine barren. Several hundred more acres needed to be purchased to meet the commission's final goal: 2,000 acres of ecologically healthy pine barrens surrounded by several hundred acres of buffer land.

Five burns have taken place since 1991, each supervised by Stephanie Gebauer, director of research and management for the preserve. The first covered nine acres; each succeeding burn covered a little more area, with the 1994 fire spread across 107 acres. The preserve is surrounded by houses, and Gebauer has spent a lot of time explaining the program to their occupants. Some were horrified by the thought of forest fires in their backyards; others sat in lawn chairs to watch the burns, as thrilled by the spectacle of smoke and fire as the Dutch traders who sailed up the Hudson. "On one burn," Gebauer told us, "we had two little kids run out with buckets of water. The fire people stopped them before they could hurt themselves." One local resident, an antismoking and antipollution activist, has turned her attention to the Pine Bush burning program. "She'll probably end up suing us," Gebauer ruefully admitted.

Alas, the new Pine Bush preserve took so long to establish that in 1994 it contained only two tiny clusters of *L. m. samuelis*, one of which appeared to be in rapid decline. Just outside the preserve were two more, one of which seemed on the upswing. Gebauer hoped to raise enough money to buy the property, which off-road vehicle enthusiasts had kept in a disturbed state, enabling the lupine to flourish. In 1994, it hosted eighty-three Karner Blues.

The center of the remaining metapopulation is to the north, in the Saratoga Sand Belt, where a study in 1992 identified thirty-four colonies. Between the runways at the Saratoga County airport, for example, Cryan and Dirig discovered in 1975 one of the most thickly populated Karner Blue territories in the world. The airport had long mowed the grass bordering runways to prevent fire. Because thermoses and lunch boxes sometimes fell off the mowers, workers kept the blades high to avoid destroying them. Over the years, this practice inadvertently encouraged the growth of lupine, creating by artificial means a butterfly colony of several thousand. When approached by the Department of Environmental Conservation in the mid-1980s, Saratoga County quickly agreed to stop mowing the grass during butterfly season. The airport usually did not mow then, so the agreement had little practical impact. Still, workers grumbled when forced to use Weedwackers instead of much faster mowers to trim the grass around the runway lights.

In Warren County, at the northernmost tip of the Sand Belt, the city of Queensbury encountered the butterfly on property intended for a new police station. As with the airport, the Department of Environmental Conservation asked the town to protect the lupine. Mowing seasons, blade height, a ban on dumping snow (the icy cover might not melt in time)—the conditions seemed simple enough. But after a recent election shuffled the town officialdom, talks stalled, leaving the butterfly's fate in the balance. A few miles north of the Pine Bush, surveys turned up lupine on a proposed office complex in the town of Clifton Park. The developer, DCG Development, agreed to set aside the lupine-growing part of the property, about 3 of its 140 acres.

Just up the freeway in Wilton, home of the Treatment Exclusion Zones, negotiations continued with property owners. One, Marcel Zucchino of Encore Electronics, a manufacturer of electronic components, agreed to tend the lupine in his factory's backyard; but the owners of Johnson's Auto Crushers, a nearby junkyard, were unenthusiastic enough to refuse to speak with us. (We did peek into the lupine area, though, and noticed that workers had apparently stopped dumping tires there.)

Meanwhile, the squabble over Scourge continued, albeit at lower intensity. Wilton town councilmember Cannone received fewer complaints from people in the Treatment Exclusion Zones in 1994, even though it was another banner year for bugs. Part of the reason, he told us, was that Wilton was now spraying mosquito larvae in those areas with a bacterial agent called Vectabac. (The town used Scourge everywhere else.) But another reason for the reduced volume of complaints, he said, was that "people have learned that it's pointless to yell at us—we're not the ones responsible." Spraying costs have risen about 20 percent with the new regime, he estimated. "It's more time-consuming and involves more legwork and more effort, but it's not that bad. If we're involved in saving the butterfly, that's what we have to do, I guess."

A county official showed us around the local Boy Scout camp, a butterfly zone. Campers had fenced off the lupine patches and erected warning signs. The national council of the Boy Scouts thought Camp Saratoga was underused, our guide said. It wanted to sell the land and use the proceeds to benefit urban children. Our guide opposed the plan. He was happy that the Karner Blue lived on the grounds, because its presence seemed likely to impede the sale. A mile outside Camp Saratoga, he stopped his truck and took us to a butterfly area that someone—he asked us not to repeat any names, including his—hoped to develop. Two Karner Blues fluttered by. The official tried to catch them in his cupped hands. "Missed," he said. "[The owner]'s fit to be tied. He's trying to figure out what to do." And so the process continues, a chain of negotiations, surveys, and compromises that will subtly but permanently alter the shape of human activity in this part of upstate New York. And not just there, either. The consequences of saving the Karner Blue are accumulating in a band of North America more than a thousand miles across. Here are some of them:

One metapopulation in New Hampshire is struggling to survive in a pine barrens near Concord. The butterflies are split between two small sites near the Merrimack River, one beneath a power line, the other at the Concord municipal airport. The Nature Conservancy, the big private land trust, is one of several groups trying to link the two groups of butterflies by securing the acreage between them. A thin, mile-long corridor of cleared land, the property is split into three lots. In January 1992, Fish and Wildlife agreed to buy a conservation easement from the owner of one lot, protecting it from development. But the other two lots are owned by a nearby industrial park, which may expand. In addition, they are divided by Regional Drive, a paved road that could be a significant barrier to the Karner Blues. In 1983, entomologist Dale Schweitzer examined the Karner Blues in New Hampshire, determining that for reasons unknown they are apparently unwilling to fly over roads. (Karner Blues elsewhere are not afraid to do this.) "If they don't cross the road," said David Van Luven of the local chapter of The Nature Conservancy, "we'll have to do manual movement"—that is, carrying the butterflies across the asphalt. It was possible, he said, that their observed unwillingness a decade ago was a fluke. "Maybe they'll do it now," he said in a voice that suggested crossed fingers.

In Indiana, the butterfly has a stronghold in the Indiana Dunes National Lakeshore, on the shore of Lake Michigan between Gary and Chicago. A packet of sand dunes mixed with bogs and marshes, the park is, according to Schweitzer, the "most natural setting anywhere in the world to support a large [Karner Blue] population." With controlled burning, Schweitzer believes that it can stay that way. The adjacent Midwest Steel plant also has butterflies on its land. When the company sought in 1992 to expand a landfill on its property, surveys—required for properties that might harbor endangered species—turned up a single Karner Blue. A second survey found more than a thousand eggs on dead lupine stems. Because moving waste off-site would cost up to $1 million per month, Midwest Steel moved the butterfly. Workers dug up more than 1,600 of the deeply rooted lupine plants with a stump-puller and transplanted them to a new site, where a special lupine irrigation system had been installed. The company also planted more than 3,200 nursery lupine plants and sowed about 8,000 lupine seeds. Overall, the move cost about $1.5 million— money Midwest Steel was glad to spend, given the alternatives. About 60 percent of the plants survived to the spring of 1994, as well as dozens of Karner Blues.*

Although Wisconsin has more Karner Blue locations than any other state, biologists were unable to find more than ten butterflies in half of them during recent surveys. Without active manage-

---

*The experience of Midwest Steel is an example of what is known as a formal consultation. The Endangered Species Act requires federal agencies to consult with the Fish and Wildlife Service when a federal project affects an endangered species. Midwest Steel needed a permit from the Environmental Protection Agency to expand its landfill. In the eyes of the law, granting that permit is in itself a federal project. The EPA had to consult with Fish and Wildlife, which suggested the lupine-moving operation. Few such consultations result in the outright cancellation of a project, a record often cited as evidence that accommodating endangered species' needs will not be expensive. But even successful consultations come at a price, as the $1.5 million spent by Midwest Steel demonstrates. And the lack of cancellations may, as some suggest, be better regarded as evidence that the agency is not demanding enough protection for listed species.

ment, the small sites will dwindle rapidly. The larger ones, on the other hand, can support functioning metapopulations. The most important of these is the ninety-three-square-mile Fort McCoy military training facility, run by the U.S. Army. In 1991, Mark Leach, a graduate student at the University of Wisconsin, observed more than a thousand Karner Blues and fifty-seven patches of lupine there. A military base may be the perfect place for humans and lupine to coexist. Artillery practice sets off occasional fires; tank practice, a grinding, crushing occupation, also clears away brush and small trees. Because the butterfly cannot survive a close encounter with a tank, Fish and Wildlife has not yet agreed to let the army manage its butterflies with mechanized artillery. "We have areas of lupine identified," base spokesman Marv Clark told us. "There are signs around the areas saying what they are. They aren't exactly fenced off, but you can't go in there." We asked what would happen to the butterfly if the base was closed during the conversion to a peacetime economy. "I never thought of that," he said. "From what they tell me, I guess this place would be deep forest in ten years."

That's not all. A game reserve in Michigan that needs burning, a beach park in Illinois partly closed in the summer—the list of confluences between humans and Karner Blues runs on and on. Every time we picked up the phone and made another call to Wisconsin or Ohio or New York, it seemed, we stumbled onto another butterfly story. None were earth-shattering, but no matter *where* we looked, there was always another butterfly story. Track them all down, and one would have a complete picture of all that has endangered *L. m. samuelis* and all that must give way if that endangerment is to stop.

Added together, the present efforts to save the Karner Blue from extinction will not bankrupt society. But neither will the cost be small enough to be borne without a second thought. Even so, these efforts will only present the butterfly with a better chance of hanging on in its present, greatly debilitated state. They will not bring it back to where it was at the time of the Mohawks, let alone its plenitude a century ago, at the height of eastern deforestation. The butterfly is a completely different creature now. To restore it to full ecological health requires returning some of what we've taken—a complicated business indeed.

O N E D A Y in Albany, we were escorted to the butterfly reserve at the Crossgates Mall by Laura Sommers, the biologist who had been denounced in Wilton. We parked behind the Caldor store and walked along a sandy trail beneath some power lines. Knapweed grew thickly along the trail. The knapweed, which drives out lupine, was the lichenous color of an old plastic toy soldier; waves of it lapped up against the fence that enclosed the butterfly area. Every few hours, uniformed security guards patrol the perimeter. Sommers unlocked a gate and we walked up the most open, least tree-choked sand dune we had seen anywhere near Albany. Crickets leapt from their roosts at our feet.

To the surprise of everyone, the site has retained a healthy, if crowded, colony of Karner Blues. The dune is quite steep on the side of the reserve facing the Caldor store. Aspen and sumac rustle at the peak, perhaps eighty feet above the surrounding terrain. A vista of black asphalt rewards those who climb to the top. Traffic makes a constant low rushing sound. Here *L. m. samuelis* lives on an island of sand surrounded by a fence, which in turn is surrounded by a pool of blacktop, which is in turn surrounded by a sea of humanity. It is trapped as effectively as if it were in a zoo.

This reserve will never be managed with controlled burns—it is too small, and a fire would likely kill all the butterflies. To keep the area open, the mall hires people to cut trees, mow invading weeds, and feed brush into a whirling, chewing machine called a "brush hog." To judge by a casual visit, they do a good job. But to maintain this population of Karner Blues, they will have to do that good job forever. *Forever* is a sobering thought. A store in the mall advertised trinkets from the television series *Star Trek: The Next Generation*. The show takes place in the twenty-fourth century. *Forever* means that even as the starship *Enterprise* warps through interstellar space, a shopping mall in Albany, New York, will be hiring people to cut down aspen and knapweed. A distant descendant of today's security guard will patrol the fence.

This prospect seems absurd to people like John Cryan, the Pine Bush activist. Even the much larger Albany Pine Bush Preserve, a few miles to the northwest, will depend on people like Stephanie Gebauer for centuries to come. "That's not saving a species," Cryan said to us. The butterfly would be alive, he conceded. But it would be like a patient kept alive for years in an intensive-care unit, too sick ever to leave. "Something like that," he said, "is not why Bob Dirig and I fought to save the Karner Blue butterfly. That's not why we filed suit—to have it preserved as a captive species on a little island surrounded by asphalt."

Species are not truly safe from extinction, biologists say, unless they are part of an ecosystem that is free to operate by its own rules. In the case of the Albany Pine Bush, that means expanding the preserve enough to handle big natural fires. Ten to twenty thousand acres would be necessary, according to Thomas Givnish of the University of Wisconsin–Madison, one of the three biologists whose recommendations were behind the establishment of the preserve. In Albany, such a reserve could not be assembled without displacing roads, stores, parking lots, industrial facilities, and housing developments—one reason that Givnish did not advocate it. But he emphasized that the current preserve, created after such struggle, is not really big enough.

Moreover, Givnish told us, one reserve, no matter how large, "will not cut it." The butterfly, he said, "occupies a narrow climatic belt from Minnesota to New Hampshire that's only a couple hundred miles wide from north to south. That means that large portions of the range of the butterfly are near its limits, where the physical or biological conditions will often be inhospitable. It's always getting wiped out at any individual place. So it would be foolhardy if one was planning for the global persistence of the species to depend on the Albany Pine Bush. You might get a once-in-a-millennium fire or have the local deer herd get out of control and munch down the lupine plants. There's all sorts of things that could happen." To avoid putting all the butterfly eggs in one basket, he said, the Karner Blue needs a series of big reserves. Four or five, Givnish thought, would do the trick. The total might run as high as 100,000 acres—about 150 square miles.

How much would such a reserve cost? No one can give an exact answer, because the cost would depend on a host of variables that are difficult to specify, including the location of the land, the real estate market at the time, the willingness of owners to sell their property, and the amount of public land that might be converted to the reserve. Suppose, though, that half the reserve comes from property that is already in a park or national forest—an extremely generous assumption, given the relatively small amount of pine barrens that are now protected in this way. That leaves government to acquire fifty thousand suitable acres somewhere between Wisconsin and New York. We called assessors in areas that might have suitable habitat, like Monroe County, Wisconsin, which contains the military base; St. Joseph County, Indiana, east of the Indiana Dunes National Lakeshore but far from costly Chicago and Gary; and Rensselaer County, New York, on the other, less-developed side of the Hudson River from Albany. None had large tracts of completely undeveloped land, but Rensselaer County had the cheapest abandoned farmland—about three thousand dollars an acre at the time that we called, according to William Film of the Rensselaer County Clerk's Office. Buying fifty thousand acres of such land would cost $150 million. "That's rock bottom," Film said, "if you can find it. Farmland in the Midwest is twenty times more expensive."

Even that might not be enough. Past taxonomists had trouble classifying the Karner Blue because it differs subtly in coloring and behavior from east to west. Those differences are linked to the slightly different genetic information carried by each population. Coded into DNA, this information represents possible ways for the Karner Blue butterfly to adapt to changing conditions. As a consequence, biologists such as Givnish would like to prevent the disappearance of this genetic variation. Members of individual metapopulations should be able to mate, which would encourage the flow of genes from one end of the butterfly's range to the other. Ideally, the sanctuaries should be adjoined by bits of land that could serve as stepping-stones between them, in the view of Alan Haney, a pine barren and oak savanna specialist at the School of Natural Resources at the University of Wisconsin–Stevens

Point. New Hampshire and Minnesota, the two edges of the Karner Blue range, are more than thirteen hundred miles apart. Haney agreed that an archipelago of butterfly reserves between them would require hundreds of thousands of acres. Securing that archipelago by purchasing the land would require buying expensive farmland in the Midwest, not just abandoned upstate New York homesteads. The cost would be billions of dollars. It would be even more if we insist on including the territory currently occupied by Chicago, Toledo, Albany, and the other cities that sit on land that once contained Karner Blues. The human upheaval would be large, too, because it would not be easy to set aside that land without pushing out some people. But spending that money and moving aside those people may be necessary to protect and restore *L. m. samuelis* to complete health—if, that is, society is going to be serious about the task.

That money and effort would be directed at just one subspecies. It would do nothing to resolve the plight of the Kanab ambersnail (*Oxyloma kanabensis*), a freshwater mollusk found only in Kanab, Utah. Almost the entire species lives in Three Lakes Canyon, a valley north of town. Thirty acres on the canyon floor are covered by the eponymous lakes—an oasislike spot in dry southern Utah. The canyon floor is owned by Brandt A. Child, a semiretired civil engineer from Bountiful, Utah, who bought the land in 1990 with his retirement savings, intending to turn it into a trailer park for elderly vacationers from the East Coast. A survey that year pegged the number of Kanab ambersnails on his property at about 100,000. Late that year, Child began construction. The following February, the U.S. Fish and Wildlife Service informed Child of the snail's presence and told him not to use earthmoving equipment, effectively ending his plans for the trailer park. Child was unable to build on his land or sell it. Later that same year, a teenager dumped ten domestic geese and one domestic duck into the lakes after a disagreement with his parents about keeping the birds. Geese and ducks like to eat snails. Fish and Wildlife quickly removed the birds. An FBI investigation into the incident included pumping the birds' stomachs for incriminating snail shells. (None were found.) The land still sits there—waiting,

Child told us, for someone foolish enough to purchase it. Until the lakes are protected, the snail's status will be insecure.

Building an archipelago of Karner Blue refuges and safeguarding lakes for the Kanab ambersnail will not help the Florida scrub jay (*Aphelocoma coerulescens coerulescens*), a special population of an otherwise widespread bird that is restricted to central Florida, especially the highlands. Highlands is a relative term—their highest point is scarcely three hundred feet above sea level. Still, that was enough to keep this part of Florida out of the water 2 million years ago, when high seas drowned the rest of the peninsula. Marooned on their piece of Florida, these scrub jays developed much more closely knit families than scrub jays on the mainland. Instead of flying away to find mates, juvenile birds hang around the parental nest, sometimes for several years, watching out for snakes and hawks and helping to feed the next generations of babies. Family units spend most of the day at home, in a well-defined territory that the birds defend, squawking angrily, against all comers. The jay's future is uncertain, ecologists say, because it is restricted to Florida oak scrub—the low tangle of palmetto, stunted oaks, and prickly pear cactus that grows only in the sand dunes of central Florida. Unfortunately, central Florida is highly in demand for retirement communities; it is also some of the best orange-growing land in the world. As a result, Florida oak scrub is often described as one of the most threatened ecosystems in the United States. At least eleven of its denizens, including *A. c. coerulescens*, are on the federal list of endangered or threatened species. Restoring them to good health would involve tearing down retirement homes and uprooting orange trees—prospects guaranteed to cost a lot of money and make some people unhappy.

Setting aside land for the Karner Blue butterfly and the Kanab ambersnail and the Florida scrub jay will not help the king salmon (*Oncorhyncus tshawytscha*) on the Elwha River in Washington State. The river was once home to the S'Klallam Nation. Indeed, the river was so important to its inhabitants that their legends claimed the Creator had fashioned the first S'Klallam from the dirt of its banks. Now those banks are buried beneath the reservoirs of two hydroelectric dams. In the eighty years of their existence, the dams have laid down more than 4 million cubic yards of sediment and destroyed the run of king salmon that used to spawn in the Elwha. The salmon can be brought back, claim ichthyologists (fish specialists), by removing the dams. Let the river run its old course from the base of Mount Olympus to the Strait of Juan de Fuca, they say. The fish will return. Congress has been debating the notion of dismantling the dams and compensating the current users of their electric power. The action would cost up to $200 million.

Saving the Karner Blue butterfly and the Kanab ambersnail and the Florida scrub jay and the king salmon will not improve the chances of the California gnatcatcher (*Polioptila californica californica*), a small, nondescript bird that is picky about its housing arrangements. It lives exclusively between Los Angeles and northern Baja California, on land that is undeveloped, not too high, not too steeply pitched, and, for the most part, near the ocean—which is to say that *P. c. californica* inhabits some of the most expensive real estate in the world. The number of people in southern California has quintupled since 1940, a rate of growth rivaling that of Bangladesh; in the 1980s alone, more than 3.5 million people swarmed in. Inevitably, the rise in the acreage devoted to the urban, suburban, and rural habitat of *Homo sapiens californica* has caused almost everything else to lose ground— including *P. c. californica*, which has relinquished about 60 to 90 percent of its habitat (nobody knows exactly how much the bird had in the beginning). Plans are afoot to preserve hundreds of thousands of acres, some of which developers could otherwise turn into lots worth $200,000 or more. The preserves would cost billions of dollars—but they would not save the Alabama beach mouse or the Virginia northern flying squirrel or the Iowa Pleistocene snail or the Texas blind salamander or the Kentucky cave shrimp or the Hawaiian 'akiapol'au bird or the northeastern beach tiger beetle of Connecticut or the piping plover of Rhode Island or most of the hundreds of other imperiled species in North America.

Viewed as individual cases, almost all these species can be saved. The great majority of them were harmed by human actions, and these actions presumably could be at least partly undone without insurmountable difficulty. Recall the parable of the cooked frog. If each past human decision turned up the heat a notch, so to speak, the temperature of the pot now could be lowered without causing a disaster. One notch for one pot would not save all biodiversity, though. Thousands of species are in trouble. Not every one will be as costly and difficult to save as the Karner Blue, but enough will be that saving them all could not be accomplished without sacrifices from every American. We could not turn down the heat on *every* pot without turning up the heat on our collective economic pot. Sometimes the sacrifices would be small, sometimes large; sometimes obvious, sometimes subtle. But they would always occur.

At this point someone might say, Who cares? Do we really *need* another gas station? Another parking lot? Another shopping mall? Is it desperately important to have more golf courses and banks and convenience stores? At first glance, the answer seems easy: no. We do not need *one* more convenience store. But that doesn't mean we can easily do without *all* convenience stores. People build convenience stores, housing developments, and all the rest not to create glitzy monuments to glass, steel, and vinyl siding but to serve ordinary human purposes like raising families and living in pleasant houses. These desires do not go away when you block the corner store. Indeed, stopping that one store might be beneficial. A patch of beauty might be spared; meanwhile, the people who would have built the store or worked in it might find more environmentally benign employment. But adopt a policy of no more stores and people will be out of work and unable to find the things they need. Then shut down the banks, the golf courses, the shopping malls, the parking lots, and the gas stations and watch the costs to people's hopes and dreams rise to ever more unacceptable heights. The Cooked Frog Problem, in other words, cuts two ways. Saving all species everywhere would cook our society to death.

The practical impossibility of saving everything in no way implies that Americans should do nothing or would want to ignore all endangered species. People often work hard for goals that they know cannot be fully achieved. Although human beings are unlikely to boil themselves alive, they are demonstrably willing to raise the temperature of the water they sit in, sometimes to uncomfortably high temperatures, if there is a good reason for it. To ask people to make such sacrifices, the goal needs to be clearly explained, its value established. That means facing the questions Laura Sommers was pelted with in Wilton. Why should the citizenry go to so much trouble to protect a butterfly? If it is going to cost a lot of money, why should Americans save any biodiversity at all? What would be lost if it vanished? What would be gained by going to the trouble of protecting it? When all is said and done, how hot should we let the water get to protect our natural heritage?

WE VISITED Wilton a few weeks after the meeting between Laura Sommers and the angry citizenry. By then, the town and the state had come to terms. Big balloons floated above lupine sites and the spray planes were twisting around them. It was the same day that the county official gave us a tour of the butterfly zones. He took us through the trails of the Boy Scout camp in his truck. Although the day was hot and his vehicle without airconditioning, we did not open the windows because the mosquitoes were too intense. In some places, we found it impossible to stand outdoors for more than a minute. Less than a mile away was another lupine site, part of an old farm. Planes had avoided it. Across the street sat a row of modest ranch houses with little brick-edged flower gardens and sprinklers on the lawn for children. Here, the insects were not bad at midday. We knocked on doors until one was opened by a young woman tethered to a child. We asked her what she thought of the spraying controversy.

"I hope that butterfly's worth it," she said. "I haven't been outside after dusk in a month."

Chapter Five

REASONS PECULIARLY
OUR OWN

W HEN WHOOPING CRANES walk, their heads bob and their feet pull up to astonishing heights. In bright sun, their feathers are so white that their shadowed bellies seem blue. Whooping cranes are not completely white, though. Their wings are tipped with long black pinions and their skulls are hugged by red berets of rough featherless skin. They also have slim black legs that kink like ideograms. Sometimes whooping cranes like to stand in water for hours. When they see things far away, they stretch themselves into pale spikes almost five feet tall. In this stance, they look too spindly to move with agility, but then they pull their heads down and their bodies seem to fill out and they stride across the land with the awkward grace of children walking barefoot through sharp pebbles. Despite their dandified airs, whooping cranes eat slimy things like lizards, worms, and crayfish, plunging their long bills avidly into the muck at their feet. When they come up, swallowing, you can see spatters of mud on their elegant throats.

Experts call whooping cranes "whoopers"; taxonomists call them *Grus americanus*, the American crane. They belong to the same order as quails, coots, and rails; a sure way to annoy a crane expert is to ask how closely they are related to storks, herons, and egrets. (They aren't, except for being birds.) Cranes are Asian creatures that spread into North America hundreds of thousands of years ago. Whooping crane bones and fossils have been found from the west coast of California to the east coast of Florida, and in thirty-three of the states between, not to mention Canadian provinces and Mexican states. The species was probably not seen by Europeans until 1722, when a British traveler named Mark Catesby was presented with a whole whooper skin by a Native American he met in the Carolinas. He was told, Catesby reported, that "they make a remarkable hooping noise." And they do—a buglelike call often written as *Ker-loo! Ker-lee-oo!*

Whoopers like to scatter themselves across the landscape. Single pairs occupy areas hundreds of acres in size and chase off intruders. In nesting season, they hardly make a sound except to warn of danger. Couples mate for life, migrating year after year from their winter quarters to the same northern rookery. Nests are made of heaped grass and can be five feet in diameter. The female usually lays two creamy spotted eggs that are about four inches long. The birds take turns sitting on the eggs, which are rarely left untended. In May 1883, an egg collector named J. W. Preston found an occupied nest near Eagle Lake in northern Iowa. The whooper on it leapt to its feet and ran close to Preston, dragging its wings as if they were broken. When this failed to distract him, the bird threw sticks and moss at him. After that, too, failed, Preston recalled, "with pitable mien it spread itself on the water and begged me to leave its treasure, which, in a heartless manner, I didn't do." Eleven years later, ornithologist Rudolph M. Anderson and his son spotted a whooper nest in almost the same spot. The birds simply ran away. Man and boy watched them disappear into the marsh. It was the last time anyone observed a wild pair nesting in the United States.

Not many of these magnificent beasts are left. The ones we visited were in Florida, subjects of a program to reintroduce the species to a state in which it thrived until driven away by hunters and houses. In January 1993, the Fish and Wildlife Service conveyed fourteen young birds to the Three Lakes Wildlife Management Area, a 55,000-acre spread not far south of the theme park megacomplex in Orlando. That part of Florida is backwoods ranching country, hot, sandy, and flat; to appreciate its charms, it is helpful to be accompanied by a biologist. The one who drove us was

Stephen Nesbitt of the Florida Game and Freshwater Fish Department. After turning off a two-lane highway, we jounced in Nesbitt's pickup truck through what had once been a cattle ranch. Then we got out and walked along a trail. Nesbitt told us to watch out for snakes. At the end of the trail was a small wooden shack on stilts. Inside were a few chairs and some scraps of paper. Three slits about a foot high permitted occupants to survey a fenced-off area perhaps 75 feet across and 125 feet long. Strutting around inside was an appreciable fraction of all the whooping cranes on Earth.

Unaware of us, the birds walked with the intelligent gravity of the benign aliens in a science fiction film. Their yellow gaze was cool, quick, and remote. Legs bent widdershins, straightened, bent again. We had a list of questions for Nesbitt, but it was hard to keep track of them around the cranes. After a while, we gave up and simply watched. They had just grown their adult plumage, shifting from buff to white; five had died in the three months since the birds' introduction, but the other nine were healthy. In the middle of the enclosure was a pond the size of a living room. Whoopers pranced at its edge, plucking small wriggly shapes from the slop. The birds' tail feathers shook like cheerleaders' pom-poms.

Nesbitt had been working with cranes since 1974 and planning this introduction since 1980. But his devoted labor has played just a small part in the long human struggle to save the bird from oblivion. Ornithologists realized a hundred years ago that *G. americanus* was rare. Their slowly mounting concern led in 1937 to the creation of the Aransas National Wildlife Refuge, preserving almost fifty thousand acres of whooper habitat on the coast of Texas near Corpus Christi. A year later came the first official census of the species. The results were a shock: eighteen birds at Aransas, eleven more at a second site in Louisiana. Twenty-nine whooping cranes in all the world! Alarmed, the Fish and Wildlife Service, the Canadian Wildlife Service, and the Audubon Society joined forces in 1945 to save *G. americanus*—the first such large-scale effort, and one that launched today's endangered species program.

The crusade was needed. By 1949, no whooping cranes lived outside Aransas; five years later, the number of whoopers had shrunk to twenty-one. Because nobody knew how to save the species, researchers from the Patuxent Wildlife Research Center in Maryland and the Canadian Wildlife Service spent almost three decades learning how to slip eggs from whooper nests and fly them in special hand-carried incubator suitcases to laboratories, where they are hatched in a cage. The newborns are raised in pens with stuffed cranes that serve as parents and young chickens that serve as foster nestmates (young cranes are aggressive, and their real nestmates are too valuable to be pecked); out of sight, ornithologists stick their hands into crane puppets to teach the birds how to eat and drink. All the while, military officers, airline industry executives, oil company officials, water utility engineers, ranching lobbyists, conservation enthusiasts, and hosts of others have created a dance of their own—an intricate web of negotiation that spares the cranes from most human impact.

Today the whooping crane is the centerpiece of no less than three big nature preserves: Aransas, now up to 54,829 acres; the 11,072,000-acre Wood Buffalo National Park in Canada, where they breed in the summer; and the 8,000 acres of easements and set-aside land in the Platte River Trust in Nebraska, where the birds sometimes stop on the journey between. (Nesbitt hopes the new population will eventually occupy about 22,000 acres in Florida.) Most important, the whooper population had grown by the summer of 1994 to 288, the beneficiaries of the longest and most concentrated effort to prevent extinction that has ever occurred.

We asked Nesbitt why he and others had spent so much time on *G. americanus.* "Just look at them," he said, gesturing to the enclosure. A whooper was spreading its wings: satiny circumflexes seven feet across. "I'm not comfortable with that kind of question," he said. It was easy to understand his distress. Questioning such work smacks of mercantile calculation and seems to presuppose a cynical, negative answer. Still, it is reasonable to ask why so much time and money and attention has been lavished on a few birds, if only to make the reasons explicit. Saving cranes is one of many worthwhile endeavors competing for our attention and resources. So it's important to ask why we should save the whooping crane, as opposed to doing something else. For that matter, why save the Karner Blue butterfly? Or the American burying beetle? Indeed, why should we save *any* species?

ONE OF THE FIRST people to worry about these questions was William Temple Hornaday, the influential director of the New York Zoological Park. Hunter, taxidermist, polemicist, student of animal morals, advocate of the white man's burden, enthusiast for phrenology and temperance, Hornaday was a passionate man who got under a lot of people's skins. Of all his enthusiasms, biodiversity was foremost: he spent more than forty years railing against the loss of species. "Today," he wrote in 1913, "the thing that stares me in the face every waking hour, like a grisly spectre with bloody fang and claw, is *the extermination of species*. To me, this is a horrible thing. It is wholesale murder, no less. It is a capital crime, and a black disgrace to the races of civilized mankind."

"I am no mild-mannered, white-bearded scientist," Hornaday sneered—truthfully. Born in 1854, he traveled to Africa and Asia as a young man, looking for examples of species he had never seen. When he found one, he shot it. He stuffed the bodies and sent them to museums. In 1882, he became the chief taxidermist of the Smithsonian Institution. Five years later, the museum asked him to report on the status of the bison. Finding the species on the edge of extinction, he launched a campaign to save it that continued for decades, increasing his notoriety. When the New York Zoological Park—popularly known today as the Bronx Zoo—opened in 1896, Hornaday was its director. He used his position to lobby Congress to preserve the bison. When Uncle Sam established a bison refuge in Montana, Hornaday stocked it from the Bronx Zoo collection. The program was a success, and Hornaday more than anyone else is responsible for the animal's continued survival.

Other conservationists had pushed to stop deforestation and development, and some had worked hard to save endangered species. Hornaday alone fought full-time for biodiversity. His Permanent Wild Life Protection Fund was the first group in the nation, perhaps the world, dedicated specifically to halting extinction. His *Our Vanishing Wild Life,* a 411-page tract published in 1913, was probably the first book devoted to the biodiversity crisis. A year later, he produced the second: *Wild Life Conservation in Theory and Practice.* Now, at the other end of the century, Hornaday's analysis of the problem does not seem sophisticated. And his solution—stop all hunting!—sounds naïve. But nonetheless, his books, speeches, and articles told Americans in simple form why they should care about the fate of other species.

In Hornaday's view, other species have an abundance of uses, direct and indirect. Humans exploit species directly in many ways. Hornaday's example was the white-tailed deer, a source of meat then endangered by overhunting. If the deer vanished, nobody would have any venison. On the other hand, Hornaday argued, the nationwide deer population, properly managed, could, without threat to the species, produce an annual crop of 2 million animals—"an immense volume of free wild food," in his terms. Because each adult deer provided a minimum of ten dollars' worth of meat, he said, this program would increase the national well-being by $20 million a year. Meanwhile, unchecked avarice was destroying the species. How, he asked, could we throw away this resource?

This argument may seem odd today, when few Americans depend on game, but it resounded powerfully at the turn of the century. And its essence is still beyond dispute—other species are a treasure. Families dining at the table consume the fruits of such species as *Bos tauris* (the European domestic cow), *Lactuca sativa* (lettuce), *Lycopersico esculentum* (tomato), *Cucumis sativus* (cucumber), and *Allium cepa* (onion). The grinders on the sideboard contain the berries of *Piper nigrum* (black pepper). After dinner, the family takes a stroll, during which they see *Bellis perennis* (the English daisy), *Mysosotis sylvatica* (the woods forget-me-not), and *Taraxacum officinale* (the common dandelion). These hardly exhaust the list, of course. Think of cornstarch, roses, indigo, rubber, coffee—even the flour that makes our daily bread.

Of all uses for other species perhaps the most intriguing is as a source of drugs. Bark from the white willow gave us salicin, an ancient version of aspirin; the Grecian foxglove provided digoxin, a cardiac medication; bear bile is the origin of ursodiol, a gallstone dissolver; deadly nightshade led to atropine, an eye dilator and anti-inflammatory; the velvet bean produced L-dopa, a treatment for Parkinson's disease; and everyone knows the story of penicillin, the bacteria slayer discovered accidentally in a mold. There are scores more of these tales—plants alone are responsible for at least 119 drugs in use today around the globe. Among the most heartening recent discoveries is a Japanese soil bacterium examined in the laboratories of Merck & Company, a big drug company based in Whitehouse Station, New Jersey. Chemical compounds within the microorganism led researchers to the drug ivermectin, which destroys the worm larvae that cause river blindness (onchocerciasis, as it is technically known), a horrible disease that until recently ran uncontrolled through parts of Africa and Latin America. Distributed free under the name of Mectizan by Merck and the World Health Organization in affected areas, ivermectin has spared countless people from misery.

These tales are no accident. Each species, biologists say, has a unique package of genes, which, when unwrapped by scientific manipulation, may reveal the key to new pest-resistant crops, new pigments for artists, new treatments for AIDS. "The honeybee is like a magic well," Edward O. Wilson once told a congressional committee. "The more you draw from it, the more there is to draw. And so it is with any species, which is a unique configuration of genes assembled over thousands of years, possessing its own biology, mysteries, and still untested uses for mankind." The potential in each species may indeed be huge—Wilson has calculated that the genetic information encoded in the DNA from the common mouse, if represented as ordinary-size letters, would almost fill the fifteen editions of the *Encyclopaedia Britannica* printed since 1768.

Comparisons to encyclopedias are fitting, for biologists frequently liken the world's biodiversity to a library in which the vast majority of books have never been read. And even those that have been read are unlikely to be exhausted, according to Thomas Eisner, a chemical ecologist at Cornell University. "Even species that are well known chemically," he has argued, "are bound to contain unknown chemicals discoverable only by future techniques." Reading the books in the species library once will not be enough, in other words. Each generation will profit from reading them over and over again, new nuances appearing each time. The analogy to works like *King Lear* and *Hamlet*, sources of endless new theatrical inspiration, is surprisingly exact.

These benefits—dinner, diversion, and drugs—by no means exhaust the usefulness of other species. In addition to direct services (benefits that flow straight to people), biodiversity also contributes indirect services (benefits that flow to other species or physical factors that are in turn beneficial to people). William T. Hornaday, again, was among the first to make the point. One of his examples was the avian appetite for insects. Because birds eat insects, he said, they should not be slaughtered. Alive, each quail "devoured 145 different kinds of bad insects, and the seeds of 129 anathema weeds." Dead, the quail was nothing but a meager dinner. Hornaday could not understand why people were hunting quails to near extinction.

More important, possibly, would be the species wiped out along with the quail. Peter Raven of the Missouri Botanical Garden has estimated that the loss of one species of plant eliminates en passant ten to thirty other species. An oft-told example comes from the island nation of Mauritius. The tambalacocque, a rare tree, has a green fruit, known as a drupe, covered with a tough skin. In 1977, the ecologist Stanley Temple suggested that the scarcity of tambalacocque trees was due to the loss of the dodo, a Mauritian bird that vanished in the seventeenth century, soon after the island was invaded by hungry Europeans. Enough records survive to let us know that the bird was a kind of flightless fifty-pound dove with a featherless face and a strongly curved bill. Its gizzard contained stones suitable for grinding fruit. Temple proposed that the fruit of the tambalacocque could not germinate unless its thick skin had been abraded by passing through a dodo gizzard. When the dodo was exterminated, the tambalacocque was doomed. Only thirteen of these trees remained, Temple reported, each more than three centuries old. As an experiment, he gave some of their seeds to turkeys. After they had passed through the birds, the seeds germinated—the first new tambalacocques, Temple thought, since the dodo.

The dodo and the tambalacocque tree are but two components of the fathomlessly complex mechanism that we call biodiversity. Beyond the support they provide for one another, species play a vital role in such essentials as maintaining the quality of the atmosphere (forests act as air filters), controlling the climate (vegetation takes in carbon dioxide from the atmosphere), regulating freshwater supplies (trees absorb and release water), generating soil (microorganisms crumble rock), and disposing of wastes (American burying beetles inter dead mice). To deprive ourselves of these ecological functions would be suicidal. Although removing any single part of biodiversity is unlikely to lead to cataclysm, ecologists say, the full consequences of an extinction cannot be known in advance. This demands prudence, lest we unknowingly bring disaster on ourselves. "If the [living world], in the course of eons, has built something we like but do not understand," wrote the celebrated conservationist Aldo Leopold, "then who but a fool would discard seemingly useless parts? To keep every cog and wheel is the first precaution of intelligent tinkering."

In *Extinction*, Paul and Anne Ehrlich likened humankind to airline passengers on a plane from which the management has popped off many of the rivets on the wings. The airline, archly dubbed Growthmania Intercontinental, assures one and all that the manufacturer included plenty of extra rivets and that Growthmania can sell them for two dollars apiece. "Any sane person," the Ehrlichs wrote, would "make reservations on another carrier." But that isn't possible on Spaceship Earth—it's the only passenger line around. "And," the Ehrlichs reported, "frighteningly, it is swarming with rivet poppers behaving in ways analogous to that just described." Rivets, of course, stand for species; rivet popping means assisting in their extinction. Leading rivet poppers, to the Ehrlichs' way of thinking, included the President of the United States and most other politicians, such businesspeople as utility officials, automobile makers, and timber-firm executives, almost all of the world's economists and practically every engineer, the Pope and everyone else of any note in the Vatican, the editors of *The Wall Street Journal*, and a fair selection of scientists, including, surprisingly, those in charge of the Entomological Society of America. All are setting the planet up— inadvertently, to be sure—for the awful moment when one too many rivets are removed, the plane suddenly disintegrates, and in a whorl of torn metal humanity comes flaming down.

A PLANE whose every rivet may hold the key to our fate—can anyone doubt the power of this image? Just as vivid are those like it, the cogs and wheels that must be preserved, the genetic library with its unread books. Biodiversity is necessary, these pictures say. It is of utmost practical importance to us; we destroy it at our peril. And, indeed, this belief is true—for biodiversity *as a whole*. But that is not the same as saving individual species. Indeed, these images, when their implications are carefully examined, provide reasons *not* to save most individual species. Consider the example of the whooping crane. Hunters shot them and collectors snatched their eggs and skin and milliners put their feathers into hats. It was also part of an ecosystem, feeding and being fed upon, that benefited humanity by its presence. The bird had some direct and indirect uses, in other words. But does that mean it had—or has— any important *value*?

Value is a word with many meanings, and the answer to this question depends on the chosen definition. When Wilson, Ehrlich, Raven, and other ecologists speak of the direct value of biodiversity as a source of food or drugs, or of its indirect value as a provider of ecological services, they are describing its usefulness for some human purpose—its utilitarian value. The question is, then, does the whooper actually possess this kind of value in any significant quantity?

In principle, such questions are not difficult to answer, because utilitarian values can be measured and tied to numbers, usually dollars; or they provide a means for ranking things, telling us when one is more or less important than another. Hammers have utilitarian value, one can say, and the price people are willing to pay for them reflects, in part, that value. More intangible goods can have this kind of worth, too. The utilitarian value of a beautiful lake at the end of a hike cannot be easily measured in dollar terms, but people have their favorite hikes and their favorite lakes. Clearly, other types of value exist, but utilitarian values dominate the discussions about why endangered species must be saved.

As for the utilitarian value of the crane, hunters were less than unanimous on its edibility, suggesting that the bird was no delicacy; worse, these dubious benefits were hard to obtain, because whoopers were so wary that they were difficult to bag. On the other hand, the bird's skin and eggs were interesting to collectors, selling for two dollars and eighteen dollars, respectively, in 1890. Still, its numbers were low enough that a single obsessed individual could have bought the entire species to corner the market on whooper skins and eggs, suggesting that at the time its total commercial value was not overwhelming. People sometimes used its long wing bones for flutes, but the market for bone instruments is insignificant. And nobody has proposed that the bird will provide a cure for cancer or any other disease. Even if someone did, the species has four close relatives, one of which, the Eurasian crane, is common. The genetic information unique to the whooper is thus small and unlikely to be of much import.

The one exception to this unremitting lack of direct value is the bird's ability to draw tourists, ourselves included. How much is that worth? Every year, 75,000 to 100,000 people visit the Aransas refuge. For the majority, the center of interest is the forty-seven-foot, six-inch wooden tower built by the Fish and Wildlife Service at the edge of the territory occupied by what is called, inevitably, the "tower pair." Equipped with binocularlike viewing devices, the tower can hold up to twenty people. Because visitors like to watch for a while, lines often form at the base.

Outside the refuge, charter boats carry passengers to observe the cranes and other waterfowl. One such service is Captain Ted's Whooping Crane Tours, run by Ted and Bobbi Appell. "You're *guaranteed* to see the crane," Bobbi Appell told us in the middle of an enthusiastic sales pitch for the tour that convinced us, at least, to think about the next flight to Corpus Christi. Customers are taken through the marshes on the *Skimmer*, a custom bird-watching boat with a draft of just eighteen inches. For twenty-five dollars, Captain Ted's provides unlimited coffee, a Continental breakfast, complimentary "spotting scopes," and a handy bird-watching checklist. From November 1 to the end of the cranes' stay at Aransas in late winter, the *Skimmer* runs at least once a day, six days a week, carrying about eight thousand paying customers a year.

The economic value of these visits is hard to quantify. Brent Giezentanner, manager of the refuge, once guessed that visitors to his domain add $5 million each year to the local economy. Not all of this sum can be attributed to the whooper, though. Many visitors come in the summer, when cranes are breeding in the north; and Aransas always has other attractions—alligators, armadillos, and almost four hundred species of birds, more than any other national wildlife refuge. Even Captain Ted's tours are not completely dependent on the whooper. Between April and July, while the cranes are gone, the tour switches its focus to some rookery islands with different birds—and charges the same twenty-five dollars.

But even if the entire $5 million were attributed to the whooping crane, one must ask whether that sum is greater than the profit from doing something else at Aransas. (If this question smacks of mercantilism, so be it: appealing to the whooper's economic value as a reason to save the bird is also mercantile.) Oil and gas exploration at the refuge has been vigorous. Suppose the whooping crane was the only thing standing in the way of extracting $10 million in oil profits each year from Aransas? If whoopers should be saved because they provide $5 million in direct benefits, then they presumably should be eliminated if they block humanity from receiving the greater benefit of $10 million in petroleum profits. (If the objection is raised that the oil companies, not humanity, would receive the profit, a check from those companies for $5,000,001 would presumably settle the matter.)

Clearly, this reasoning is oversimplified to the point of caricature. The whooping crane will be there in perpetuity, whereas the oil would last for only a few decades. On the other hand, the land, now cleared of cranes, could be used for houses and other human purposes; coastal Texas is one of the fastest-growing areas in the nation. But the larger point is apparent. If one of North America's premier endangered species has only modest direct value, how much should we assign less well known species?

Not much. The hunt for miracle drugs in biodiversity illustrates the problem. Between 1955 and 1982, the Developmental Therapeutics Program at the National Cancer Institute screened several hundred thousand species of plant, marine organism, bacterium, fungus, and protist for what researchers called "anticancer activity." The procedure was complex in detail but simple in principle: researchers ground up a small sample of the organism and administered it to cancer cells. If the cells reacted, the scientists separated the organism into its chemical constituents, which were tested separately in a procedure analogous to sifting through a set of ever-finer sieves. Michael Grever, a former associate director of the program, told us that such random screening, at either the NCI or private drug firms, led to about one-quarter of today's cancer drugs.

The work was difficult, according to Saul A. Schepartz, another screening-program administrator. Testing plants, for example, involves collecting their roots, leaves, and seeds, often in remote places, transporting them intact to laboratories, chemically preparing extracts, and then placing them on cancer cells in a petri dish. Although screening discovered a fourth of today's cancer drugs, they were harder and more expensive to find than the other three-fourths. "The program was basically discontinued [in 1982] because there hadn't been much success," Schepartz said.

Nonetheless, a second program began in September 1986. "It's the sort of high-risk, low-payoff thing that's appropriate for government to do," said Schepartz, who is now associate director of the Developmental Therapeutics Program. "Companies have been in and out of the [NCI screening] organization. They come in and essentially discover that it probably doesn't pay commercially. That's fine—one role for government is to take these long-shot risks." Intended to search out treatments for cancer and AIDS, the second screening program uses new methods to improve speed and reliability. By June 1994, the NCI had collected 115,896 samples from almost 100,000 species. It had tested more than 63,000 extracts against cancer and AIDS.

Nothing exciting had yet turned up for cancer, but several anti-AIDS compounds seemed promising. One, a traditional plant medicine from Samoa, had the drawback of belonging to a chemical family notorious for promoting the growth of cancer tumors. ("From animal tests," says Gordon Cragg, who supervises the program, "we think it is not actually carcinogenic, but it is difficult to convince anyone of this. People say, 'Maybe in animals you don't see it, but put it in humans and it might behave differently.' ") Another compound comes from *Ancistrocladus korupensis*, a vine in Cameroon; it is now in the early stages of testing. Alarmingly, a third candidate—extracted from *Calophyllum lanigerum*, a Malaysian tree—was almost abandoned after the investigators who collected the first sample were unable to find a second. The original tree had disappeared into its native swamp, and investigators could not find the anti-AIDS compound in other members of the species. Despairing botanists eventually discovered chemically similar compounds in a cousin to the first tree, *C. teysmanni*. Each of the candidates is exciting in potential, NCI investigators told us, though they cautioned that the odds are strongly against any individual substance's becoming a useful drug.

We asked Gordon Cragg recently what would happen to the Developmental Therapeutics Program if every plant species in the rain forest vanished tomorrow. "What a horrible thought," he said. He paused. "Well," he said slowly, "if the rain forest was cut down, we would look at other places." We asked what they would be. "I've read that there's one and a half *million* species of fungi. There're countless species of bacteria. Our first program screened a couple hundred thousand species in twenty years. Even if we got up to screening a hundred thousand in one year, we could keep our random screening program busy for a long time with just fungi and bacteria. Now, I wouldn't want to cut down the rain forest for any reason. Losing it would have a significant effect on our chances of discovering new agents—but I don't think its existence is absolutely necessary to find cures."

Nobody has performed a comparable effort to screen plants and animals for their palatability, although the thousands of years that agriculture has existed could be considered a long-running version of such a program. Of the 250,000 species of plant, no more than 3,000 are regarded as a food source. The remainder are unlikely to hide culinary treasures; as the World Conservation Monitoring Centre noted in *Global Biodiversity*, its mammoth compilation on the subject, "most have been sampled at one time or another." The core of human food needs is met by only fifteen to twenty species: wheat, corn, cattle, and so on. Although it is important to maintain genetic diversity among these species, and even wild cousins to help future farmers ward off new pests, saving the vast majority of plant species cannot be justified by appealing to their edibility; similar reasoning applies to animals. And although some five hundred insect species are part of human diets, the countless millions of other insects will never show up on people's menus.

Of course, none of this takes into account the indirect benefits of biodiversity—the way other species help us get breathable air and drinkable water. But here, too, the benefits tend to come from biodiversity in toto, rather than from individual species. Again, the whooping crane is an example. The species does not fix nitrogen, aid in water retention, or create soil. Individual birds may act as a check on local populations of crabs, frogs, clams, and snails. But the importance of that check would depend on the number of birds. For the last few millennia, according to the crane scholar Robert Porter Allen, they probably did not number more than thirteen or fourteen hundred. (Later calculations have put the total even lower, at five hundred to seven hundred birds.) Small numbers of predators like grizzly bears have a significant ecological effect, but no one casts the whooper in such an important role. Indeed, its importance to its surroundings is small enough that the Fish and Wildlife Service believes that the crane's reintroduction to Florida will not have significant environmental impact.

Nor is the whooper alone in its ecological inutility. Through photosynthesis, plants are the world's major sources of organic carbon molecules, the chemical building blocks of life. But because so many species produce these molecules in so many different ways, huge numbers would have to vanish before the world experienced a failure of photosynthesis. Only a single specimen exists of a plant named for Peter Raven—*Arctostaphylos hookerii ravenii*, Raven's manzanita. Will its extinction really have an impact on the provision of ecological services? The prospect seems unlikely. Similarly, many species eat plants, converting those organic molecules into the proteins that make up muscle, feathers, and insect carapaces. These creatures, too, are largely replaceable one by another—fungible, as social scientists say, at least in this respect.

Dismissing the ecological importance of individual species goes against the appealingly familiar notion that each one is an irreplaceable strand in a seamless "web of life." Many Americans, buffeted by the chaotic disruptions of existence in the late twentieth century, seem to find comfort in thinking of nature as an orderly, organic weave, every thread part of the whole, and all irreplaceable. In the 1970s, this thinking generated an outpouring of ecophilosophy for the common man, as exemplified by the lovely vision that "everything is connected to everything else"—to cite the first of biologist Barry Commoner's famous Three Laws of Ecology. But this picture has been tested and found wanting. Indeed, some ecologists question whether ecosystems actually exist as such. "There are the self-perpetuating, self-regulating systems you see in popular accounts," Daniel Simberloff told us, "but I am unaware of any rigorous proof that [such perfectly meshed systems] occur frequently in nature." Biological communities, he argued, are little more than creations of contingency: collections of organisms that happen to share the same living quarters. Species interact with one another, but so do the denizens of an apartment complex, and nobody thinks the building will fall down if one family leaves.

Look again at the pleasant story of the dodo and the tambalacocque. Although the bird's ability to help the tree reproduce has never been in question, other scientists soon challenged the implication that the tambalacocque was doomed without the dodo. "The story was presented well in the [original] paper," explained Mark Witmer, the Cornell University graduate student in ecology who reexamined it in the 1980s. "But the evidence wasn't there." Not all the tambalacocques on Mauritius are more than three centuries old, he pointed out in a 1991 article written with another skeptic, British ornithologist Anthony Cheke. Moreover, other biologists had raised new trees without passing the seeds through the gizzards of large birds. The evidence against the link between the species is not absolutely conclusive, Witmer told us, but he was dismayed to see the tale treated as absolutely factual. "It's everywhere," he grumbled. "It's gotten into the popular mind." Waspishly, the Witmer-Cheke paper listed sixteen textbooks and ecology papers that cited it as gospel.

The metaphor of the web of life is not completely mistaken. Some organisms are deeply linked, wild eastern blue lupine and Karner Blue butterflies being examples. And a few species are vital to many others because they control entire ecosystems. Examples of such "keystone" species include beavers, whose dams create a watery habitat used by many other organisms; damselfish, which dominate reef life because they eat coral; mangroves, home of the species that Simberloff and Wilson experimented on; and starfish, which keep down the mussels that would otherwise overwhelm many Pacific tidal areas. But these are rare and are overwhelmed by the legions of the fungible. "If the California condor disappears forever from the California hills, it will be a tragedy," wrote David Ehrenfeld, an ecologist at Rutgers University. "But don't expect the chaparral to die, the redwoods to wither, the San Andreas fault to open up, or even the California tourist industry to suffer—they won't."

Indeed, changes in communities happen all the time, and cataclysm is not the universal result. When the Pilgrims landed, the most common tree between southern Massachusetts and northern Georgia was the American chestnut. In many places, the tree covered three-quarters of the land. The chestnut blight, an Asian fungus, appeared in New York City in 1904 and spread rapidly.

Within four decades, almost all mature chestnuts in the East were dead. The species was replaced primarily by several types of oak. The same area had just experienced the demise of its most common bird, the passenger pigeon, which may have accounted for more than a third of all the birds in the forest. Although these losses changed the forest drastically, they had so little obvious deleterious, ecosystem-smashing effect that now, decades later, some scientists have had to remind their colleagues not to think of apparently undisturbed eastern forestland as pristine.

Because we usually do not know which species are the keystones and which are expendable, isn't our ignorance itself a reason to save them all? And what about the huge number of species that have yet to be discovered—doesn't prudence demand that we stop their extinction?

Alas, the answer to these questions is no, because they exemplify the long-recognized logical fallacy of *argumentum ad ignorantium*. "The fact that you do not know the value of a species," explained Elliot Sober, a professor of philosophy at the University of Wisconsin–Madison,

> by itself, cannot count as a reason for wanting one thing rather than another to happen to it. . . . If we literally *do not know* what consequences the extinction of this or that species may bring, then we should take seriously the possibility that the extinction may be beneficial as well as the possibility that it may be deleterious. It may sound deep to insist that we preserve endangered species precisely because we do not know why they are valuable. But ignorance on a scale like this cannot provide the basis for any rational action.

The fallacy is highlighted by considering the possibility that a species may be one that we *don't* want to save, according to Mark Sagoff, a philosopher at the University of Maryland, in College Park. The AIDS virus, he pointed out, "apparently originated in a species of monkey in Africa. Who could deny that the world would have been spared great agony had that species a century ago gone extinct?" The monkey would thus be an example of biodiversity having a bad consequence. Often we focus on bad consequences and seek to minimize their occurrence—look at the campaigns to force chemical companies to certify that products are benign before they are allowed on the market. Because we do not know the uses of many species, treating biodiversity in the way environmental activists would like to treat chemicals would suggest automatically banning species we don't know about. The idea is ludicrous, but that is the point. Arguing that ignorance forces a decision is always ludicrous.

But are we really ignorant? Not all species will prove to be cancer cures, but some surely will. Screen enough species through programs like that of the NCI, and we will eventually find them. Doesn't merely knowing these cures are out there mean that we should not throw away even the slimmest possibility of discovering one? And that we should therefore save everything? True enough—if saving everything were free. But protecting all species would be a fantastically costly enterprise, as demonstrated by the expense of protecting the Karner Blue. Doing so would stop our lives in their tracks. "My Aunt Tillie," Sagoff noted, "used the same argument for saving everything in her 'you never know' drawer against the day when she might need it. She eventually had no room for herself."

In sum, biodiversity as a whole has overwhelming utilitarian value, but most individual species do not. The reasons for saving the 10 million rarely apply to the one. The whooping crane might be worth saving for its value to tourists. But that type of value surely does not extend to the Karner Blue butterfly or the American burying beetle. Nor does it extend, one presumes, to the Socorro isopod, or the tidal shore beggar's tick, or the small whorled pogonia. Should we therefore sweep them aside? We discard useless pieces of paper as they build up around the house— why not useless species, which have built up around the planet? Why not get rid of any species that end up getting in the way? If the value of the oil beneath Aransas soars, why shouldn't we kill the last whoopers?

This logic is compelling, but people have rarely embraced it. Time and time again, human beings have hesitated, axe raised, and decided to remove endangered species from the executioner's

block. Even if they have no utilitarian value, people work to protect them. To judge by these actions, people must disagree with
the logic above, which would license us to wipe out most other
species. This suggests, in turn, that the entire discussion of utilitarian value, though often invoked as a reason to conserve
biodiversity, is a red herring. We humans do not worry about losing endangered species in the same pragmatic way that we might
worry about losing our wallets. The prospect of letting the
whooper go fills us with a different kind of disquiet—a feeling
that has led some conservationists to argue that other species have
a right to exist.

OUR EFFORTS to understand that disquiet led us to David
Ehrenfeld, the ecologist at Rutgers University. It was an auspi-
cious occasion for such a conversation: Ehrenfeld, the founding
editor of the journal *Conservation Biology*, was attending the sev-
enth annual meeting of the Society for Conservation Biology, and
the halls and rooms around us were filled with people who lived
and breathed biodiversity. The conference was at Arizona State
University, in Tempe, and Ehrenfeld was dressed appropriately:
cowboy hat, cowboy boots, cowboy string tie. We asked him about
the whooping crane—why should we save it? "You probably can't
justify saving the whooping crane on grounds of its benefits to
people," he said. "But that doesn't mean we should stop trying to
prevent it from going extinct. Suppose we don't believe we need
it. The species is useless. Should we throw it away?"

To Ehrenfeld, the inability to find much direct or indirect
worth in species like the whooping crane merely illustrates the
poverty of that kind of argument. Invoking the utilitarian value of
biodiversity sets up a metric to measure its importance and opens
the possibility that the whooping crane may come up short—that,
in other words, the most efficient use of the Aransas preserve
could be as a wallowing ground for the industrial-entertainment
complex. "I'm sure that you could construct an airtight practical argument to transform Aransas into a cesspool," Ehrenfeld

said. "Getting rid of the cranes might well be the smart thing to do."

Appeals to such "prudential" arguments, as philosophers call them, won't save many species, he agreed. "If other species were really a major source of new drugs, they would be a major source of profits, and the companies would really be chasing after them. They aren't. Why should they? Drug companies aren't run by fools—if they could make a lot of money out of the rain forest, they would have an army of researchers there now." The arguments about the genetic treasures that might be found in every species were exasperating, Ehrenfeld allowed. He picked up his briefcase and rested it on his lap. "If we think we should save the whooping crane because it will cure cancer," he said, "we're kidding ourselves."

Why, then, should we save the whooping crane, or biodiversity in general?

"That's the question, isn't it?" he said. "You won't find the answer in economics."

For Ehrenfeld and other prominent conservation biologists, species should be preserved for reasons that have nothing to do with their usefulness to human beings. "Value is an intrinsic part of diversity," he has written. "It does not depend on the properties of the species in question, the uses to which particular species may or may not be put, or their alleged role in the balance of global ecosystems. For biological diversity, value *is*."

Ehrenfeld laid out these ideas in *The Arrogance of Humanism*, a book that has been awarded the status of a classic in conservation circles since its publication in 1978. Among other points, it argued that the Greek thinker Protagoras was wrong—man is not the measure of all things. To judge the worth of another species by its value to humanity is simply an instance of what Ehrenfeld dryly called "humanism," in analogy with racism and sexism. Separating the value of biodiversity from all consideration of its impact on *Homo sapiens*, Ehrenfeld suggested a different reason for conserving species: because they exist and have existed for a long time. "Long-standing existence in Nature," he wrote, is deemed to carry with it the unimpeachable right to continued existence. Existence is the only criterion of the value of parts of Nature, and diminution of the number of existing things is the best measure of decrease of what we ought to value. This is, as mentioned, an ancient way of evaluating "conservability," and by rights ought to be named the "Noah Principle" after the person who was one of the first to put it into practice.

Why save the whooping crane? The Noah Principle gives a simple answer: Because it's there. Because it has been there for a long time, and that lengthy history gives it the right to stay around. Because losing species that have long been on Earth lessens the total value of the planet.

Invoking the Noah Principle to defend the whooping crane, a bird of obvious beauty and grace, would raise few objections. The Karner Blue butterfly, delicate and pretty, is similarly easy to defend. But what about less obvious cases? The American burying beetle is fascinating, but most people would not think it lovely. What about cockroaches and flies? And what about species that are actually harmful to humans? Does even the smallpox virus have a right to exist? Yes, according to Ehrenfeld. Stopping the extinction of the smallpox virus, he has written, would be the "ultimate example" of the Noah Principle.

Smallpox, the variola virus, may be the worst killer in history. It targets only a single species: *Homo sapiens*. Although it wreaked terrible havoc in Europe for centuries, its most savage outbreaks were triggered by European contact with the Americas. Some demographers today believe that when Columbus landed the Americas had more people than Europe. Smallpox, more than anything else, changed that. Exceeding even the huge death toll in North America, epidemics in Central and South America killed millions within a few decades of Columbus's landing. That didn't exhaust the virus. Variola swept through cultures and communities throughout the nineteenth century, felling colonists and Native Americans alike.

In 1967, the World Health Organization launched a program to eradicate smallpox, which then infected 2.5 million people a year.

It was wonderfully successful. The last case in the wild occurred in October 1977. After the disease was eliminated, variola populations still existed in secure laboratories, including one at the University of Birmingham, in Great Britain. In 1978, it inexplicably escaped, infecting a medical photographer whose office was on the floor above. All of modern medicine was helpless to save her. A second victim was the laboratory supervisor, who killed himself in remorse. Appalled, many governments destroyed their remaining stocks of variola. By 1983, it remained only at the Centers for Disease Control, in Atlanta, and at the Research Institute for Viral Preparations, in Moscow. After the virus genome was mapped, WHO called for the last variola to be destroyed on December 31, 1993—the first controlled, deliberate elimination of a species. (Actually, viruses do not reproduce sexually and thus do not fit the classic definition of a species. But researchers refer to variola as a species in this context.)

In August 1993, an international virology conference in Glasgow debated the move. One side argued that extinction would rob humankind of a chance to acquire precious knowledge, because the way viruses work is just beginning to be understood. The other side pointed out that researchers will have their hands full with other terrible viruses, such as HIV, Ebola virus, and the emerging family of hantaviruses. Neither side paid much attention to the Noah Principle. Ultimately, they postponed the execution until June 1995.

Neither side paid much attention to the Noah Principle, for good reason. By denying that species may be distinguished on prudential grounds, it provides no practical guidance in a world distinguished by choice—it is a switch that is always stuck on *yes*, no matter what else may be happening. Ehrenfeld is the first to agree. For those like himself who reject human-centered approaches to life, he has written, "there is simply no way to tell whether one arbitrarily chosen part of Nature has more 'value' than another part, so like Noah we do not bother to make the effort."

People can avoid making the effort only by granting biodiversity total preeminence—an act that has implications far beyond buying Rainforest Crisp breakfast cereal and Enviro-Mints. Taken to its logical extreme, the "unimpeachable right to continued existence" would move biodiversity to the top of our government's budget priorities, displacing health, education, welfare, defense, and even other environmental programs until each species' every need was fulfilled; call on the government to police and reform economic activities, banishing any that are in conflict with biodiversity; and require, not implore, citizens to check their own behavior, ensuring that the way we live no longer endangers species in any way. Aransas must be set aside to protect the whooping crane; the land occupied by highways, mines, and pipelines must be turned back to the American burying beetle; if need be, Albany, Buffalo, Detroit, and Chicago must be dismantled if this would ensure the survival of the Karner Blue butterfly; the variola virus must be saved.

Extreme as this picture may look, the language of "unimpeachable rights" demands such actions. Performing them, though, casts us into unsteady terrain. Widespread smallpox vaccination is no longer practiced. As a consequence, the escape of the virus into the general population could lead to thousands of deaths. The Noah Principle does not accept the legitimacy of these fears—a stance that one suspects few Americans would endorse, if only because it prevents us from reaching decisions by reason.

The Noah Principle will never hold sway. Not because of human greed, though that is certainly important. Not because we can't afford to enforce it fully, though that certainly is true. But because it does not answer to the spirit of the great conservationists themselves—people like Robert Porter Allen, the Audubon Society ornithologist who, more than anyone, saved the whooping crane from annihilation.

IN NOVEMBER 1946, Allen went to Aransas National Wildlife Refuge as the representative of a whooping crane project jointly sponsored by the Audubon Society and the U.S. Fish and Wildlife Service. At that time, twenty-five whoopers lived there. Almost nothing was known about their habits. Allen went to Aransas to learn them. For weeks, he walked the refuge as winter closed in, hoping the reclusive birds would let him come close. They never did. Noting that whoopers did not avoid cattle, Allen built a wooden bull with a rust-colored canvas coat as a blind. Holes in the nostrils let him peer out. He spent weeks hiding inside his Trojan bull, hoping whoopers would come close by. They didn't— they knew what real bulls looked like. That spring, the whoopers migrated, as they always do. Allen carefully assembled an almost-invisible network of blinds and waited for the birds to return. When they did, he spent joyful weeks observing families of one of "the biggest, rarest, and most wary birds in the world going about the business of everyday life only 150 feet away."

Allen was determined to solve the great whooper mystery: where it flew in the summer. Just before the birds went north that first year, Allen drove to the North Platte River in Nebraska, where the cranes were known to stop. The locals greeted him with enthusiasm. Allen had shared his love for the species with photographers from the magazines *Life* and *Natural History*, and the resultant imagery had stirred the Midwest into whooper madness. Hundreds of Nebraskans went on a twenty-four-hour whooper watch. The North Platte *Telegraph-Bulletin* asked its readers to phone Allen ("who is headquartering at the Hotel Pawnee . . . awaiting just such an alarm") if they saw the birds arrive. Radio stations issued daily whooper bulletins. Allen was besieged with phone calls in his hotel. Eventually, he found the birds, buzzing them with a borrowed plane as he snapped away with his camera. The cranes' arrival in Saskatoon, Saskatchewan, their last known stop before the breeding grounds, was splashed across the front page of the local *Star-Phoenix*. STAR-PHOENIX PHOTOGRAPHS RAREST BIRD IN WORLD, WHOOPING CRANE, read the headline. It was printed in red ink.

Allen thought he had the migration route down—except for the northern terminus, where the birds disappeared to breed in the great Canadian wilderness. He spent the summers of 1947 and 1948 flying over Saskatchewan, Alberta, and the Northwest Territories, hoping to spot the twin white flash of a whooping crane pair. Months of effort produced no result, and he gave up. Word reached him in June 1954 that whoopers had been spotted at the mouth of the Sass River, deep inside Wood Buffalo National Park, a huge, roadless, and almost inaccessible reserve at the northern edge of Alberta.

Because mounting an expedition takes time, Allen could not fly to Canada until the following summer. His first attempt to explore the area where the whoopers had been spotted ended in failure when the Sass River proved impossible to canoe. In nearby Fort Smith, he managed to inveigle a helicopter pilot into taking his party up the river, leapfrogging its impassable parts and dropping them off at a landmark a few miles from where they thought the nearest cranes were. Mosquitoes, rising in clouds of frightful density, made the walk to the breeding grounds miserable; the watery ground vibrated with their larvae. The men couldn't find the cranes and returned to the landing site. The next day was a repeat of their mosquito-ridden failure, as was the day after that. Slowly, Allen realized the pilot had set them down in the wrong place. They had no idea where they were. He radioed for help. They learned they were indeed on the Sass River, but miles from where they should have been. Eleven days passed as they waited for another helicopter. Summer commenced; blackflies joined the ranks of the mosquitoes. It developed that a helicopter was not available. The increasingly grouchy men walked along the near-impenetrable banks of the Sass. The first one and a half miles took thirteen hours of terrible labor to cover. When they straggled into Fort Smith, twenty-nine days had passed.

Two days later, Allen embarked on a third expedition, this time accompanied by one other researcher, Ray Stevens. It had turned out that a helicopter was, in fact, available. To their relief, the pilot took them to the correct place. It was a mess—moss and lichen in a mucky carpet beneath a snarl of spruce, tamarack, and dwarf birch. In the constant mist, visibility was often less than a hundred feet, sometimes less than fifty. The two men stumbled through the marsh, mosquitoes buzzing in their ears, trying to match up the maze of ponds they were splashing through with the one on the map. All at once, they saw a whooping crane, then another. The birds immediately flew away. Allen and Stevens looked for another week but never saw them again. By then, the two men were exhausted and filthy and bug-bitten. They were also elated: they had walked the species' breeding ground. A reporter from the New York *Herald Tribune* awaited their return to Fort Smith. Allen's journey was front-page news.

Several days later, Allen made a final plane trip over Wood Buffalo. He saw the pair again. With them were two fledglings. Young whoopers—at last! The pilot made a tight banking turn to make a second pass. Allen yelled with joy.

That shout expressed his passion for whoopers and other threatened birds, like the roseate spoonbill and the American egret. His campaign for the whooping crane turned it into the poster child for biodiversity, the symbol of everything natural that might be lost. The swell of excitement about the whooper that he created led in the 1960s to the first federal programs to protect endangered species, and in 1973 to the Endangered Species Act itself—results, it seems fair to say, greater than any he would have dreamed possible. (Allen didn't live to see it, though; he died in 1963.)

Why did Allen spend his life crusading for birds? Not because he thought they would provide a cure for cancer. Indeed, his books are full of scorn for people who measure value in dollars and cents. Nor did he devote those mosquito-filled summers to protecting the crane's unimpeachable right to exist. Saving the whooping crane, in his view, was not especially "natural." Even before people came to the Americas, nature had reduced the species to fewer than two thousand individuals, suggesting it was an evolutionary loser. We humans, Allen thought, "have singled out the Whooping Crane for survival for reasons that are peculiarly our own, in the face of the possibility that Nature had already greased the skids to its ultimate destruction."

Reasons that are peculiarly our own—Allen was referring to something of almost embarrassing obviousness. He wanted to save the whooping crane because he thought the big white creatures were grand and fascinating in and of themselves. Because the prospect of losing the species forever was sad. Because the birds occupied a piece of his heart that belonged to nothing else. Because, in sum, *he* valued them, a feeling shared by almost everyone who has ever seen a whooper.

Philosophers have a long tradition of thinking about value. Human beings, most say, are evaluators; human choices, the embodiment of all values. "Whatever has *value* in our world does not have value in itself," Nietzsche urged in a famous passage from *The Gay Science*. Rather, it "has been *given* value, as a present. And it was *we* [humans] who gave and bestowed it." If every person on Earth suddenly vanished, they would take with them every scrap of goodness, beauty, and morality, as well as all evil, ugliness, and wrong. Brute matter alone would be left. Humans alone can bewail the fate of the passenger pigeon, as Aldo Leopold put it. If humankind had vanished, no pigeon would have mourned. Only people can do these things.

Human beings commonly champion objects and goals with little or no utilitarian value, as Mark Sagoff, the philosopher, has noted. They attend religious services, volunteer at hospitals on weeknights that could otherwise be spent watching videos, take used automobile oil to disposal places even though they will never get caught dumping it in the bushes, take time to vote despite knowing that their input will make almost no difference to a national election. People do these things because they have value in a second, nonutilitarian sense, value that consists of some intangible but vital quality such as goodness or nobility of spirit. So why shouldn't Americans add saving species with little utilitarian value to the list of actions they perform to create and maintain this other kind of value? Indeed, "it is the useless species we most need and want to protect," Sagoff claimed.

> Whales are an example. Whale oil is no longer in demand for illumination. Those of us who deplore the hunting of whales are not concerned with sustainable harvests or with long-run yields of blubber. Nor are there obvious ecological reasons to protect whales: in their absence, the seas would not fill up with krill. Plainly, hunting whales is appalling for moral and aesthetic reasons.

Because prudence will save so few species, caring about biodiversity becomes, as Sagoff told us, a question "about right and wrong, and should be treated as such first and foremost."

The Noah Principle embraces the same view, of course, but does so by creating what thinkers since Kant have called a "perfect duty" toward all species. Such a duty, Sagoff wrote, "does not admit of exceptions in order to accommodate wants, interests, or inclinations." A classic illustration of a perfect duty is that we must not enslave others, even if becoming a slaveholder would free us from poverty. By contrast, we do not have a perfect duty to help the poor. "Obviously it is distasteful, to say the least, if you gorge yourself while the world starves," Sagoff told us. "So some compassion is called for. But you don't have the *duty* to give up all of your own aspirations to help them."

The problem with creating a perfect duty to biodiversity is twofold. It is *unethical*, because trying to save every species perfectly would force our society to destroy many or all of its other accomplishments, an act of self-immolation that the ecologically concerned cannot force on others, who may have different but equally worthy goals. And it is *impracticable*, because this perfect duty is impossible to fulfill, even if our society were willing to turn back three hundred years of its history.

On the ethical side, the desire to protect biodiversity must not overwhelm other human goals. It would be wrong, for instance, if we allowed concern for the environment to destroy someone's aspirations to educate their children, or to provide good health care for their family, or to live in a safe, comfortable home. We can make it harder to do these things, but at some point we risk doing wrong in trying to act right. "You're not supposed to starve your children to build the cathedral," Sagoff told us. "Nor should you ignore your spiritual duties to buy them all fancy cars. Fulfilling either obligation absolutely means ignoring the other. Sometimes you can do pretty well on both. But sometimes they conflict, and you have to make a choice of which good thing you're going to give the most to."

Reverence for biodiversity, in other words, stands alongside other values, and we must negotiate among them. Finding ways to do that did not discourage Sagoff. "We have a lot of ways that we deal with questions of right and wrong," he said. "Americans balance moral and ethical imponderables all the time." No matter how we do it, though, we must recognize that protecting endangered species is an imperfect duty, bound by the need to respect our ethical duties toward others.

On the practicable side, saving every species is akin to maintaining a completely risk-free, absolutely unpolluted environment. Creating such a pristine environment, Sagoff wrote in *The Economy of the Earth*,

> is meritorious from a moral point of view, and a society acts virtuously in attempting to eliminate pollution, just as it acts virtuously in attempting to eliminate poverty. Yet a society that stops short of committing enormous resources to efforts of this kind does not necessarily violate moral obligations. A virtuous society, of course, makes it a policy to go the "extra mile" to eliminate the causes of poverty, pollution, and other evils. But we are permitted, at some point, to take economic costs and technical feasibility into account.

Acknowledging that a problem is moral, in other words, does not mean abjuring practicable concerns. Everyone may agree that, from an ethical point of view, protecting the whooping crane is a good thing to do. But they can also agree that the same protection is, pragmatically speaking, a costly, even losing, economic proposition. The two viewpoints are not mutually exclusive, and both must play a role in making choices. "To balance the ethical with the prudential," Sagoff has argued, "is to recognize that the way toward ideals which are morally valuable, like the protection of nature, must be *practicable*. . . . A prudent regard for our interests determines when virtuous action would be supererogatory: that is, morally praiseworthy, but impracticable and above and beyond the call of duty."

Casting the value of biodiversity in this way suggests a middle road: greater protection than that mandated by utilitarian values alone but less than the perfect duty demanded by the Noah Principle. Both of the other two approaches, however, have the distinct advantage of simplifying the process of choice. In principle, abjuring all but utilitarian values would enable us to turn the protection of biodiversity over to economists, eager to measure the dollar value of anything. The protection of biodiversity would be reduced to a series of benefit-cost calculations. Species would have to pay their way or face extinction. At the other extreme, putting the Noah Principle into practice would turn the task over to biologists, eager to defend the ecological worth of every creature. The protection of biodiversity would be reduced to a series of engineering decisions, designing arks to save every species without regard to cost. In either case, we have a roadmap to decisions.

Rejecting these extremes leaves us in a quandary. We are forced to admit the value of both economics and ecology, and must struggle to reconcile mutually incompatible goals that are often equally praiseworthy. The only advantage of this stance is that it means recognizing the human condition. On the individual level, people make these painful decisions every time they choose between saving for their children's education and for their own retirement. On the level of society, people choose among moral goals through the creation of laws.

In Robert Allen's day, the law imposed few duties toward biodiversity. When he traveled to Aransas, his expenses were paid by his employer, the National Audubon Society, a private organization; when he convinced the helicopter pilot to fly him near the whooper's breeding grounds, he used persuasion, not the coercive force of the state; and when he exhorted others to join his crusade, he drew on the love for the crane shared by his fellow biologists, naturalists, and citizens in Canada and the United States—but he could not order people to change the way they lived. People helped him because they thought saving the crane was good and virtuous, not because they had a legal obligation to participate.

Since that time, laws like the Endangered Species Act have expanded our obligations, pushing them closer to the realm of perfect duties. Moving away from the old balance is surely good in principle, because in the past our legal system did not nudge us to remember our natural heritage and thereby may have helped to encourage thoughtless waste. At the same time, one can wonder whether our laws today strike the proper balance among goods (that is, whether they are ethical), and whether they respect the importance of having appropriate means (that is, whether they are practicable).

A clue to the answer came during our visit to Florida. After visiting the cranes, we drove to a restaurant a few miles away with Stephen Nesbitt, the biologist. The restaurant looked like any farmland eatery: faded tablecloths of red-and-white plaid, a plethora of calendars on the wall, pickup trucks in the parking lot. The room was full of burly men who looked as if they worked outdoors. To our surprise, heads swiveled in our direction when we entered. The object of the stares was not us, the two strangers with notebooks, but Nesbitt, in his Game and Freshwater Fish uniform.

Although every table had at least one diner, many had enough open chairs to accommodate us. We moved toward one, but Nesbitt demurred; he thought sharing a table with locals might lead to an unpleasant incident. The waitress watched us leave and did not say a word. After driving several miles down the road without finding another restaurant, we turned around and retraced our route. Passing the first restaurant, we continued back to St. Cloud, some thirty miles away, where we finally had lunch.

Along the way, it occurred to us that matters had gone awry. Ranchers, farmers, loggers, and the like live in rural places because they love the outdoors and its inhabitants. Nesbitt was a biologist for precisely the same reason. Yet Nesbitt's uniform set them off. Something about the simple presence of someone associated with government-organized efforts to preserve wild areas attracted hostility from the very people who live there. Nesbitt seemed to accept the anger as normal. When we pored through the history of our efforts to preserve biodiversity—the history, in essence, of the Endangered Species Act—we understood why.

Chapter Six

"THE AWFUL BEAST
IS BACK"

R ARE IS the day when sitting U.S. attorneys general take
time from administering the Department of Justice to in-
tervene personally in a lawsuit. Rarer still are the occasions when they argue cases themselves in the chambers of the
Supreme Court. And most rare of all are the days when they ask
the nine justices to inspect a dead fish. On April 18, 1978, though,
Griffin Bell, attorney general for the Carter administration, did
exactly that. A big man with a raspy, deeply southern voice, Bell
interrupted his oral argument to withdraw a test tube from his
jacket pocket. "I have in my hand a darter," he proclaimed, "a
snail darter." The snail darter, a freshwater fish no bigger than a
human thumb, had been placed on the endangered species list
three years before; the case involved a dam that would destroy its
only known habitat. Bell handed the fish to the bench. The test
tube made its way along the line of nine justices, each of whom
solemnly peered at its contents before passing it to a neighbor.
Stopping a dam that would provide thousands of jobs for the sake
of this insignificant fish? Ridiculous! The attorney general stood
back, satisfied, as laughter filled the court. The laughter was
halted by the quiet voice of Justice John Paul Stevens. "Mr. Attorney General," he said, "your exhibit makes me wonder. Does the
Government take the position that some endangered species are
entitled to more protection than others?" Bell's smile disappeared.
The justice was asking whether the law protected such magnifi-

cent creatures as bald eagles and grizzly bears but not lowly beings like the birdwing pearly mussel or the snail darter. Bell had no answer. By scornfully displaying the test tube, he had clearly demonstrated that he regarded some species as not deserving of legal protection. Conceding this, however, would open the door to another question: on what basis would Bell draw the line?

Rare too is the day that the Supreme Court considers a case like *Tennessee Valley Authority v. Hill*. Established in 1933 to control floods in and provide hydroelectric power to the poor rural communities in southern Appalachia, the TVA eventually built sixty dams, reservoirs, and flood-control projects in four states. *TVA v. Hill* concerned the sixty-first: the Tellico Dam, a $110 million project on the Little Tennessee River, fourteen miles downstream from its confluence with the Tellico River and about thirty miles southwest of Knoxville, in the eastern part of the state. Opposition to Tellico, local and national, had been intense for years. Nature lovers argued that the dam would obliterate the last free-flowing stretch of a once-beautiful river; anglers, that it would ruin the best trout fishing east of the Mississippi. Worst of all, Tellico would drown scores of religious and archaeological sites—the area had been home to the Cherokee Nation and its capital, Tanasi, until Uncle Sam drove them away in 1838. Proponents of the dam claimed that it would provide construction jobs, attract industry to a poor area, create a beautiful lake for recreation, and be the center of a brand-new small city. In addition, the dam was more than 90 percent complete; throwing away the construction costs would be unconscionable. None of these arguments mattered. The snail darter, not scenery, recreation, and history, was at issue in *TVA v. Hill*. Closing the floodgates of Tellico would inundate its sole known habitat, and the species would vanish within weeks.

Despite Stevens's close questioning, Bell was confident that the dam would prevail, as were most of its other backers. They could not imagine a world in which a tiny fish could stop an almost-complete dam. But that is exactly how the world turned out to be. The Supreme Court gave the victory to the snail darter, flabbergasting the members of Congress who had passed the Endangered

Species Act only a few years before. The official surprise was, so to speak, unsurprising. The Endangered Species Act sprang less from informed policymaking than from the simple aspiration to save everything—to banish extinction from the face of the planet, or at least from the United States. *TVA v. Hill* demonstrated that turning this appealing aspiration into a duty would be harder and more fractious than anyone initially realized. Indeed, even those who fought to broaden the government's role in guarding endangered species have been surprised at how expansive that role has become. And nobody anticipated how impracticable the duty to save everything would be.

THE ROOTS of the political effort to protect biodiversity go back to October 1956, when Ray C. Erickson, a federal wildlife biologist, met with thirty-three other people in a conference room in Washington, D.C., to discuss the whooping crane. Although Robert Porter Allen's exploration of its breeding grounds had created enormous public interest, the bird was not faring well. That year, the total number of wild whooping cranes stood at just twenty-four. Fearing the loss of America's favorite endangered species, the Fish and Wildlife Service asked to meet with ornithologists, conservationists, zoo and museum directors, and officials of the Canadian Wildlife Service. Erickson had rarely seen such a tense gathering. Everyone there had devoted years to saving the crane, and all agreed that the situation was dire. But they were angrily divided over how next to proceed. One side, led by little-known wildlife managers, argued that the species could be saved only by capturing all the young birds, breeding them until their numbers rose, and then releasing them into the wild. The other side, dominated by the renowned Allen, believed that despite the low population figures, the crane was capable of rescuing itself. Seizing the birds would be too risky, Allen argued, because it might injure them. And the thought of the whooping crane surviving only in captivity was vile. The first group responded that the second group's sentimental inaction would only hasten the death of the species. Tempers flew. "It wasn't a very tranquil meeting, to say the least," Erickson later recalled. It lasted for seven hours, and it ended, he said, in a "heated stalemate."

Erickson had a plan that he had hoped would be acceptable to both factions. Why not conduct some initial breeding experiments on the greater sandhill crane, a whooper relative that was not endangered? If the results were good, the methods could then be transferred to the rare whooper itself. "But there was so much discord at the meeting," he said, "that I didn't think it was prudent to bring [the idea] up at the time." Indeed, his proposal was not fully aired until 1961, when the incoming Kennedy administration circulated a memorandum urging agency heads to give serious consideration to new ideas from their staffs. "That was the wedge I used to get attention," Erickson said. With a few thousand dollars from the agency, he set up breeding pens at the Monte Vista Wildlife Refuge, in south-central Colorado. It was the first federal project to focus on endangered species.

Several years' work on sandhill cranes and other species convinced Erickson that the service should try to incubate eggs taken from birds in the field rather than try to induce captured birds to mate in captivity.* Because Allen still opposed tinkering with natural processes, Erickson was unable to win approval for his scheme. By luck, Senator Karl E. Mundt, Republican of South Dakota, had an aide who worried that his children would never see a whooping crane. Mundt was impressed by his aide's arguents— and by the large color photograph of the bird that Erickson hurriedly produced so that Mundt could hang it on his wall. In 1965, the senator squeezed out $350,000 for an endangered-wildlife research program at the Patuxent Wildlife Research Center, near Laurel, Maryland. At last, Erickson had the funds, the facility, and the manpower to get things done—at least for the whooping crane, and possibly for a few other species.

Establishing an endangered-species program was not easy. Ex-

---

*Examining the censuses taken at Aransas, Erickson had noticed that the arriving whooper families usually consisted of two adults and one young. Nesting whoopers generally hatch two chicks, but the stronger pushes out the weaker, which dies. Erickson reasoned that taking one egg would guarantee the survival of that chick, while leaving a second that would not be threatened by its sibling.

cept for a few well-known examples like the whooper, Erickson
didn't know what creatures were in trouble or why. Nobody had
compiled a catalogue raisonné of the nation's vanishing biodiversity. The closest approach was a card file on threatened wildlife
begun in 1960 by the IUCN, the Swiss-based alliance of private
environmental groups. Because the IUCN data skipped around the
entire world, Erickson realized that the agency would need to create its own, more complete inventory for the United States. Thus
was born the Committee on Rare and Endangered Wildlife Species (CREWS), a group of Fish and Wildlife biologists. Hastily assembling what information was at hand, CREWS produced a
tentative list in January 1964; by the next August, the tally was in
sufficiently good shape to be called a "preliminary draft." It gave
a brief natural history of 62 animals—36 birds, 15 mammals, 6
fish, and 5 reptiles and amphibians—and described the threats
faced by each. CREWS sent out hundreds of copies of the draft.
Responses flooded in, and the inventory grew. It contained 142
species in 1968, when it was first published officially. By 1973, the
list filled 289 pages and included 70 birds, 44 mammals, 55 fish,
and 18 reptiles and amphibians.

All the while, Fish and Wildlife considered the even more
vexing question of what to do about the animals on the list. Back
in 1964, Dan Janzen, then director of Fish and Wildlife, had announced his retirement. As his successor, Interior Secretary Stewart Udall chose John Gottschalk, head of the Fish and Wildlife
office in Boston. Presciently, Udall told Gottschalk that endangered species would become an issue of paramount importance. He
suggested that Gottschalk ask the departing Janzen to review the
problem and suggest solutions. Janzen's memorandum outlined a
three-step process. The first step, he wrote, was to establish an ob-
jective definition for *endangered*. In compiling its lists, CREWS had
simply used its own judgment; Janzen thought this was too unsci-
entific. The second step was to identify the threats—hunting, habitat loss, and so forth—facing listed species. The last step was to
develop a plan to watch over each species on the list. Because habitat transformation was the major threat, Janzen argued, protecting
species would in many cases mean conserving that habitat.

Janzen's last step, arguably the most important, was certainly the hardest. Before 1964, Fish and Wildlife could safeguard land only by persuading Congress to pass special legislation conferring protected status on a given area. That year, however, Congress created the Land and Water Conservation Fund, which took in revenue from recreational user fees, surplus land sales, and a tax on motorboat fuel. The legislation authorized Fish and Wildlife to use the money for a variety of purposes, including, happily, "the preservation of species of fish or wildlife that are threatened with extinction." Unhappily, the fund had a peculiar catch. Fish and Wildlife could buy land with the money only if the purchase was authorized under a law *other* than the one establishing the fund, and no law had ever given that power to the agency.

New Fish and Wildlife director Gottschalk decided to buy some property anyway. He proposed taking $3.1 million from the Land and Water Conservation Fund in fiscal 1965 to acquire habitat for the whooping crane, the Mexican duck, the Florida sandhill crane, and several rare Hawaiian birds. (Although the sandhill crane was not imperiled, a subspecies, the Florida sandhill crane, was in trouble.) After Gottschalk submitted the plan to the Bureau of the Budget, he was asked how the purchase could be justified legally. Gottschalk in turn asked the Interior Department solicitor—the head lawyer of the department—whether he could get away with it. "Probably," the solicitor in effect said, "but you'd be a lot better off with an actual law giving you the power to buy the land." From that point, the Interior Department pursued a double track. On the one hand, Gottschalk tried to brazen through the budget request; on the other, his boss, Secretary Udall, attempted to induce Congress to pass legislation awarding him the authority to make the request.

Following the first track, Gottschalk testified in February 1965 before a caustically skeptical House subcommittee chaired by Winfield Denton, Democrat of Indiana. Denton went line by line through the habitat-purchase plan, not troubling to conceal his contempt for the fuzzy-headed bureaucrats who wanted to spend millions of dollars in real money to buy land for a bunch of useless birds. Of Gottschalk's $3.1 million, Denton noted, $1.1 million would buy five thousand acres of whooping crane habitat. "According to your records," he said, "there were only thirty-two [adult] whooping cranes in the spring of 1964, so the acquisition of this land would be at a cost of about $35,000 per bird. Do you think that the expenditure of funds on this basis could be considered as wise use of the taxpayers' money?"

It wasn't just a few birds, Gottschalk remonstrated. At issue, he said, was "the prevention of one entire species of animal from disappearing from the face of the earth."

Denton was unimpressed. He knew long division and didn't like what he saw when he applied it to Gottschalk's proposal. Saving the Florida sandhill crane, Denton calculated, would cost taxpayers $1,400 per crane; the Mexican duck, $5,800 per duck; the Hawaiian birds, a bargain-basement $100 apiece. All in all, he figured, this was some pretty expensive poultry. The subcommittee bounced the entire plan, telling Gottschalk that he would have to persuade Congress to pass a law specifically allowing the Interior Department to buy habitat.

On the second track, Secretary Udall was working to do just that, and more. Three months later, Congress debated a bill that would not only empower Fish and Wildlife to buy habitat, but called on the Agriculture, Defense, and Interior departments to protect endangered species and their habitat on land under their jurisdiction. Federal land was now managed, Udall told a congressional committee, to maximize the returns from logging, mining, agriculture, flood control, hydroelectric power, and so on. Often such uses of the land, praiseworthy in themselves, conflicted with preserving biodiversity. Therefore, he said, the bill he was proposing included "a clear policy statement as to the precedence of species protection." Capitol Hill enthusiastically agreed. "It would be most unfortunate and a waste of money," one Senate report on the bill argued, "to carry out an endangered species program designed to conserve and protect the species and their habitat and find that other Federal agencies are not taking similar steps in regard to the species and habitat found on their lands."

The Endangered Species Act of 1966 sailed through Congress with almost no objection. The law authorized the Secretary of the

Interior to compile a list of domestic fish and wildlife species menaced by extinction. It gave Fish and Wildlife permission to spend $15 million to buy habitat for those species. It told the Agriculture, Defense, and Interior departments that Congress wanted them to preserve the habitats of endangered species on the lands under their jurisdiction, "insofar as is practicable and consistent with their primary purpose." And it instructed the secretary of the Interior to "encourage other Federal agencies to utilize, where practicable, their authorities."

Practicable was a safety valve. To Udall's way of thinking, it provided room for balance where balance was needed. Take the federal prairie dog program, for example. Because prairie dogs gobbled up cattle feed, government agencies spent a lot of time poisoning them. The poison also killed black-footed ferrets, which were critically endangered. Whenever practicable, the program should be modified or curtailed if it could hurt ferrets. Similarly, federal game managers often tried to give game fish free run of a river by poisoning the fish that competed with them for food— "trash fish," in the angler's lexicon. Under the act, the game managers should think twice before poisoning a stream full of endangered fish. The idea was to give endangered species a high priority in federal programs and on federal land, but not *sole* priority. There was no explicit prohibition on killing them, and the secretary's power to "encourage" other agencies was only that, without any recourse if persuasion failed.

Udall hoped that the 1966 act might, by itself, provide enough protection to ensure the survival of endangered species. He soon learned that entrenched federal bureaucracies would treat "insofar as is practicable" not as a means for balance but as an invitation to ignore the law. Because Fish and Wildlife could not ban outright the killing of endangered species, other parts of the government got away with paying lip service to conservation. And even Fish and Wildlife was no model of rapid action—it failed to acquire any habitat until 1968, when it picked up 2,300 acres for the National Key deer, a subspecies in the Florida Keys. "All we had was persuasion and [the ability to buy land], and probably they were adequate, if sincerely applied," said Jack Berryman, then the head of Fish and Wildlife's Division of Wildlife Services. "But more was needed."

To some conservationists, the whale imbroglio was the last straw. Congress amended the Endangered Species Act in 1969, expanding the list to include endangered species found outside the United States and prohibiting the importation of products made from them. In July 1970, the Interior Department proposed adding eight whales to the list, including the almost extinct blue, right, and humpback whales. Three of the others—the finback, sei, and sperm whales—were the chief remaining prey of commercial whalers. Because listing the sperm whale would effectively ban the profitable market in sperm-whale oil for submarines, the Pentagon and the Commerce Department fought the action. Knowing that the decision to list a species was supposed to be a purely scientific judgment, they claimed their objections were not commercially motivated. Instead, they harped on the provision in the law that species on the list had to be in imminent danger. The three whales, although greatly reduced by overhunting, did not face *immediate* extinction; their position would not become truly unrecoverable for another few decades. As a result, Fish and Wildlife director Gottschalk concluded in September that, technically speaking, the finback, sei, and sperm whales did not belong on the list.

Regarding this as an affront to common sense, Interior Secretary Walter J. Hickel decided to list them anyway, which involved publishing a notice to that effect in the *Federal Register*. Two days before Thanksgiving, Hickel submitted the final rule to the printers, who would publish it after the holiday. Unfortunately for Hickel's federal career, this flamboyant man had also sent a letter to President Richard M. Nixon protesting his Vietnam policies. The letter made headlines on the day before Thanksgiving, and Nixon summarily fired Hickel. Seeing opportunity in Hickel's downfall, the Pentagon and the Commerce Department pressured Hickel's second in command, E. U. Curtis Bohlen, a passionate environmentalist, to withdraw the listing. In a deadpan voice

Bohlen told us that, with the holiday weekend approaching, "I somehow couldn't get around to it." The rule was published on the following Wednesday.

Like many environmentalists in those days, "Buff" Bohlen, as he is known, had impeccable Republican credentials. The nephew of Charles E. "Chip" Bohlen, an ambassador to the Soviet Union and major State Department figure, Buff graduated from Harvard, served in the Korean War, and worked for more than a dozen years in the State Department. In 1969, he became undersecretary of the Interior, a position that let him influence policy on endangered species. The whale fight, Bohlen thought, showed that the government had to be able to say no. Fish and Wildlife must be able to ban killing endangered species outright. And listing couldn't be delayed by spurious objections—the Pentagon had been able to come up with a substitute submarine oil without much trouble. When Bohlen set down all the changes he wanted in the law, they filled twenty pages. Realizing it would be better to begin anew, Bohlen threw away his amendments and wrote a completely new Endangered Species Act. In February 1972, President Nixon sent Bohlen's bill to Congress, arguing that the old law "simply [did] not provide the kind of management tools needed to act early enough to save a vanishing species." In so doing, the President set into motion a process that rapidly went out of control.

BY ALL REPORTS, Richard Nixon was not a committed environmentalist. On the other hand, he was not a green-basher, either. "I came up in February or March [1969] and had my interview with the President," recalled Nathaniel P. Reed, who became the Interior Department's assistant secretary for Fish and Wildlife. One of Reed's priorities was to stop ranchers from using the coyote-killing chemical 1080, because it also killed wildcats, eagles, and many other species. "I told him I wanted 1080 off the public land," Reed said, "and he looked up and said, 'My wife has always been on me to get that stuff off the land. I don't know what it is, but you can have my assurance of support.'"

"His [Nixon's] position was a fairly crass one, I guess you'd say," John D. Ehrlichman, then the presidential assistant for domestic affairs, explained to us. "In his view, the environmental issues were one of those class of issues that had no political magic. They had the potential for costing a lot of people jobs, and that was bad, but they also were something that a small number of people cared passionately about, so it was an issue that wasn't going to go away." Ehrlichman added, "He said to me, basically, 'You look out for this subject. Keep us out of trouble. Do what you think is right. If you have any questions, you come up to me.'"

Ehrlichman had no questions about Bohlen's revised Endangered Species Act, which looked like "feel-good" legislation—something that would let everyone in Washington, D.C., the President included, stand up for bald eagles and whooping cranes without any practical downside. As a consequence, the initial congressional reception to Nixon's call for legislation was nonpartisan, enthusiastic, and idealistic to the extreme; legislators fell all over themselves to submit stronger versions of an Endangered Species Act. The House Merchant Marine and Fisheries Committee held hearings in March and April 1972 on fourteen bills; the Senate Commerce Committee later worked on three more.

For all the fanfare, the bills did not greatly differ from Bohlen's version; all exalted the human need to preserve the world's natural heritage and instructed Fish and Wildlife to go to work. Not that Capitol Hill regarded the matter as urgent—eighteen months after Nixon introduced the legislation, no law had been passed, though the halls of Congress continued to ring with proclamations of nonpartisan goodwill. Senator John Tunney, Democrat of California, was still trumpeting in July 1973 that allowing "the extinction of animal species is ecologically, economically, and ethically unsound." Across the aisle, Senator Charles Percy, Republican of Illinois, responded within the hour that "for too long there has been insufficient means to protect and preserve all the valuable species of wildlife that contribute so much to the quality of life as we know it." The new law, rumbled Congressman Melvin Price, a powerful and conservative Democrat from Illinois, would do nothing less than "protect man from himself."

Few members of Congress paid attention to the text of the legislation they extolled, and fewer yet noticed the evolution of a tiny phrase in what eventually became Section 7 of the final bill, which outlined the federal government's duties toward endangered species. One target of Bohlen's wrath was the Interior Department's inability to do more than "encourage other Federal agencies to utilize, where practicable, their authorities" to protect endangered species. Accordingly, his proposed law said those agencies "*shall* utilize, where practicable, their authorities" to safeguard biodiversity. In legal terms, the rephrasing was a small but important stiffening of the language—the equivalent, according to Paul Lenzini, then the chief counsel for the trade association of the state fish and wildlife agencies, of telling other federal agencies to carry out their ordinary duties but "do the best you can to avoid endangering any of these critters." It was, Lenzini thought, a "sensible" approach.

Sensible wasn't enough, in the view of Frank M. Potter, Jr., then counsel for the Merchant Marine and Fisheries Committee. In Potter's view, he was in the right place at the right time. Most of the House members treated Merchant Marine as if it were "off in the wilderness," he told us. The only commercial interests paying attention were shipbuilders, "who didn't care much one way or another" about endangered species. "We were able to operate in relative obscurity," he said. "As long as people consider you benign and irrelevant, you're likely to get a lot of four hundred–to–thirty votes." That was good, because Potter intended to slip some surprises into the legislation. To Potter's way of thinking, "the business-as-usual mentality" wasn't "terribly concerned" about biodiversity. "It's too easy to say, 'We'd like to do this but we can't right now.'" It might be all right in theory for the law to have a balancing mechanism, but in practice, Potter believed, endangered species always lost. The solution was not to come up with some allegedly better balancing mechanism; it was to have no balancing mechanism at all—a Noah Principle law. "We wanted," he said, "to make the mesh in the net as fine as we could get away with."

"We" meant Potter and the man he called his "coconspirator": Lee M. Talbot, then the senior scientist at the newly formed

Council on Environmental Quality. Formerly an ecologist for the United Nations and the Smithsonian Institution, Talbot had grown up in an environmental family: his father knew Aldo Leopold, the great conservationist, and his mother was the daughter of the first director of the Biological Survey, the bureaucratic ancestor of the Fish and Wildlife Service. Talbot had stumped for endangered species since the 1950s; as head ecologist of the Smithsonian Institution in the 1960s, he testified on behalf of the first Endangered Species Act. In the 1970s, he wrote the Marine Mammal Protection Act; in the 1980s, he became the director general of the IUCN. At this time, Talbot, like Potter, saw an opportunity to put some bite in the law. And Talbot, like Potter, thought that the whale battle had demonstrated that it was a bad idea to leave any wiggle-room. Although Talbot respected Bohlen's intentions, he thought the administration's draft law "was pretty damn weak." Since few in Congress seemed to be paying real attention, Talbot, working inside the administration, and Potter, working on Capitol Hill, decided to plug the holes themselves. "I had targeted everything that was too weak," Talbot said, "and Frank had picked up things I hadn't, so what we did from our two branches was work out a step-by-step process to kill off those things."

The most important task was to get rid of all vestiges of the word *practicable*. As is customary, the House and Senate had considered separate versions of Bohlen's bill in 1972. When Congress, distracted by the fall elections, failed to act, each chamber reintroduced it the next year. But as the bills marched through committee hearings and back to their respective chambers for a vote, Potter and Talbot worked them over. In the House version, which Potter shepherded from committee to Congress, *practicable* was banished; in the Senate version, it was limited to one mention. Without any appeal to practicability, federal agencies would no longer have an exit.

Almost as important, Potter and Talbot revised the preamble of the bills, which laid out their purpose. As revised, the goal of the legislation was, in part, to conserve and protect "the ecosystems upon which endangered and threatened species of wildlife depend." Because ecosystems cover land, the preamble in effect committed the entire federal government to a mandatory program of habitat protection. "That's where we really stuck it to them," Potter said.

"As that bill drifted through the Hill and the other agencies and OMB [the Office of Management and Budget], there were probably not more than four of us who understood its ramifications," Bohlen said. "It was only sometime after its passage that people realized its implications. We certainly didn't advertise it. Why should we have? It was not our intent to ring alarm bells." Discussions centered on other features of the legislation: adding threatened species to the list, listing species even if they faced danger in just part of their range, removing the $15 million cap on habitat acquisition, and outlining an extensive program of cooperative agreements with the states. The act now covered all species, not just vertebrates, and made it a federal offense to "take"—harass, harm, pursue, hunt, shoot, wound, kill, trap, capture, or collect, in the definition of the law—listed species (except plants on nonfederal property). Each bill passed with little opposition.

Because the House and Senate versions differed, the two chambers had to meet to forge a single mutually acceptable piece of legislation. To Potter, Talbot, and Bohlen, the House-Senate conference was the last obstacle to a strong law. To their pleasure, the ramifications of Section 7 and the preamble continued to escape attention from the kingpins of "business as usual." The only holdover from the "practicable" era, the single mention in the Senate version, was struck out during the conference with little protest or notice. "The people from the Senate didn't care all that hard," Potter said. "We, though, knew exactly what we were doing." The result expanded the duties owed endangered species by all federal agencies—and left no "practicable" way out.

When the conferees presented the final bill to their respective chambers, the floor votes were lopsided. Not a single senator cast a ballot against the bill and only four members of the House of Representatives did. President Nixon signed the Endangered Species Act on December 28, 1973.

Few members of Congress, Paul Lenzini told us, had the "fog-giest idea" of what they were doing. "There was no idea that their ox was being gored," he said, "so they all voted for it." Even Bohlen, the act's original author, didn't appreciate the financial implications of his work. When his initial bill was passed through the Office of Management and Budget, he was asked the cost of enforcing it. "I said it just rearranges things a little bit and I can't believe it will cost much more than we're currently spending." Did he really think that? "My tongue was in my cheek a little," he told us, "but I had no idea ultimately how much money would be needed to implement it."

In the short run, the act did cost relatively little, because noth-ing happened. Lynn Greenwalt, newly appointed the director of the Fish and Wildlife Service after eighteen years in the agency, approached the new Endangered Species Act with caution that verged on terror. To begin with, the law applied to all species. As a biologist, Greenwalt knew that most species are insects, plants, and fungi. He also knew that this would come as a surprise to Capitol Hill. "They weren't thinking about dung beetles," he said to us. "They were thinking of huge grizzly bears and bald eagles and stately monarchs of the air." Congress could not possibly un-derstand the implications of its own words.

More important, the act just didn't *look* like other legislation. On its face, Section 7 of the law gave a little-known branch of the Interior Department near-absolute powers over the 30 percent of the country owned by Uncle Sam, and considerable leverage over any part of the rest that had a project regulated or financed by the federal government. Greenwalt liked to proclaim in a down-home voice that "even a fellow from the sticks" knew that these projects are everywhere. Offshore-oil leases, deep-sea mining operations, veterans' hospitals, hydroelectric dams, interstate gas pipelines, federal highways, coastal housing developments—the Endangered Species Act could, in principle, reach its fingers into all. Telling Fish and Wildlife to slam on the brakes when any such project hurt an endangered species was equivalent to creating a new blue-print for growth across much of the nation. Conservationists later hailed the law as "prescient," but Greenwalt doubted that Congress had in mind such sweeping changes. If it had, Greenwalt's agency, a haven for guys with gimme caps who liked to work outdoors, would hardly be the one chosen to implement those changes. As an advocate of protecting biodiversity, Greenwalt believed that redirecting economic growth was a good idea. But he also thought that the quickest way to lose his power would be to let Capitol Hill find out he had it.

Greenwalt's belief was not mere cynicism, for Congress provided ample proof that its members had never considered what saving the country's natural heritage would require. For instance, yet another little-debated provision of the law required the Smithsonian Institution to write down the plants that its botanists believed should adorn the endangered species list. In January 1975, the museum published its candidates: almost 3,200 species. Other petitions flooded in, too. By that fall more than 20,000 species of plant and animal had been nominated, each of which had to be individually evaluated. The agency's listing department then had a staff of seven professionals. Following the bureaucratic procedures necessary to list a single species took one professional almost a month of eight-hour days. At that rate, processing the candidates would take five centuries.

With visions of bureaucratic gridlock dancing in his head, Greenwalt begged for more staff and more money. To fulfill Congress's stated intent, he told the House Merchant Marine and Fisheries Committee in October 1975, Fish and Wildlife would need to triple its biodiversity staff over the next few years. The total endangered species budget—for listing species, conducting research, consulting with other federal agencies, and generally administering the law—was then $7.5 million; Greenwalt needed three times that. Habitat acquisition was a separate matter, for which Congress had appropriated $6.9 million in 1976. For 1977, Greenwalt told the committee, he needed $115 million; $189 million more would cover the next four years. (In fact, Congress appropriated $41 million for that five-year period.)

When Greenwalt testified the next year before the House Appropriations Committee, his request included $2.5 million to purchase habitat for the Mississippi sandhill crane, a subspecies of the sandhill crane. Once again, a head of Fish and Wildlife faced a hostile congressional committee chair, in this case Sidney Yates, another powerful and conservative Democrat from Illinois. Why on earth, the incredulous Yates asked, was Fish and Wildlife going to spend so much money on these birds? Only forty cranes were left, Greenwalt told him. An interstate highway was about to pave over their last known habitat, to which they had clung for millennia. Yates asked, "Can't we transfer them somewhere?"

"Not very feasibly," Greenwalt said.*

With such mixed signals coming from Capitol Hill, it is no surprise that Fish and Wildlife laid low for a while, then proceeded with the caution of a draftee sent to inspect a minefield. After the act was signed, the agency did not list any new species for a year. Then Greenwalt released his first suggested additions to the endangered list: three species of kangaroo, native only to Australia. He waited until 1975 to propose the first species that actually resided in a U.S. congressional district. The additions were a mixed bag: the grizzly bear, dropped from the list in 1969 because it was not threatened in Alaska and Canada, now relisted because it was threatened in the lower forty-eight states; the Scioto madtom, a catfish found only in one small area of Ohio and not seen since 1957; the American crocodile, subject of a long-running conservationists' campaign; the bayou darter, endemic to Mississippi but immediately in conflict with a Soil Conservation Corps project, which was modified to resolve the problem; and three Hawaiian birds—the Hawaiian creeper, Newell's Townsend's shearwater, and the po'ouli—that remained chiefly on parkland. "We were not trying to pick fights with the first ones," Greenwalt said, "and I don't know what we would have done if there had been a fight. We were just trying to develop the regulations to list them. If we didn't do it carefully, we could get everything undone for us."

"Carefully" meant staying away from cases like *TVA v Hill*—something the agency did not manage to do.

---

*Despite Yates's misgivings, the Appropriations Committee gave Greenwalt $4.2 million for the Mississippi sandhill crane—more than he had asked for. On the other hand, Congress raised the total endangered species budget, including funds for habitat acquisition, to only $24 million, less than one-fifth of what Greenwalt had said was needed.

THE TENNESSEE VALLEY AUTHORITY first considered the Tellico Dam back in 1936, when the site was the last, and least important, on a list of about seventy potential projects in the Tennessee River watershed. Despite Tellico's low priority, Congress appropriated funds for construction in 1942. The War Materials Production Board stopped the project four months later, saying the construction materials were needed to fight Hitler. The TVA spent the next twenty-five years trying to get it started again. In the view of some critics, the agency acted as if losing Tellico had been an affront to its collective pride that could not be forgiven until the dam was reauthorized. Nonsense, the TVA in effect said. It wanted Tellico for purely altruistic reasons. The project would be the centerpiece of a sprawling industrial, commercial, and residential development that would create a glittering new community of fifty thousand souls. On that basis, Congress reauthorized the dam in 1966, to the horror of the ad hoc coalition of citizens fighting Tellico. Amid cries of "boondoggle" and "white elephant," the coalition sued the TVA in 1971 over the inadequacy of its environmental-impact statements and halted the project for twenty months. Construction resumed in 1973, after the TVA corrected its oversight by producing a new statement that documented Tellico's destructive effects in loving detail.

That August, David Etnier, an ichthyologist in the zoology department of the University of Tennessee in Knoxville, snorkeled with a colleague in the lower reaches of the Little Tennessee. Etnier did not like Tellico and had testified to that effect in the lawsuit. Believing that further litigation might be in the offing, Etnier wanted to examine the area more closely. Unlike most of the river, a part of the reservoir site named Coytee Springs was not good for trout fishing, which meant that the state government hadn't surveyed it carefully. Etnier swam there, face mask pointing toward the river bottom, snorkel tip pointing toward the sky. Breaststroking through the shallows, he noticed a small fish on the stony bottom. That he spotted it at all was a testament to the ichthyologist's professional eye, for the fish was almost the same color as the gravel on which it rested. Etnier swam a bit closer. The fish moved a few inches, settling on a patch of sand. With expert care and speed, he scooped up the sand beneath the fish—and, with it, the fish itself. About three hundred species of fish are known in Tennessee. Etnier keeps a mental card file of them in his head. Flicking through it, he did not see the fish in his hands. That meant, he said, his catch was "something completely new to science." After swimming back to shore, he dropped it into a jar of formaldehyde.

From its body shape, Etnier knew that the fish was one of the North American freshwater fish commonly known as darters, because of their penchant for darting away at the last minute from exploring hands. More than 150 species in four genera are known, at least 90 of which are found in Tennessee; local fishing buffs often use them as bait. They are related to perches. This darter, Etnier saw, was a member of the genus *Percina*. But unlike other *Percina*, it had four broad chestnut stripes on its back. Otherwise, it seemed undistinguished. He returned the next day to the same place in the river, watched the darters for a while, and collected a dozen more specimens. Unusual for darters, their diet seemed to consist largely of small soft-bodied freshwater snails. This *Percina*, Etnier concluded, must be a "snail darter." To *Percina*, he eventually appended the species name *tanasi*, in honor of the Tellico-imperiled former Cherokee capital.

Congress passed the Endangered Species Act that December. A few months later, Hiram G. Hill, Jr., a student at the University of Tennessee Law School, learned about the new species from a friend who was one of Etnier's students. Hill, like Etnier, was unenthusiastic about the prospect of transforming a marvelous trout stream just fifty miles from Knoxville into another slice of fast-food Americana. He dropped by the zoology department and asked whether the species was in trouble. Yes, Etnier said. It had been found only in that part of the Little Tennessee, which had clear, swiftly moving waters. The dam would turn the spot into a reservoir, stopping the current and making the water cloudy. Tons of silt would settle onto the bottom, burying the snails that the darter depended on. Intrigued, Hill turned the plight of *P. tanasi* into a term paper for his environmental law course, which was taught by an energetic young professor named Zygmunt J. B. Plater. Plater then turned his student's paper into a new lease on life for Tellico's opponents.

Plater and Hill asked Fish and Wildlife in January 1975 to list the snail darter on an emergency basis as a federally endangered species. Keith Schreiner, head of the service's Office of Endangered Species, didn't like the attempt to force his hand. "I pleaded with the snail darter's protectors not to do this," he told us. "It was inevitable that the outcome would be to weaken the act, and I didn't want to save the snail darter at the expense of the law." Schreiner's begging fell on deaf ears; Plater was determined to be, in Schreiner's bitter words, "the snail darter savior." Six weeks after receiving the petition, Fish and Wildlife published in the *Federal Register* its intention to declare the fish an endangered species. TVA inundated the agency with complaints, but to no avail—the dam would, after all, bury the fish's only known habitat. On October 9, 1975, the service officially added *P. tanasi* to the endangered species list, identifying Tellico as the sole threat to the species' existence. Finishing the dam, the service ruled, "would result in total destruction of the snail darter's habitat." Henceforth, according to the law, no action of the federal government would be permitted to harm that habitat. The TVA paid no attention. Construction proceeded apace.

Infuriated, Hill, Plater, and Donald S. Cohen, an assistant dean of the law school, continued the fight by forming the Tennessee Endangered Species Committee. They raised money by printing bumper stickers, holding potluck dinners, selling T-shirts, and exploring the outer reaches of their credit card limits. The T-shirt quickly became notorious. It was modeled on the poster for the movie *Jaws*, which depicted a huge shark, mouth agape, rising from below to menace a swimming figure. On the shirt, the snail darter replaced the swimmer; beneath it, the jaws and nose of the shark formed the ominous acronym TVA. Hundreds were sold. The Tennessee Valley Authority ignored the ruckus. The inevitable lawsuit was filed early in 1976.

Many conservationists were not quick to join the crusade. Because something about the words *snail darter* lent themselves to ridicule, the battle over what was invariably dubbed a "two-inch minnow" was a public-relations disaster. "The national [environmental] groups said it looks like extremism and quite unbalanced," recalled Plater, who subsequently moved to Boston College Law School. "I said, if that were the case, we never would have brought the suit. I said, it's a clear example of the fact that you can have environmental benefits *and* economic benefits. There was no need for the twenty-fifth dam within fifty miles. There is no natural river left—there is now more shoreline in Tennessee than in all the Great Lakes." As for the "two-inch minnow" derided by talk-show hosts, he said, "It's a caricature. It's not a minnow; it's a perch. It's not two inches long; it's two and a half inches long. Most important, TVA sunk money into the project *knowing* it was there."

By the time the lawsuit went to trial, the dam was more than three-quarters finished. The TVA had already committed $78 million, including $29 million appropriated by Congress *after* legislators had been apprised of the dam's detrimental effects on an endangered species. In the view of TVA head Aubrey Wagner, the Endangered Species Act "required Federal agencies to take *reasonable* measures . . . to conserve endangered or threatened species of fish, wildlife, and plants." Abandoning a dam so near completion to save a tiny fish, Wagner thought, was not only unreasonable; it was flat-out crazy.

To Wagner's dismay, Tellico's opponents were quite willing to have their mental health questioned. Plater in particular battled nonstop for the fish, demonstrating in the process that a single obsessed person can fight city hall, provided that he is willing to work relentlessly, suffer ridicule, and sleep on activists' couches in Washington for weeks on end. At various times, he told us, the opponents of the snail darter threatened him with death, disbarment, and defunding (the University of Tennessee received grants from the TVA). Plater wouldn't stop. When a district court judge refused to stop construction, Plater, Hill, and Cohen appealed. The appellate court overturned that decision, at which point the TVA appealed. After the Supreme Court agreed to hear the case, Attor-

ney General Griffin Bell chose to argue the TVA's case himself.*
That was when he produced what he regarded as the substance of
the dispute: a two-and-one-half-inch perch in a test tube. In best
country lawyer style, he pulled the dead snail darter out of his
pocket.

To Donald Cohen, who watched while Plater argued their case,
Bell's gesture was simply a routine piece of courtroom theatrics.
Waving the test tube, he was playing the role of the reasonable fellow beset by loony minnow aficionados. Cohen was pleased when
the tactic backfired, and the attorney general was asked by Justice
Stevens whether some species are entitled to more protection than
others. The question put Bell into a quandary. If building Tellico
would drown the last breeding ground of the bald eagle, few
voices would be heard in favor of the project. So Tellico was not
more important than *any* species; it was just more important than
the snail darter. Yet that implied some process for distinguishing
between important and unimportant species, and the Endangered
Species Act had none. Unwilling to pull new law out of thin air,
Bell made a fateful reply. No, he said, the government was not
taking the position that some species are better than others. All
species, in sum, are equal in the eyes of the law, be they eagle,
bear, pearly mussel, or snail darter.

Bell spoke for a few more minutes and sat down to hear the defenders of the fish argue that it might provide a cure for cancer.
Leaving the courtroom, Bell was surrounded by reporters and
cameras on the Supreme Court steps. The test tube was still in his
jacket. He displayed the fish, and a thicket of lenses bore down on
it. "And *then*," he told us, "later on, I was investigated by some
environmental groups to see if I had violated the law by killing a

---

*Bell's decision was based in part on an unusual circumstance: the federal government
both supported and opposed the dam's completion. The administration of President Gerald
Ford had backed the TVA and its appeal to the Supreme Court. The incoming administration of President Jimmy Carter reversed course and told the new attorney general to
push for the snail darter. Ridiculous, said Bell. The government could not petition the Supreme Court to reverse the decision of a lower court and then tell the assembled justices
in oral argument, "Oops, sorry we bothered you; the lower court's decision was actually
okay." In a bizarre compromise, Bell's legal brief against the fish included an appendix arguing in favor of it. To his displeasure, Plater cited the dissenting appendix to bolster the
snail darter's case before the Supreme Court.

snail darter." He laughed. "I tell you," he said, "it's a weird time we live in."

Weird indeed. Years later, Bell still seemed to be amazed by what the Supreme Court said in June 1978, when it released its decision in *TVA v. Hill*. By a vote of six to three, the Court gave the nod to the snail darter. The law said nothing, the justices noted, about any balancing of competing values when considering the protection of biodiversity. The legislative debate over the Endangered Species Act, as well as the act itself, the Court concluded, "shows clearly that Congress viewed the value of endangered species as 'incalculable' "—a term with a working definition of "infinite." Obviously, the Court pointed out, no one can offset the loss of infinite value with something of merely finite value. Simple logic therefore dictated halting Tellico. If that sounded unreasonable, the justices said, that was too bad. Congress had discussed the legislation extensively, and the "plain intent" of the ensuing legislation was "to halt and reverse the trend toward species extinction, whatever the cost."

Whatever the cost—the Court was saying something of almost embarrassing obviousness. By enacting a law that eliminated the practicable, Congress had with little discussion or debate created a perfect duty to biodiversity. Although Allen believed that people care about endangered species "for reasons peculiarly our own," the act embraced the Noah Principle, which abjured human aspirations. The nation's natural heritage must be saved, no matter what. The implications of that commitment soon stared Congress in the face—and it blinked.

EVEN BEFORE Griffin Bell displayed a dead fish to the Supreme Court, a few members of Congress had suspected that they might have signed a blank check when they voted for the Endangered Species Act. Already two lawsuits had challenged projects in Indiana and Mississippi on behalf of endangered species, and a petition to list the furbish lousewort, a plant with an absurd-sounding name, had led to a public battle over the Dickey Lincoln Dam in Maine. More and more it seemed to legislators that saving all endangered species might require sacrifice. To avoid this unpleasant prospect, Senators John Culver, Democrat of Iowa, and Howard Baker, Republican of Tennessee, introduced a bill in early 1978 to amend the Endangered Species Act by creating an escape hatch—a high-level committee that under certain conditions would be able to exempt a project from the strictures of the law. The idea was to prevent a hail of lawsuits by setting up a mechanism to resolve disputes outside the courts. Then came the ruling in *TVA v Hill*, and everything changed: Tellico was in Howard Baker's state, and Baker was the minority leader of the Senate.

The Senate voted overwhelmingly to establish the Baker-Culver committee. When the House considered a similar amendment to the Endangered Species Act that fall, John Duncan, the Tennessee Republican whose district included Tellico, decided to take no chances. He proposed an additional amendment specifically exempting the dam. A resounding majority said aye. Members of each chamber met in conference to iron out the differences between the House and Senate versions. Although Duncan's proposed exemption didn't survive, the Baker-Culver amendment did. It created what is officially known as the Endangered Species Committee: the secretary of Agriculture, the secretary of the Army, the secretary of the Interior, the head of the Council of Economic Advisors, the administrator of the Environmental Protection Agency, the administrator of the National Oceanic and Atmospheric Administration, and a representative from the governors of the affected states. Convened when all attempts failed to resolve conflicts between a federal project and an endangered species, the Endangered Species Committee can permit the extinction of a species, as long as the benefits of the project "clearly outweigh" the benefits of all alternative courses that would avoid harming the species. The group was promptly nicknamed the "God Committee," after the only power able to overrule Noah. In exchange for dropping the Duncan amendment, the Tennessee delegation got the next best thing: a commitment that *P. tanasi* would be the committee's first order of business.

Baker apparently had little doubt in his mind about what would happen when the God Committee considered Tellico. Reason would prevail, and an almost-finished dam would not be stopped because of some tiny fish. One can only imagine this powerful man's outrage when the God Committee ruled against the dam on January 23, 1979—unanimously. His own creation had turned against him! Worse, Secretary of the Interior Cecil Andrus, chair of the committee, made it clear that Tellico had never stood a chance. "Frankly," he said, "I hate to see the snail darter get the credit for stopping a project that was ill-conceived and uneconomical in the first place."*

Less than one week later, the infuriated Baker responded by introducing legislation that would exempt Tellico directly and abolish the Endangered Species Committee that he himself had created. When the plan was killed in committee, Baker went to the Senate floor in June with an attempt to amend a bill that made some minor adjustments to the act, hoping to expunge the committee by this route. Supporters of the act stood firm; Baker lost the floor vote.

The Tennessee delegation was not to be denied. A few days later, the House considered the $10.8 billion Energy and Water Development Appropriations Act of 1980. The bill was a routine but important vehicle for funding the type of projects that detractors refer to as "pork," including, in this case, a new office building for the Senate and a pay raise for congressional staff. In the middle of a stream of amendments, John Duncan, the Tennessee congressman who had already tried to exempt Tellico, slipped in language that again authorized TVA to finish the dam, regardless of any other law. Duncan did not even read his amendment completely to his colleagues; he simply spent thirty seconds explaining

---

*At the same meeting, the committee approved an exemption for the Grayrocks Dam in Wyoming, which had been enjoined by a lawsuit because construction menaced the whooping crane's migration stop downstream in the Platte River. As Duncan had for Tellico, Teno Roncalio, Republican of Wyoming, proposed amending the Endangered Species Act by adding a declaration that Grayrocks was in compliance with the law, no matter what it did. The House approved his amendment; when the House and Senate met in conference, the final bill instead directed the Endangered Species Committee to consider the Grayrocks Dam at the same time that it worked on Tellico. Just before the meeting, the parties to the lawsuit came to a settlement, and the God Committee granted the Grayrocks Dam an exemption, in part because of this agreement.

what he wanted. Nobody objected, and the amended bill was accepted without a recorded vote.

Duncan's sleight of hand infuriated the Senate. With Baker, Culver of Iowa had proposed the God Committee, but unlike Baker he thought people should abide by its decisions. He angrily demanded that the Tellico exemption be tossed aside, an idea that passed the Senate by a narrow margin. Members of the House and Senate met in yet another conference to iron out their differences, but this time the two chambers were at loggerheads. The House insisted that the Duncan amendment stay in; the Senate, that it be eliminated. The whole multibillion-dollar platter of pork was menaced by this unrelated amendment about a fish. The conference sent the bill back to both chambers, with an amendment granting the Tellico Dam an exemption. The House stuck by Duncan, passing his amendment by a large margin. This left the matter in the hands of the Senate and the increasingly infuriated Howard Baker. Baker took the podium in September and expressed his opinion of the whole matter. "Mr. President," he said,

> the awful beast is back. The Tennessee snail darter, the bane of my existence, the nemesis of my golden years, the bold perverter of the Endangered Species Act is back. He is still insisting that the Tellico dam on the Little Tennessee River—a dam that is now 99 percent complete—be destroyed. . . . Frankly, Mr. President, I am beginning to question his motives. This two-inch terror kept the lowest profile of all God's creatures for thousands of years until a relatively short time ago, but now he seems to enjoy the publicity. Perhaps if we gave him a cover story in *Time* or *Newsweek*, or got him a feature on the *CBS Evening News* or an interview with Barbara Walters, his lust for fame might be fulfilled and he would leave us alone.

Baker's impassioned cry for ichthyological justice did not settle the matter. Immediately after, Senator J. Bennett Johnston, Jr., Democrat of Louisiana, explained the facts of pork.

> If you want an energy and water resources bill, in my judgment, we are going to have to drop the snail darter. We are going to have

to build the Tellico dam. Why is that? Because the Senate was closely divided 53 to 45 on the question last time. The House brought it up and reconsidered and by a vote of 156 ayes and 258 nays voted against the Senate amendment and then voted to insist on their language. They made it perfectly clear that no Tellico—no bill.

In a vote of forty-eight to forty-four, the Senate approved the Duncan amendment.

On November 29, 1979, TVA engineers cut the steel cables that held open the floodgates to the Tellico Dam. Blocked, the waters of the Little Tennessee rose up the sides of the valley. In three or four weeks, officials said, the reservoir would reach its full size of 14,000 acres. Tanasi would vanish. So would *Percina tanasi*.

ON NOVEMBER 1, 1980, almost exactly a year after the floodgates closed, David Etnier, discoverer of the snail darter, trudged the banks of South Chickamauga Creek, a badly polluted tributary of the Tennessee River about sixty miles downstream from the Tellico Dam. Boots on feet, seine in hand, he and several students lugubriously examined what life remained in the stream. The process was routine: dip seine, inspect catch, return fish to water, dip seine again. Etnier had spent his professional career in this way. Until that day, though, he had never caught an extinct fish. Incredibly, a live snail darter flopped in the folds of the net. Etnier's surprise would be hard to overstate. The Little Tennessee had been a river of striking clarity; the South Chickamauga was a mess. It had never occurred to Etnier that the snail darter could live in both. Polluted water not being in short supply in the Tennessee Valley, Etnier quickly thought of twenty other turbid streams in which to look. He found the fish happily living in three of them. Etnier recommended that the Fish and Wildlife Service change the status of *P. tanasi* from endangered to threatened, which it did in July 1984. Within a decade, he was suggesting that the species might be delisted altogether—although, he stressed, the possibility remained something for the distant future.

Tellico has not proven to be a complete disaster. TVA sold 11,102 acres around the dam in 1982 to the Tellico Regional Development Agency, a state body, which took charge of developing it. In the next decade, the development agency was able to sell 5,415 acres, about half the land. Not much of it ended up going to the manufacturers who the TVA had claimed would pour into the area; keeping open the parkway to their nonexistent facilities remains, the development agency has confessed, "a serious operational and financial problem." Most of the sold property ended up as a retirement community called Tellico Village. Sales and property taxes from Tellico Village helped keep afloat Loudon and Monroe counties during the 1991–1992 recession, although the revenue to the localities is less than the cost of the dam to the nation as a whole. Tellico Village, we were told, is full of snowbirds—retirees from the North. They arrive in campers with out-of-state license plates. Few seem to be aware they live in a former battleground.

During the debate that followed the *TVA v. Hill* debate, Congress had the opportunity to reconsider the legal duties owed biodiversity. In the middle of discussing the amendments that created the God Committee, Senator Jake Garn, Republican of Utah, offered his own revision of the law. "As a society, and as a Congress," he told his colleagues,

> we have competing responsibilities. Beyond the need to protect the environment, we are also responsible for the provision and preservation of aspects of our society which are judged desirable by the American people. These include food and water, electricity and other forms of power, and the materials we use to make everything from hospital beds to golden spittoons for Las Vegas casinos. Some of the uses to which we put our physical wealth are honorable and noble; others are certainly not that useful.

But, he said, society had to negotiate its way among them, rather than have the government follow only one value, no matter how important. That is why balance, in his view, had to be returned to the law. Congress balked at Garn's amendment, in part because its members hoped the God Committee would provide a way to meet those competing responsibilities.

That hope has not been fulfilled. Notwithstanding the fears of some members of Congress that the escape hatch would turn into a revolving door, the God Committee has met *once* since Tellico Dam; in three other cases, a party has applied for an exemption but did not proceed beyond the preliminary stages of the appeal process. And despite a string of later amendments, the original strategy of Potter and Talbot remains largely intact. Because federal agencies routinely used the notion of balance to ignore biodiversity, the two men had wanted a law that would exalt endangered species to a height impossible to ignore. Thinking that pushing the legal language to the limit would command attention, they decided to fix an inadequate balancing mechanism by jettisoning the notion of balance altogether. The result was a law equivalent to the Noah Principle. No one could have been more surprised than Talbot when the Supreme Court took the letter of the law seriously and assigned complete preeminence to biodiversity.

Allowing the protection of endangered species to overwhelm other human goals, as called for by the Endangered Species Act, would be unethical, in the sense that we have used this word. But that may be a problem only if we take the act literally. What we wish for may be impossible, Aristotle noted in the *Nichomachean Ethics*, but to be on solid ground what we choose to do must be possible. A wish to save all endangered species may be ethically tenable if we choose practicable means for striving to come as close as we can to the goal. Across the nation, people are grappling with those means, with the efforts varying widely from place to place and problem to problem. No attempt is typical, and so we chose to visit an ambitious, pathbreaking effort to save biodiversity in an entire region: the Balcones Canyonlands near Austin, Texas.

Chapter Seven

THE "IS" AND THE
"OUGHT"

O N MARCH 13, 1993, Interior Secretary Bruce Babbitt
stood among the ashe junipers and oaks of the Austin
Hill Country and inadvertently echoed former Attorney
General Griffin Bell—he held up for public inspection a jar containing an endangered species, in this case a Barton Springs salamander. In all other respects, the two occasions were different.
Babbitt was in Texas to praise the Endangered Species Act, not to
bury it; appropriately, the salamander was alive, not floating in pre-
servative. The amphibian was one of the many species whose sal-
vation would be accomplished by a comprehensive regional plan
then being worked out by an Austin-based team of scientists, developers, environmentalists, and government officials. Getting
these diverse, often clashing, interests to work together hadn't been
easy, and the secretary was in Austin to cheer them on. "You're at
the ten-yard line," he said. "You're going to create a national
model if you can take that ball and get it across the goal line."

The football metaphor was oddly chosen, for Babbitt was extolling a process that was supposed to bring the parties together,
rather than pit them against one another in a fierce struggle. The
secretary had come to the Hill Country in his hiking boots and
work jacket to say that central Texas—and, by extension, the nation as a whole—is big enough for humans *and* nature. Neither
needs to lose. A balance can be struck, he argued, that will allow
development to continue and endangered species to flourish. Ev-

erything can have its place; all needs can be accommodated—beliefs that Babbitt articulated with the passion that had made him the most popular secretary of the Interior for years.

Meeting with local business, environmental, and political leaders at the lodge of a wildlife preserve, Babbitt held up the Austin plan as an exemplar of how the current system could help the nation protect its natural heritage. Known officially as the Balcones Canyonlands Conservation Plan, it would conserve the habitat of more than three dozen species, seven of which were on the federal endangered list, save local rivers, preserve groundwater supplies, and protect the magnificent scenery of the Hill Country—all the while allowing Austin to continue growing. The plan had yet to be submitted to the Fish and Wildlife Service, the Interior Department agency that reported to Babbitt. Still, he said, it was a "national model."

The secretary, a native Westerner, brimmed that day with the optimism of the West. Expectations were high. Schemes like the one in Austin were sprouting up all over the country. The Endangered Species Act was going to work, he believed, and it was going to happen on his watch. With Austin leading the way, the plans hewed the same straightforward path to the goal line: study the relevant endangered species, determine what it needs to recover, then lay out the necessary actions to meet those needs. The key was good science, and the Austin plan was scientifically exemplary—a tribute to the growing intellectual prowess of ecology and conservation biology.

But it was exemplary in another way, too. In laying out the means for saving all the species in Austin's backyard, the scientists, as required by law, paid no attention to the practicability of following their recommendations. In other words, all the ecological fieldwork, computer simulations, and geographic information systems behind the Austin plan ignored the values of the people whose lives it would change. It foundered for that very reason. After being presented with the program, those same people decided, for good or ill, that saving all biodiversity was too much to ask.

AUSTIN, TEXAS, is a geological border town. To its east stretches the blackland prairie, the kingdom of tall grass, now mostly plowed under for agriculture. To its west rises the Edwards Plateau, the great uplifted sheath of limestone that leads to the drylands of the Southwest. A few miles from Austin, prairie and plateau meet at the Balcones Canyonlands, a network of intertwined geological fractures that runs along a rough north–south line more than a hundred miles long. Eroded by wind and water, the canyonlands have become a jumble of gorges whose rippling walls reminded early Spanish visitors of the tiered balconies of their own cities—hence the name Balcones. The Balcones Canyonlands lie on the southern and eastern edges of what Texans today call the Hill Country. Flopped like a rumpled rug across twenty or so central Texas counties, the Hill Country gleams with rivers, springs, and dam-made lakes—a marvelous playground just west of the city.

Austin itself is located in the middle of Travis County; the western half of the county, a place of rugged slopes and open forest, is the gateway to the Hill Country. Everyone in town has a soft spot for this part of the county, as we were told by Robert Brandes, a third-generation Austinite whose landowning family long allowed neighbors free access to its property. And Austin itself, Brandes told us firmly, "is still the best town in America, despite everything." Blessed with a pleasant climate, fiercely proud of its cuisine, vibrant with a raucous music scene, home of the state's legislature and its leading public university, Austin has acquired a reputation for down-home cosmopolitan liberalism that is hard to reconcile with the stereotypical image of Texas. The sentimental heart of the city is at its southwestern edge, in Barton Springs Pool, where warm, gushing springs have been converted into a sort of gigantic public swimming pool that is thronged on sunny days with children, retirees, University of Texas students, and middle-aged people playing hooky. "There's an outdoor life here that I—everybody here, really—couldn't bear to lose," Brandes told us. "It's worth fighting for."

Brandes and many other Austinites were alarmed when the city grew like Topsy in the 1980s. The number of people in the Austin area jumped to three-quarters of a million during that decade, a rise of 50 percent. Backed by money from the savings-and-loan frenzy, then at its height, the housing industry exploded, too. The most desirable land was in the hills of western Travis County. Heeding the voices begging for new houses and apartments, landowners there turned fields and hillsides into real estate. With astonishing speed, a wave of homes and apartment buildings washed over the area, followed by an undertow of fast-food places, convenience stores, and gas stations. Austinites were not the only ones to feel threatened. The new homes seemed likely to wipe out the area's few remaining black-capped vireos.

Small, black-headed, olive-winged, the black-capped vireo (*Vireo atricapillus*) once nested from southern Kansas through northern Mexico, spending the winter along the Pacific coast of central Mexico. Intensely territorial, the vireo always stakes out a bit of land it can call its own. When young birds leave the parental nest, they fly up to ten miles away, looking for a place to live. It isn't easy to find: the vireo, a picky sort, nests and forages in the mixture of young oaks, sumacs, and shrubbery that rises up in this part of North America after some form of disturbance, such as a wildfire or erosion in a canyon. When the oaks grow taller and the sumacs are replaced by juniper, the vireo moves on to other patches. Like the Karner Blue, the vireo lives in a constantly shifting mosaic of habitat, the pieces shuffled by environmental turmoil. Good habitat is highly prized: vireos return from their wintering grounds to the same area until it is overgrown.

The disturbance that creates vireo habitat need not be "natural." More than likely, Native Americans burned so much land to make bison pasture that they helped the bird spread into Oklahoma and Kansas from its ancestral range farther south. According to Joe Grzybowski, a vireo expert at the University of Central Oklahoma, in Edmond, Americans today sometimes play a similar role. One of the bird's strongholds is Fort Hood, an army installation about sixty miles north of Austin. Artillery practice sets off fires, Grzybowski told us, and the birds thrive in the vegetation that grows up afterward. Where routine tank maneuvers create open trails, vireos nest along the edges of those trails.

The vireo and the Karner Blue share another feature: victimization by Smokey Bear. Campaigns against forest fires inadvertently stopped the creation of new habitat in some areas. In others, agriculture and cattle ranching wiped out prime habitat, plowing it under or grazing the land to a frazzle. Another problem is a species that accompanies contemporary human expansion the way phoretic mites hitch a ride on the American burying beetle: the brown-headed cowbird, the bête noire of ornithologists, the bird that bird lovers love to hate. The female cowbird lays her eggs in other birds' nests, often removing some of the host's own eggs in the process. When the cowbirds hatch, the chicks, large and aggressive, capture so much food and parental attention that the host's own offspring starve. Indigenous to the Great Plains, cowbirds were relatively uncommon before the European settlement of that area. Today, ornithologists say, it is one of the most important threats to birds on this continent. The reason is that cowbirds live on the edge of the forest but place their eggs in nests within. As people clear the forest, cowbirds follow, feeding in the open areas and gaining access to other birds in the interior. In some places, Grzybowski has observed cowbirds in nine out of every ten vireo nests. With cowbirds spreading throughout their territory, vireos are victimized year after year.

The result, predictable in every way, has been a drastic decline in the species. The vireo disappeared from Kansas in the 1950s. In Oklahoma, it has two remnant populations, only one of which has a chance of survival. Healthy populations survive in southern Texas and northern Mexico, but in north and central Texas the vireo is barely hanging on. Fewer than a hundred pairs live in the hills west of Austin. If people didn't stop building there, the natural beauty of western Travis County and the vireo would be swallowed up together.

AMONG THOSE worried about the destruction of Travis County's natural heritage were the agents of the U.S. Fish and Wildlife Service. The agency first awarded official attention to the black-capped vireo in 1982, when it assigned the bird to Category 2 (some evidence of endangerment, not enough to support listing). Three years later, the bird rose to Category 1 (strong evidence of endangerment, but unlisted due to lack of money and labor). The service proposed adding it to the endangered species list in December 1986. After waiting for public comment, as the law requires, Fish and Wildlife formally listed the vireo ten months later.

Conflict immediately erupted. Steiner Ranch, a 4,500-acre spread fifteen miles northwest of downtown Austin, was then being converted to a gigantic planned community. The developer was Hughes Interests, owned by Al Hughes, a real estate and savings-and-loan tycoon with holdings in Houston, Dallas, and El Paso. Hughes Interests had spent several years collecting the sackful of city, county, and state permits necessary to put up a community that would eventually cover seven and a half square miles with as many as 14,000 homes. But the bulldozers had hardly driven onto the property before Hughes ran into vireo trouble.

To build the first chunk of Steiner Ranch, a 188-acre parcel on a ridge above Lake Austin, Hughes needed to cut a road between the construction site and Route 620, which bordered the property. Because the construction would affect some streams, the company applied in the fall of 1987 for a permit from the Army Corps of Engineers, which watches over the nation's rivers and wetlands. The Corps replied that building the road might endanger the vireos that were known to nest on the property. Because the vireo was on the endangered species list, the Corps would have to consult with Fish and Wildlife before issuing the permit. In practice, this meant that Steiner Ranch construction supervisor Donald Bosse would have to hire a biological consultant, who would survey the property and report the location of vireos and vireo habitat to Fish and Wildlife. Bosse had never encountered the Fish and Wildlife Service in a lifetime of building. He was dismayed to learn how expensive dealing with bird habitat could be.

Fish and Wildlife instructed the Corps to tell Hughes that it could get the permit only if the company set aside 115 acres of vireo habitat—"prime buildable land, too," Bosse said, "nothing bad about it"—along with funds to survey it and manage it and write reports about it. The total cost was about $1.8 million. Moreover, Hughes had to slow down work after April 15, when the vireos would be returning from their wintering grounds in Mexico. When the birds arrived, Bosse said, "We had a whole list of restrictions. The permit said we could use equipment of a certain type and certain decibel level in certain places, and certain types with another decibel level in another place, and some parts of the year we could do this, and some parts of the year we could do that. It was a whole list of very complicated things, and it made building the road into quite a headache. And so you can imagine our reaction when Earth First! came in and asked us not to do what we were allowed to do by the permit."

Earth First!—one of America's most radical environmental groups, as indicated by the exclamation point—had been active in Austin for five years. Launched in Arizona, the organization was decentralized to a fault; while some West Coast chapters earned the wrath of other environmentalists by putting spikes in trees (making them dangerous to cut up in sawmills), the Texas contingent was, relatively speaking, a respectable member of the community. Learning about the road from the Sierra Club, a dozen members of Earth First! met with Bosse and Clifton Ladd, Hughes's environmental consultant. Steiner Ranch, the activists said, was destroying vireo territories—the equivalent of bulldozing a human being's house. This had to stop.

Bosse and Ladd pointed out to the activists that the company had offset any potential loss by setting aside 115 acres of good land, an action endorsed by the Fish and Wildlife Service. When Earth First! said that Fish and Wildlife should not have accepted the deal, Bosse and Ladd argued that heavy construction equipment could not be used after April 15, when the vireos returned from their wintering grounds, and that therefore the birds would not be disturbed. Everything would work out, they promised. And they bought the activists some beer. These assurances did not sit well with Christi Stevens, a University of Texas student who was one of the founding members of the Austin branch of Earth First! "By April first or so," she told us, "we were out there every day with binoculars. The first day we saw black-capped vireos on

Steiner Ranch, we called up Bosse and said you have to stop. He said, 'I have a permit until April 15 and I won't stop.' "

On April 7, 1988, Stevens and two other members of Earth First! attached themselves to the road-building equipment by looping bicycle locks around their necks. Supporters waved signs and banners as an annoyed emergency rescue squad cut the protesters free and hauled them to jail for a couple of hours. Television cameras recorded the whole episode. Perhaps recognizing the potential for further embarrassing news coverage, Hughes declined to press charges.

Earth First! was unmoved by the leniency. William Bunch, an Austin attorney representing the organization, announced on April 22 that Earth First! was about to sue many developers and government agencies for violating the Endangered Species Act. "We sent out a notice of intent to sue to *tons* of people," Bunch said, "whoever was proposing to do a project in black-capped vireo habitat." By that time, the area around Route 620 was deep in the throes of real-estate dementia, a condition rampant in the 1980s. In the space of a few months, Conoco, Schlumberger, and 3M, all giant companies, announced plans to build multimillion-dollar research facilities in western Travis County, not far from Steiner Ranch; billboards sprang up like crabgrass, advertising still more projects. Bunch sent them all notices.

The most immediate target of his ire was not these Fortune 500 companies or Steiner Ranch, but another development, the Parke, on another former ranch a few miles up Route 620. Fred A. Purcell, a dentist turned developer from Austin, headed the limited partnership, 620 Investors, that bought the property in 1983. "At that time," he said, "the master plan of the city of Austin actually had a map in an appendix that was called 'Environmental Constraints to Development.' This property was the *only* piece of western Travis County that was labeled as having no environmental constraints on development. That was a big reason why I bought it." The partnership wanted to build high-density single- and multiple-family housing, a scattering of light industry, a supermarket, and, fatefully, a parking lot for the supermarket.

Building the lot involved paving over a limestone cavern called

Tooth Cave. *Cavern* may be overly grandiose: Tooth Cave is a saucer-shaped space just beneath the surface that is perhaps forty feet across and at most five feet high. Its entrance is a nondescript hole in the top of the cave that is now blocked by a metal grate. A child could explore its deepest reaches in a minute or two. On the other hand, grandiosity may be called for. The cave contains an evolutionarily fascinating collection of beetles, spiders, and other invertebrates.

Western Travis County consists principally of limestone. Circulating through fissures, groundwater wears away networks of small sinkholes in the rock. Over the years, Austinites have plugged them in countless numbers. Often they are inhabited by troglobites: invertebrates that spend their entire lives underground. Because troglobites rarely leave their home bases, the caves act as a set of islands, isolating separate populations of common species. The result has been a burst of evolutionary inventiveness that led to the creation of many highly localized invertebrate species, some found in only a few caves, a few limited to one. Tooth Cave, in this light, is a hot spot of biodiversity. Among its denizens are the Tooth Cave spider (*Neoleptoneta myopica*), the Tooth Cave ground beetle (*Rhadine persephone*), and the Tooth Cave pseudoscorpion (*Tartarocreagris texana*), a creature that resembles a small tailless scorpion. Paving over the cave entrance would destroy all three populations, because they depend on it to let in nutrients, chiefly in the form of drifting leaf litter.

Even if the cave was not directly paved over, the construction would still pose a threat, because it would attract fire ants. Famed for their massive biting attacks, fire ants are the cowbirds of entomology, the insects even insect aficionados detest. Accidentally introduced from their native Argentina to Mobile, Alabama, in the 1930s, they swept through the South, extirpating dozens of insect species in their path. Austin has a particularly virulent infestation, in which colonies with multiple queens spread in a kind of wash of fire ants across the earth. James Reddell, a biospeleologist (expert on cave life) at the University of Texas, has seen them take over several caves, destroying every living thing inside. Fire ants love construction sites and heavily trafficked places like the edges of parking lots; it would be difficult to keep them away from Tooth Cave.

Alarmed by Purcell's plans, the Travis Audubon Society asked the Fish and Wildlife Service in February 1985 to list six cave invertebrates, including those in Tooth Cave. The agency placed them in Category 1 three months later. Meanwhile, the Parke went forward, its crews slowly clearing much of the property and beginning construction. As Earth First! considered protesting at Steiner Ranch, William Bunch, the environmental lawyer, asked Fish and Wildlife what was happening to the cave invertebrates. On April 19, 1988, twelve days after the Earth First! protest at Steiner Ranch, the agency announced its intention to list them. "They told us the timing was coincidental," Bunch said.

Tooth Cave has two neighboring caves, Amber Cave and Kretschmarr Cave, the latter known to troglobite enthusiasts as the type locality of the Kretschmarr Cave mold beetle (*Texamaurops redelli*). "I knew there were sinkholes on the property when we bought it," Purcell told us. "But certainly we had no idea there was going to be any type of endangered insect that lived inside those sinkholes." It had slowly dawned on him that he might lose his shirt to protect creatures that most Americans would not hesitate to step on. "I have nothing against parks, or endangered species, or even endangered bugs," he said. "But this law was telling me—one person in Austin, Texas—to foot the bill for preserving things that supposedly benefit the whole country. Well, if they're so good, then why doesn't the whole country pay me to protect them? Why should I get stuck with the bill for it all?" Irate, he threatened to dump a load of cement in his caves.

Soon after Purcell's threat, Christi Stevens and three other Earth First! members slipped into the caves, announcing that they would not leave until the invertebrates were safely ensconced on the endangered species list. By committing an act of civil disobedience for the sake of insects, Stevens explained to us, "we were breaking new ground. We were pushing the limits of our compassion. We were out to protect the cave bugs and get across a strong message that all creatures are created equal." The protesters did not actually spend much time underground during the "cave-in," because they didn't want to squash the very troglobites whose cause they espoused. Unavoidably, though, they spent the night inside the caves, afraid of being surprised by the police if they slept outside.

On the second day, two sheriffs went after Stevens, who was occupying Tooth Cave. She crawled into its deepest, narrowest recesses, where the pudgy officers—"real coffee-and-doughnuts-type sheriffs," Stevens explained—were unable to follow. "They confiscated my water and food, though," she said. "Their cologne made my eyes water. It was so strong, I started to worry about what it would do to the cave bugs. They were clumping around in there like mad. I said [to the police], 'Don't step on the dirt; step on the rocks!' They knew by being clumsy they could get me out of there." Stevens permitted them to arrest her, spent a few hours in jail, and returned to Tooth Cave. She and the other activists stayed for another ten days—until they decided with Bunch, their lawyer, that the Fish and Wildlife Service, resisting the appearance of blackmail, would not list the species until the activists ended their siege. Stevens left the cave on September 12, 1988. The troglobites were placed on the endangered list four days later. "They told us that timing was coincidental, too," Bunch said.

The activists seemed to have won the day when Purcell agreed to hire a biologist to develop a troglobite-protection plan and donate the land around the caves to the Texas System of Natural Laboratories, a consortium run by the state university system. Yet Bunch was not reassured. True, the savings-and-loan debacle was shutting off the flow of cheap capital that had overheated Austin's real estate market. But Texas had gone through many boom-and-bust cycles before. When the good times returned, Bunch thought, speculators would again try to convert habitat to real estate, and environmental activists would again be playing catch-up, trying to stop an almost irresistible commercial juggernaut. The fundamental problem, in his view, was that the endangered species lived on private land, not government preserves. This was especially true in Texas, which has almost no public land. A real solution to the endangerment problem, therefore, had to include private property. And that, Bunch realized, meant sitting down at the table with the same people whose actions Christi Stevens was protesting. "There was going to be too much going on for us to catch it all," he said. "But there was a possibility of doing it with a cooperative approach."

BECAUSE ECOLOGICAL and political boundaries rarely coincide, the conservation of endangered species frequently spills over onto private land. To protect biodiversity, the law cannot stop at the edge of public property; otherwise, hunters could sit outside Aransas and blast away at whooping cranes. If the cranes are to be saved, hunting must be banned on both public and private land. It is hard to single out one cause of harm like hunting, however, without putting other causes into question. In ordinary circumstances, building houses on private property is hardly a criminal activity. Yet should the land contain the habitat of an endangered species, the construction could harm that species. In this way, an otherwise-worthwhile private endeavor would become a potential crime—much to the disbelief of the landowner and builder.

For the first decade of the Endangered Species Act, private parties could not avoid this dilemma. The law was virtually absolute: Thou shalt not take. As a result, they had great incentive to ensure that an official endangered species never appeared on their property. The implications were demonstrated in an extreme form by the case of the San Diego mesa mint, which the Fish and Wildlife Service proposed listing in October 1978. One of the plant's three populations inhabited a 279-acre tract on which Pardee Construction of San Diego intended to erect a 1,429-unit subdivision. Pardee had asked the Veterans Administration to provide a loan guarantee. A few days before the mesa mint was added to the list, the VA informed the developer that the plant lived on the site; Pardee promptly bulldozed the population while it was still unprotected. After a few angry letters, the company got a VA loan guarantee—no endangered species existed on the property to disrupt construction.

Recognizing the situation, Congress altered the Endangered Species Act in 1982 to create what a House report called a "unique partnership between the public and private sectors in the interest of endangered species and habitat conservation." The amendment gave private parties a way out from the absolute prohibition against taking a listed species, one that Congress hoped would end up promoting both development and conservation. Property owners like Hughes and 620 Investors create what is called a habitat-conservation plan, which lays out the actions they will take to offset any negative effects their projects may have on listed species. The plan may call for the owner to set aside and manage some of the property as protected habitat or to purchase and protect habitat elsewhere. If the Fish and Wildlife Service judges the plan financially acceptable and, more important, biologically sound, the agency issues an incidental-take permit, which promises that nobody will go to jail if a bulldozer driver inadvertently flattens a bird or a butterfly. The permit does not allow anyone to wipe out a species; only a few individuals, if that, may be taken, and these only inadvertently. But it gives developers legal protection, so long as their projects do not imperil the species as a whole.

Intended to reconcile private interests and public efforts to save biodiversity, habitat-conservation plans identify a species' needs and then, where necessary, redirect and scale back developers' projects. "If you trim away the fat, you rarely end up with an either/or situation," explained Michael O'Connell, a conservation biologist at the World Wildlife Fund and a coauthor of *Reconciling Conflicts Under the Endangered Species Act*, a book on habitat-conservation plans. The plans are not a magic solution to all controversies over endangered species, according to Michael Bean, head of the Environmental Defense Fund's wildlife program and one of O'Connell's coauthors on *Reconciling Conflicts*. But, Bean has argued, the plans are perfect when urban development threatens an endangered species' habitat. In these cases, both sides can get what they want and society as a whole is well served.

Habitat-conservation plans were not immediately popular. The law was patterned after an innovative land deal on San Bruno Mountain, a hilltop near San Francisco that houses three rare species of butterfly, two of which were on the endangered species list.

But the next plan was not put together until 1986, four years after the amendment, when private groups and local, state, and federal agencies set aside 16,729 acres for the Coachella Valley fringe-toed lizard in Riverside County, California, east of San Diego County. The third, covering five species on North Key Largo, Florida, dissolved when the state and local governments bought out the developers, eliminating the need for a permit. (Two small landowners eventually put together separate plans for their properties.) By the summer of 1988, six years after the amendments were passed, the service had approved exactly three plans. In July of that year, representatives of the city of Austin and Travis County decided to try to put together a fourth.

Initially, they had gathered at the offices of Fish and Wildlife with the unclear hope that they could figure out some way to avoid the years of legal squabbling that inevitably followed listing a lot of species on private land. According to David Pimentel, now director of Travis County's Environmental Department, the discussion eventually turned to habitat-conservation plans. "I had a vague sense of what [such a plan] was," Pimentel said. Perhaps that vagueness allowed him to accept a grandiose variation on the idea: Austin and Travis County would not try for a series of plans, each of which would cover a particular development; instead, they would assemble a single, *regional* habitat-conservation plan that would cover the entire Balcones Canyonlands ecosystem.

Conservation biologists had long promoted the idea of regional preserves. A series of individual habitat-conservation plans in an area would produce a crazy quilt of small, isolated preserves separated by developed land. Such a fragmented landscape, as ecologists call it, is a perfect environment for wild predators like cowbirds and civilized ones like housecats. The smaller the preserve, the closer its interior, where species like the vireo have a better chance of surviving, to its edge, where species like the cowbird lurk. Thus, creating preserves through a collection of individual efforts might end up setting aside lots of acreage to little effect. A regional plan, on the other hand, could put together a system of large, unfragmented reserves—a much better approach, biologically speaking. Politically, the regional approach also made sense. Instead of battling through dozens of individual conflicts, in other words, city and county would try to resolve all the issues at a stroke with a proactive scheme covering the hundreds of thousands of acres that comprise western Travis County.

Marshaling all the forces necessary for such a plan would be difficult. It would be even harder if the planners acknowledged from the outset—as Pimentel did, gulping—that the black-capped vireo was not the only endangered species in the Austin Hill Country. Like the vireo, the golden-cheeked warbler (*Dendroica chrysoparia*), the sole bird that breeds only in Texas, first caught the attention of the Fish and Wildlife Service in 1982, when the agency listed it as a Category 2 species. Warblers make their nests with strips of bark from ashe juniper, and only ashe juniper. Because the bark cannot be peeled away until the tree is at least twenty years old, the bird is perforce restricted to forests with a lot of old juniper. It further prefers to nest in tall trees along the bottom of narrow canyons, as long as junipers are around to provide the nesting material. Unfortunately, these canyons are becoming scarce in Texas, because many have been flooded by dams. The junipers, too, are harder to find than they used to be, because the Department of Agriculture for decades encouraged farmers to remove them to improve ranch pastureland. (It stopped in the 1970s.) But being backed into an ecological corner by its narrow habitat range was not the bird's main problem. Like the vireo, the warbler faced its most dangerous enemy in the apparently insatiable desire of many middle-class Americans to place their homes in the most beautiful part of central Texas. It, too, would be done in by Austin's housing boom.

Almost every wildlife professional in Travis County believed that the warbler was destined for the endangered list. As soon as it got there, the Endangered Species Act would clamp down on any activity that threatened the bird. But if the Austin plan covered the warbler *before* it was listed, the organizers would have much more flexibility, because they would not be bound by the strictures of the law. Activists liked the idea of planning ahead. So did politicians and builders, who did not want to argue through a plan for one species, only to have the arrangements upset by another. "We didn't want to sell the public on the vireo, then tell them later on that now we've got the warbler," Pimentel told us.

City and county officials met with representatives of The Nature Conservancy in September 1988, handing the mantle of leadership to that organization. They then turned to the task of building a consensus among the disparate parties with stakes in the Austin Hill Country: The Texas Parks and Wildlife Department. The Sierra Club. The Lower Colorado River Authority. Hughes Interests, developers of Steiner Ranch. The Texas General Land Office. The Travis Audubon Society. The Texas Department of Highways. The City of Austin. The Travis County Commissioners. The Nature Conservancy. The Texas Capitol Area Builders Association. Earth First! And so on. The habitat-conservation plan had to satisfy them all.

The parties gathered for the first time in October. It was, people thought, an especially propitious time for such a plan. The housing market was slumping: Austin, which issued 26,000 housing permits in 1983, handed out fewer than 3,500 in 1987. And now the commercial market was showing signs of strain. Indeed, the bonfire of savings-and-loan failures would soon consume El Paso Savings, financial angel of the Steiner Ranch project. (Eventually, Hughes Interests fell into bankruptcy, and by 1994 fewer than two hundred houses had appeared at the end of Steiner Ranch Boulevard.) The slowdown would give people time to create a plan. At the same time, they knew their endangered species problem was not going to evaporate.

Directing the planning process was an Executive Committee, carefully balanced with enough representatives of government, developers, landowners, and environmentalists to ensure a near-constant simmer of anger, mistrust, and squabbling. Its first task was to design a system of preserves that would ensure the species' survival. The next step would be to figure out how to pay for that system with a combination of taxpayer money and developer fees. Once the preserves and their financing were assured, the regional habitat-conservation plan would be submitted to the Fish and Wildlife Service, which, it was hoped, would issue an incidental-take permit. With permit in hand, landowners and developers would have a countywide set of rules for working with property, and the species in the area would have a good chance of survival.

The job of laying down,the scientific guidelines for a preserve system was handed to the Biological Advisory Team, a group of experts on the species involved. They decided that the first order of business was to collect more data. This was no surprise— scientists, being scientists, always want more data. The results would be used to create a population viability analysis for the warbler and vireo. PVAs, as they are known, estimate the chance that a given species with a given population will survive if society takes particular measures to conserve it. They try to account for the random accidents that affect species: inbreeding, genetic drift, demographic stochasticity (the chance that, say, the offspring of a small group are mostly one sex), and environmental stochasticity (the chance that, say, a big storm will wipe out most of the group). To be considered viable, a population must be capable of surviving these types of accidents. A chief question facing the Biological Advisory Team was the size of the "minimum viable population," the *smallest* population that would still have a good chance of survival. The minimum viable population is the bottom line for a species. Once that was established for both birds, the scientists needed to estimate how much land would have to be set aside to accommodate that minimum number.

Craig Pease, a biologist at the University of Texas, conducted the PVA for the vireo and warbler. "It's like building a bridge," Pease told us. "You hire an engineer to build something that will stand up under all possible scenarios." To work through the complicated mathematical model he set up in his computer, he needed all the data the other members of the team were gathering and more. Reproduction rates, preferred nesting sites, juvenile dispersal distances, sensitivity to habitat disturbance—everything went into the maw of Pease's voracious computer.

Nobody pretends that population viability analysis is an exact science. "A lot of [PVAs] aren't very good at all," said Mark Shaffer, vice president for resource planning at the Wilderness Society, who pioneered the approach in 1981. "The life characteristics of fewer than a dozen species are known well enough to be used in these models." Furthermore, he told us, they have not been empirically verified. "I don't think anyone has looked at PVAs, seen the kind of data they require [to perform a thoroughly detailed analysis], and then gathered it—still less directly tested one." Pease was the first to admit this. His PVA, he emphasized, presented scientific hypotheses, not proven facts. But in some sense, the caveats did not matter. Even if PVAs are hard to assemble, one had to be put together anyway, because it would be the foundation for the science-based system of vireo and warbler preserves that was the key to gaining the approval of the Fish and Wildlife Service.

The Biological Advisory Team gathered in October 1989 to pool its results, including Pease's preliminary population viability analysis. Most of the other scientists were not ornithologists; those who were, while familiar with the needs and habits of individual birds or populations, had never looked at the needs of a species as a whole. None of them knew the mathematical and computer methods necessary to construct a PVA, and just a few were familiar with the concept. Pease's conclusions shocked them all.

To stand a good chance of surviving at least a century, Pease suggested, each species needed five hundred to one thousand nesting pairs of birds—small numbers, as these things go. To hold this minimum population, he said, the network of preserves must include a minimum amount of suitable habitat. The easy way to calculate the necessary area would be to multiply the viable population by the territory each nesting pair required: two to four acres for the black-capped vireo, eight to fifteen for the golden-cheeked warbler. A few moments with a pocket calculator would produce a minimum preserve size of 1,000 to 4,000 acres for the vireo and 4,000 to 15,000 acres for the warbler, perhaps 20,000 acres in all. But the easy way was wrong.

Because the preserves would become islands of habitat in an ocean of developed land, Pease said, they had to be big enough to absorb all contingencies that either species might face. Planning for the warbler was relatively uncomplicated. Occupying older, little-disturbed forests, its population was mostly self-contained, needing protection only against a catastrophe that could wipe out an entire preserve—a big forest fire, for example. Pease recommended establishing two warbler preserves, for much the same reason that computer mavens recommend making a backup copy of every file: the chance of a disaster happening to both is small. Each of the two preserves should be at least 12,000 acres, Pease said. As important, he concluded, was that the preserves be created from contiguous blocks of suitable land. Research by other members of the biological team showed that warblers suffered in habitats fragmented by roads and other forms of development. (Later studies suggested that the major cause of the problem was the blue jay, which, like the cowbird, has expanded its range, and which attacks young warblers before they leave the nest.) If the preserves could not avoid this problem, Pease suggested doubling their size. The warbler thus needed, roughly speaking, between 25,000 and 50,000 acres.

The black-capped vireo was tougher. In the Austin area, the vireo, like the Karner Blue butterfly, lives in a metapopulation: disjunct colonies separated by areas of unused or unsuitable land. As tall trees replace the low shrubbery the vireo inhabits, the colonies are forced to shift location. To facilitate this move, young birds leave their natal sites to look for livable territory. Usually, they end up in other vireo colonies, but sometimes they don't. If they are unlucky and end up in unfriendly territory, they invariably perish. But if they find a place that a recent disturbance has just rendered vireo-friendly, they have a better chance of survival. These lucky birds create new colonies. In this way, dispersing juveniles act as a form of species insurance, allowing vireos to keep up with the changing natural landscape.

To maintain a viable population, the species would have to hatch enough young to withstand the inevitable annual loss of juvenile birds. If only a small area was protected, almost all the young birds would disperse outside the preserve, into people's backyards, and most of these would be lost. To reduce mortality to acceptable levels, Pease recommended a preserve of 123,000 acres—if its managers could protect all the land between the separate colonies. A metapopulation mixed in with humans would need considerably more space—perhaps as much as 864,000 acres, or 1,350 square *miles.*

Stunned, Pease's colleagues pelted him with questions. If the minimum viable population of vireos would actually occupy only 4,000 acres at any one time, how was it possible that it would need more than thirty times that area to survive the next hundred years? To Pease, the other scientists' disbelief showed that they had not thought through the consequences of the bird's pattern of juvenile dispersal. In any case, he thought, their real concern was something else: the political implication of his numbers. While the team wrote up its results, the barrage of complaints continued. "A lot of people were pounding on me," he said, "thinking if they talked to me the results would disappear." But Pease stuck to his model. Population viability analysis was an imperfect business, he admitted, but all the numbers pointed in the same direction. Intellectual honesty compelled him to say that Austin was going to need some big preserves. "We should just do the biology," he told his colleagues. "Let others worry about the political implications."

On January 26, 1990, Pease presented the Biological Advisory Team report, with his PVA intact, to the Executive Committee. Until that point, committee members had expected a plan that would cost about $30 million and conceivably tie up as much as 20,000 acres. The biologists' report quickly destroyed that illusion. Setting aside 123,000 acres—at a bare minimum! With land selling for one thousand to three thousand dollars an acre, the cost of acquiring the preserves suggested by the PVA could run to hundreds of millions, vastly more than anyone had expected. And that did not include the cost of managing the system. Worse, much of the habitat that the biologists regarded as suitable for the two birds lay outside Travis County, in Williamson, Burnett, and Hays counties—a political nightmare, because those conservative rural counties would be asked to take land off their tax rolls to create a preserve at the behest of the liberal city of Austin. "The reaction was total chaos," said Joseph Johnston, who attended the Executive Committee meetings for the Fish and Wildlife Service. "No ifs, ands, or buts about it. There were headlines all over the place."

Reeling from the biological report, the Executive Committee received more bad news three days later when Johnston's agency announced its intention to list the golden-cheeked warbler as a threatened species. The announcement brought into sharp relief an overlooked difference between the two birds. Although it would cost a fortune to build up a population of vireos that would be viable in the long run, so few birds survived in Travis County that the species actually occupied only a few hundred acres. For the time being, protecting the vireo would not tie up much property. The warbler, however, was not in such desperate straits. It occupied 43,000 acres scattered in patches through a 300,000-acre chunk of Travis and Williamson counties, a sizable piece of real estate. As long as the warbler stayed off the list, planners had some flexibility with that land. But once the warbler was listed, that flexibility would vanish, making it harder to come up with a scheme that could meet everyone's needs. Indeed, many in the real-estate community feared that all activity in warbler habitat would come to a halt on the day, perhaps less than a year later, that the warbler joined the list.

From the point of view of landowners, the best way to guarantee that long-term flexibility was to exercise what might be called the mesa-mint option: remove all traces of warbler habitat from their property. Earth First! had long charged that landowners were quietly destroying thousands of acres of oak and juniper, and with them their infestation of endangered species. Ten days after Fish and Wildlife announced its intention to list the warbler, the activists caught someone red-handed: Hillwood Development Company, owned by Ross Perot. A mixture of residential and commercial units, Perot's Four Points scheme sat athwart 333 acres on Route 620, not far from the Parke. Although Hillwood had promised to set aside 90 acres for the warbler, the firm sent out teams of migrant workers with chain saws and told them to strip oak and juniper from the property everywhere else—preparation, its representatives asserted, for using the land as a goat farm. When Tim Jones of Earth First! hiked onto the property and photographed the clearing, Perot's company had him arrested and pressed trespassing charges. The city government eventually weighed in, and Hillwood ended its clearing a few days later.

Other landowners were luckier. The next two months saw several hundred acres of warbler habitat vanish. One ingenious developer requested a surveying permit. Austin allows property owners to clear the necessary sight lines for surveying but limits the width of the cleared strips to fifteen feet. Curiously, this scheme called for a grid of fifteen-foot-wide survey lines every fifty feet that would cover the entire property, removing half the forest cover in the process. Austin denied the request, not least because the developer had already surveyed the property. But the other clearing was so rampant that the Fish and Wildlife Service granted the warbler emergency protection on May 2.

Builders immediately squawked, predicting an end to all development in the warbler zone. They were not alone in their dismay. Travis County had planned to build a 5.5-mile bike trail through the hills. Now that was in trouble. The city of Austin wanted to widen and straighten Route 2222, site of two dozen deaths and four hundred injuries in the past eight years. But revamping the road would cut into warbler habitat, so maybe that couldn't happen, either. PROTECTED BIRD HALTS WORK ON 67,000 ACRES, read the headline in the Austin *American-Statesman.*

A week later, Fish and Wildlife convened a public hearing about the warbler—the first of what Johnston described as "more confrontational meetings than you can shake a stick at." "There had been rumors that a couple of hundred people were going to show up," he said. "Instead one to two thousand people showed up, none of them happy." Because the room had only 140 chairs, the agency had to give its presentation twice. When Jim Young, assistant director of the agency's regional headquarters in Albuquerque, New Mexico, told the crowd that the Endangered Species Act banned the removal of warbler habitat on private land, rancher Robert Morris asked, "Can I just go cut a couple of [juniper] posts to fix my fence?"

"We can't generalize," Young replied. "We have to do it on a case-by-case basis. You'll have to contact us."

CONTACTING A FEDERAL AGENCY about every fence post? That was not what Kent Butler had in mind. A professor of planning at the University of Texas, Butler, with a team of other professionals, won the job of using the biologists' scientific guidelines to fashion the preserve system for the habitat-conservation plan. The Executive Committee hired him in the hope that his team of biologists, planners, economists, computer specialists, and political scientists would craft what Butler called a "turnkey plan": one so perfectly executed that it would sail through the Fish and Wildlife Service untouched.

Butler viewed his job as carving out a plan acceptable to all parties—"an ombudsman between scientists and politicians," as he put it. Although he knew that the strict requirements of the Endangered Species Act thrust species' needs to the forefront, he also believed that ignoring the practicable was a surefire recipe for disaster. No matter what the law said, the other parties—bankers, landowners, developers, home builders—would not want to treat the scientists' report like the word from on high. They would want a voice, a little input, some say-so. And, in Butler's opinion, they had every reason to get it. Since the days of Tocqueville, American political decisions have always been the product of bargaining among interest groups. But no real give-and-take could take place without compromising, even if only a little, the purely scientific recommendations of the biologists. "It was clear going into this," Butler said, "that it was not going to be a strictly biological plan."

Paying no attention to the mounting outcry over listing the warbler, Butler's team quietly drew up piles of maps: topography, land ownership, vegetation patterns, known bird locations, extant protected areas—the list was endless. After loading them all into a computerized geographic information system, they laid the maps atop one another, which let Butler see which land was suitable habitat and whether it was already protected in some way. "From day one," he recalled, "fragmentation was a serious problem." Much of the good habitat was split into isolated patches, which were vulnerable to cowbirds and the loss of young birds through dispersal. Linking up the separate pieces would be expensive, because often the land between them was built up.

Taking his maps to the biologists, Butler and his team tried out different preserve designs, hoping to get guidance. What will happen to the warbler if we put the boundary here? they would ask. How about there? What about this—will it hurt the vireo too much? Can I lose this patch of habitat over here? As Butler tried to balance the plan ever more finely among the competing interests, it moved further and further away from what the scientists believed was necessary to provide maximum protection. "It was extremely painful for them," Butler conceded. "I pushed them near the breaking point." The horrified scientists felt as if they were being asked to put their seal of approval on the species' extinction.

In June 1990, a month after the warbler's listing, Butler presented to the Executive Committee a rough outline of what was now officially known as the Balcones Canyonlands Conservation Plan. For all the compromising, the BCCP still packed a financial wallop. On Butler's maps were two "focus" areas, as he called them, each comprising 60,000 acres, suitable for the birds and other species of concern. (The cave invertebrates would need small amounts of additional land outside these areas.) Somewhere within these 120,000 acres would be the preserves themselves, which would total almost 80,000 acres. Part of the land was already publicly owned; part would be purchased by the local governments; part would be purchased by the federal government for a new wildlife refuge; and part would be protected by tightly regulating development. The price tag was steep: $86 million up front to acquire the preserves and pay the finance charges on the purchase, plus $1.5 million every year to maintain them. Butler believed that Uncle Sam would kick in about $30 million, which would pay for the wildlife refuge; the rest of the cost would have to be borne locally, through taxes and development fees.

Nobody was thrilled. The BCCP provided a third less habitat than the biologists' bare minimum, cost four times as much as the developers thought they could afford, and embroiled the politicians in a barrage of new regulation and fees that their constituents would hate. Moreover, the whole scheme would work only if the counties adjacent to Travis County agreed to provide some of the land. As the distress signals rose in volume, Butler's team tried to hold the fragile coalition together. To the biologists who protested that the warbler was getting too little habitat, they promised to look for more land, though acquiring it would raise the expense by several million dollars. To the politicians who protested that the restrictions would be so tight that they would amount to seizing people's property, they promised to think about throwing out the regulations and buying the land outright, though that, too, would raise the cost—to $115 million. To the developers and landowners who said that a $115 million plan would drive them into bankruptcy, they promised to hunt for additional sources of revenue to spread the cost more widely.

Welcome news arrived early in 1991, when the federal government outlined a proposal to establish a 41,000-acre national wildlife refuge, two-thirds of which would be in Travis County. "That land, more or less, could be counted as part of the plan," explained Johnston of Fish and Wildlife. "After that they only had to buy half as much land." Half as much land did not cut the plan's cost in half, however. To ensure that its refuges are biologically functional, the Fish and Wildlife Service by law must restrict its purchases to relatively undeveloped territory, which ruled out the area around Austin. As a result, the federal government's refuge had to be established in the most remote parts of Travis County, on land that was one-fourth as expensive as the land near Austin. Buying half the land would therefore drive down the cost of the BCCP, but not by nearly as much as people had hoped.

With the preserve planning limited to the Austin area, the task of satisfying the disparate interests got tougher. All the BCCP's attention was now focused on land that held the greatest value both to developers (because it was verdant, hilly real estate close to a major metropolitan area) and to conservationists (because it was verdant, hilly nature close to a major metropolitan area). By the spring of 1992, the two sides were still duking it out. Meetings of the Executive Committee grew so acrimonious that the stress-torn Butler, trying to hold all the pieces together, suffered a severe attack of pneumonia and almost died. "This kind of plan is not a game people play and laugh over beers about how they screwed the other guys," he said. "It's heavy, painful stuff. And there's always someone who can't compromise and is ready to capsize months of work by throwing the whole business in court."

Still, Butler persevered. In June 1992 his team presented the final draft plan, three years in the making, to the Executive Committee. The committee approved the plan and promptly dissolved itself, handing the implementation of the plan to a new committee composed of local governmental bodies. Despite all the anger, delays, and unexpected costs, Butler was optimistic. "This is a Humpty-Dumpty that's together right now," he told us at the time. Two months later, his optimism seemed to be confirmed. In a special election, Austinites overwhelmingly approved a $22 million bond issue to pay for the city's share of the preserves. The city government had its eye on some lands taken over by the Resolution Trust Company after the savings-and-loan collapse. Negotiations began soon after the election, and Austin slowly began to buy land for the BCCP. This was brave, because Fish and Wildlife had not yet approved the plan—indeed, the BCCP organizers had not even submitted it to the agency. This task was handled by the new committee, which sent the proposed preserve design to Fish and Wildlife in February 1993. The BCCP was off and running.

It didn't get very far. Even as the plan seemed increasingly close to becoming reality, other parties were quietly abandoning it, evading the onerous strictures of the Endangered Species Act with something called a bird letter. To obtain bird letters, landholders surveyed their property and submitted the results to the Fish and Wildlife Service. If it had no suitable habitat, or if that habitat had been unoccupied for at least three years, the service would send the landowner a quasi-official reply—a bird letter—acknowledging these conditions. Owners then had some assurance that developing their property would not result in charges of taking. "Having a bird letter is the difference between having a lot you can go and put a house on versus having a lot that you have to sit there and watch," said Harry Savio of the Capital Area Builders Association.

Bird letters added as much as 25 percent to the property's value—a premium, in other words, for the *absence* of any endangered species.

People with good vireo or warbler habitat could not get a bird letter, and they were in trouble. "There's lots of land out there, sitting for sale, and no one's going to buy it because the owners don't have a bird letter," explained J. B. Ruhl, an Austin attorney who represents landowners and developers. For those people, the BCCP was the intended solution. Once in place, it would free certain areas from the constraints of the act, and target others for acquisition or other forms of protection, all to be accomplished with the help of the landowners. But the big plan was taking so long—by 1993, it was into its fifth year—that landowners began to put together their own individual habitat-conservation plans, thus undermining the BCCP. Alas, the landowners' actions made economic sense. The boom had returned to Austin. People wanted places to live, and some in the building trade were declaring it the number one real-estate market in the United States. The demand for housing forced up land prices, and with them the BCCP price tag. Even with Uncle Sam buying half the land, it was up to some $130 million, plus $1 million in annual maintenance costs.

That summer, Travis County decided to put its own share of the BCCP preserves to a vote, placing a $48.9 million bond issue on the November 1993 ballot. The decision was a gamble, because at the time Travis County had no way of repaying the bonds without making deep cuts in other programs. It intended to pay for the bonds by levying fees on development that destroyed habitat but lacked the requisite legal authority from the state. The county had tried twice to obtain the authority, in 1991 and 1993, but both times the legislature failed to act. Because the Texas legislature meets only in the first half of odd-numbered years, the latest failure meant that the next opportunity would not be until 1995. Desperate to act before rising land prices put their share of the preserve out of reach, county officials decided to go ahead with the election, hoping that the legislature would eventually grant them the means to repay the bonds.

Almost every environmental and business group in Austin

joined to support the idea. Editorials in the Austin *American-Statesman* added to the chorus. Without the plan, warned Sam Hamilton, head of the Fish and Wildlife field office in Austin, "there is no certainty for landowners, for developers, or even for the species." The BCCP, said Travis County commissioner William Aleshire, would find it "near impossible to proceed . . . without approval of these county bonds."

One week before the vote, Secretary Babbitt returned to Austin to add his support again. The BCCP, he said, was the "flagship" of the Clinton administration's efforts to promote cooperation between landowners and land preservers. It was a milestone, a bellwether. It would demonstrate that people could come up with cooperative solutions under the Endangered Species Act. It would prove that the system really works. The BCCP, he said, "is the most imaginative experiment that's been undertaken since Frederick Law Olmsted created Central Park."

The secretary's pleas went unheeded. Eight days later, on November 2, the flagship sank—stove in by the very citizenry whose future it was supposed to enhance. The electoral margin was narrow, Austin mayor Bruce Todd said, but the message was clear. The BCCP had reached its end as "originally envisioned."

The backers of the BCCP, to borrow the secretary's metaphor, could not carry the ball across the goal line, fumbling away victory in a sudden, embarrassing collapse. Losing the bond issue was indeed a disaster. It knocked the county government to the sidelines, eliminating for the foreseeable future all possibility of its participation in the game. The city of Austin, which had conducted a successful bond election, was forced to continue the BCCP on its own, buying land with funds from its bonds. Because the city did not have enough money to purchase all the acreage needed for a successful regional conservation plan, the BCCP perforce devolved into a preserve system that was much smaller and more fragmented than called for in Butler's plan. Worse, the committee overseeing the new, shrunken BCCP did not agree to levy fees on development, the method by which Austin originally intended to repay the bonds. That left the city in an uncomfortable position.

By paying for biodiversity, they would be cutting into their ability to fund other programs in years to come—paying for the future of species instead of the future of schools, in other words.

The results pleased nobody. By the summer of 1994, the city had spent two-thirds of its bond money to buy seven thousand acres, less than a fifth of the amount Butler had originally proposed. And the revival of Austin's real-estate boom made the road ahead rough. "It was never intended that my $22 million [bond issue] would buy the whole preserve system," complained Junie Plummer, the city property agent in charge of acquiring the land. "There was a window of opportunity to get good deals, but I'm concerned that window is about to shut." Meanwhile, developers were creating a stream of individual habitat-conservation plans—exactly the situation the BCCP had hoped to avoid. Environmentalists, given a ghost of what they had thought they had, fought the Texas Parks and Recreation Department over public access to the preserve system—the department proposing greater access and the environmentalists calling for less. Developers filed a barrage of suits, with Fred Purcell in the forefront. Williamson County, Travis County's more conservative neighbor to the north, sued Fish and Wildlife, trying to yank the cave bugs off the endangered species list. The situation had become just as unpleasant and muddled as all sides had feared. The Austin area, said Kent Butler, was rejoining the rest of America in "litigation hell."

AUSTIN HAD all the ingredients for a successful regional habitat-conservation plan: sophisticated computer models from top scientists; ideological opponents who nevertheless wanted the project to succeed; a general wish to be proactive; and the full support of Interior Secretary Bruce Babbitt. None of these were enough, though, to avoid a hostile stalemate. What was the reason for the failure? What went wrong in Austin?

To be sure, not everyone regarded the BCCP as a failure. The tenacious Secretary Babbitt, for instance, did not concede defeat; indeed, he vigorously argued to us that reports of the plan's demise were premature. The loss of the bond issue was unfortunate, he said, but that didn't mean that Austin developers were free of the Endangered Species Act. All would have to put together habitat-conservation plans; from these smaller pieces, the whole BCCP would slowly be assembled. "It is not nearly as satisfactory in terms of the delay and complexity," he admitted. "Rather than starting on the large landscape, you build up from blocks, but it can be done. And what I'm hearing from people in Austin is that we'll be back on this financing issue." In the long run, he said, "it's not a pass into the end zone. It's three yards and a cloud of dust. We will still at the end of the day, I think, chalk up a victory on the scoreboard." The final network of preserved land, he promised, would "be what the science demanded."

Not everyone agreed. The public mistakenly believed that the BCCP would solve Travis County's endangerment problem, charged Robert Brandes, the third-generation landowner who ardently loves the Hill Country. "The plan was supposed to be an ecosystem-wide solution," he said. "It is not." It was not, in short, scientific. Brandes's attack was echoed by environmental lawyer William Bunch. "Ecological gerrymandering" was Bunch's description of the BCCP. "We took what the scientists wrote and threw it out the window," he told us, disgusted. "We got derailed. The law itself is based on science. Once they didn't use the science as the touchstone of how to do it, politics took over."

Science and politics: the two are often placed in opposition, with science the saint and politics the sinner. The Endangered Species Act embraces this notion, insisting that decisions to list species be based solely on scientific criteria. That is the view embedded in the habitat-conservation planning process, too. To obtain an incidental-take permit, the applicant must design a plan that is scientifically sound. In the real world, the financial basis of the plan is equally important, as the experience of Travis County shows, but biology is the heart of the planning process envisioned by the Endangered Species Act.

So much emphasis on science leaves little legitimate room for anything else. The only possible point of contention is whether particular assertions represent the "best" science. Bunch, for instance, believed that the Biological Advisory Team report produced the "best" science and that failing to follow its prescriptions undid the BCCP. Surprisingly, opponents of the plan also argued on scientific grounds. In suing to delist the cave invertebrates, the commissioners of Williamson County charged that the "best" science showed that the troglobites were not really species and not really endangered. The emphasis on science makes sense only if ecology is not just a method of reasoning or a body of knowledge, but also normative, a guide to right action, a prescription for the good life.

Using science in this way is a fallacy, though, as philosophers have recognized since David Hume published *A Treatise of Human Nature* in 1739. Science, as Hume pointed out, describes the world as it is. The problem, he said, is that scientific statements about "is" (the actual state of the world) often make a troublesome segue into statements about "ought" (the *preferred* state of the world). But this transition is rarely reasonable, because the domain of fact is not the same as the domain of value. As Hume put it, "the distinction of vice and virtue is not founded merely on the relations of objects, nor is perceiv'd by reason." Knowing what "is," scientifically speaking, is not enough to determine what "ought" to be, ethically speaking.

The split between "is" and "ought" is not perfect, because some statements of fact conjure up dangers so obvious that their identification becomes a call for action. For example, the statement "You are about to be run over by a car" suggests an immediate, desirable course of action: get out of the way. But the problems that confront the people of Austin, or anyone else with endangered species in their backyard, are less than a global calamity. Losing the black-capped vireo in western Travis County will probably not be catastrophic, although it may still be tragic.

The distinction between "is" and "ought" is vital. Science is a useful tool for answering questions about facts, but it cannot tell us what we should do about those facts. For example, Craig Pease's minimum viable population recommendation—one thousand pairs of black-capped vireos on 125,000 unfragmented acres—gave the species about a 95 percent chance of survival for at least a century. With the same computer model, Pease could tell Austinites what chance the bird has without any protection, based on its current population size of about one hundred pairs. (Ignore for a moment his own loud caveats about the accuracy of these projections.) Had they wanted to know what would happen in his model if they lumped the two warbler preserves into one, he could tell them that; he might even be able to tell them what would happen if they reduced juvenile mortality with cowbird control. All of these questions lie within the purview of science, and university scientists like Pease or government biologists like Joe Johnston are the right people to answer them.

Yet no matter how carefully Pease performed his analysis, he could never tell the people of Travis County what chance of extinction they *should* want. That is why the members of the BCCP Executive Committee could draw different conclusions (The reserves are too big! The reserves are too small!) from the same scientific report. The report presented the facts, but when there are disagreements over values or what to do about those facts, science cannot resolve those disputes. That is a task for the political process.

Unfortunately, the Endangered Species Act demands that species be given the highest priority, no matter what the implications. It forecloses our options by pretending that other choices do not exist. If the people of Austin choose to award them a lower priority, they will be overruled by the law. In its heart, the law accepts a risk of extinction only as close as possible to the "natural" one, which is tiny. Even Pease's biggest preserve system left the vireo and the warbler exposed to a risk of extinction that was far from that. Reducing it to the natural level would entail evacuating central Texas—a good working definition of *impracticable.*

When the other members of the Biological Advisory Team were shocked by the magnitude of his preserves, Pease counseled them to "just do science." They were troubled by this notion, and rightly so, because in the peculiar world of U.S. biodiversity, "just doing science" involves making choices for entire communities. Invariably the choices will be arbitrary, because scientists have no claim to represent the values of other people. As imperfect as it is, politics has a more legitimate claim to that representation than does science.

Contrary to the ideal envisioned by the Endangered Species Act, the BCCP ran aground because the latitude for politics was too *little*, not too great. Kent Butler might say that he knew the plan could not be purely biological, but the ultimate authority for deciding how far his team could stray from the Noah Principle was the biologists at the Fish and Wildlife Service. Behind the battle in Austin and wherever else economic growth encounters a listed species, federal biologists have been transformed into ecological mandarins, with the power to govern projects ranging from fence posts to highways to dams. They have the power to make compromises in the name of Native American hospitals, shopping malls, orange growers, or even developers; or not to make them in the name of beetles, butterflies, or birds. The science of ecology, by way of academics like Craig Pease and government employees like Joe Johnston, has become the arbiter of both the "is" and the "ought." Although that position is mandated by the Endangered Species Act, it has never been accepted by the people whose lives are governed by the law. Presented with the best scientific alternative, the citizens of Travis County rebelled, because there was little attempt to connect it with their values. And that is what went wrong in Austin.

SHORTLY AFTER the Biological Advisory Team presented its report in 1990, a BCCP team met with Fish and Wildlife officials, including Michael Spear, director of its Region 2, which includes Texas. Present were several members of the state's congressional delegation. The delegation proposed a swap. In exchange for an incidental-take permit, the builders, landowners, and developers on the Executive Committee would buy a black-capped vireo preserve of no less than 125,000 acres. Unfragmented, undeveloped, and already chockablock with vireos, it would fit the biologists' vision of the perfect preserve. The only catch was that the preserve would not be in Travis County, but more than two hundred miles southwest, near the Rio Grande. Land is cheap there, the BCCP team members said. For $10 million—a fraction of the cost of the BCCP—we can deliver a vireo park that would be several times bigger than would be possible to construct anywhere in Travis County.

Spear needed just a few minutes to say no. Writing off the Austin population of the vireo would restrict the bird's range, something the staff biologists would never accept. Every vireo metapopulation, he told the Texas delegation, must be protected. That is the best ecological course of action, and that is what the law demands. The Texans left, and Austin set out to save the species in its own backyard, where the habitat was already fragmented, partly developed, and losing vireos rapidly.

From a scientific perspective, Spear's response was eminently reasonable. Restricting the bird's range would reduce its genetic variation and thereby increase its chance of extinction. From a legal perspective, the Endangered Species Act could not let this occur in the name of some supposed practicability. Nor could the species be harmed in the name of an alleged ethical balance just because some real-estate people wanted to build homes in a city that was experiencing a desperate demand for housing. Because species must be protected no matter what the cost, human interests must give way. Thus, the birds in the Austin Hill Country had to be saved.

But how? The habitat-conservation planning process failed to work as Babbitt had advertised it would, and not for a lack of effort or money. The federal government has focused its efforts away from the city, where land is cheaper. Developers are funding much of the effort to preserve some vireo habitat, but nobody has indicated a willingness to fill the gap left by the defeat of the county's bonds. And yet the birds must be saved—the Endangered Species Act will not be satisfied with anything less. And the same thing may be repeated many times in many other places: all biodiversity must be saved, yet all biodiversity cannot be saved; human interests are not to be respected, yet human interests will always be respected. Clinging to the Noah Principle is an example of what Mark Sagoff dryly called the attempt "to cast social and environmental policy in the optative mood." The word *optative* is a grammatical term that means "wishful" or "dreamy." In our dream of perfection, Sagoff warned, "the perfect society to which we aspire in theory may become a powerful enemy of the good society we can become in fact."

Surrounding the new Balcones Canyonlands National Wildlife Refuge are dozens of private ranches. The landscape favored by black-capped vireos—young oaks, sumacs, and shrubbery scattered through open areas—is much like a well-managed ranch with plenty of room for grazing and shelter for cattle. For that very reason, ranchers near the reserve have recently taken to deliberately *mis*managing their land, a perverse by-product of the Endangered Species Act's insatiable quest for perfection. "If you do something to attract those birds to your property," said Deborah Holle, a wildlife biologist at the refuge, "and then want to raise goats or sell your property, Fish and Wildlife will say you can't do anything now. The way it is, it would be kind of silly to help the birds out. The [ranchers] have to be realistic."

Harry Savio, of the Capital Area Builders Association, has seen more. "I've talked to guys who strip every tree [from their land] and deep-plow it, keep it free of vegetation until they build," he told us. "Guys in this area have taken every [juniper] off their property. They see a seedling, they run and rip it out."

When we visited Austin a while ago, we, too, saw more. Driving along the verdant slopes of the Hill Country, we found it hard to believe we were in a metropolitan area of three-quarters of a million people. Views of apparently untouched canyons, splendid in afternoon light, would make anyone want to have a home in those hills. The people who have those homes also want the other comforts of American civilization: banks and burger joints, diners and doughnut shops. All were springing up in the Hill Country. As roadside billboards attested, much of the land was owned by developers with visions of housing tracts and office parks; utility companies had made plans to provide those developments with the basic services essential to modern living. Coming around a bend, we spotted a large sign that advertised the immediate availability of a commercially zoned piece of land. In square black lettering, the sign proclaimed its simple message:

FOR SALE BY OWNER
$1,500,000
Approx: 10 Acres • 1700 Plus Frontage

Below, in capital letters, was the most important piece of information:

NO BIRDS

The property owner had a bird letter.

Chapter Eight

NOAH'S CHOICE

And the Lord said unto Noah, Come thou and all thy house into
the ark, for thee have I seen righteous before me in this
generation.

Of every clean beast thou shalt take to thee by sevens, the male
and his female: and of beasts that are not clean by two, the
male and his female.

Of fowls also of the air by sevens, the male and the female; to keep
seed alive upon the face of all the earth.

For yet seven days, and I will cause it to rain upon the earth forty
days and forty nights; and every living substance that I have
made will I destroy from off the face of the earth.

And Noah did according unto all that the Lord commanded him.

—GENESIS 7:1-5

IN SOME WAYS, Noah had it easy. The materials he needed
to build his Ark were at hand and the design, provided by
the Supreme Deity, was guaranteed to be sufficient for the
task. Two by two, the creatures walked aboard, filling the vessel
just to capacity. When the parade finished, Noah had fulfilled his
obligations. He had saved "every living substance." There had
been no need to exercise judgment or agonize over tough choices.
He and his sons just stood on the gangplank and let everything in.
When no creature was waiting outside, he shut the door and
waited for the rain.

In the role of modern Noahs, we face momentous choices. We
want to load endangered species on our ark, but the task must
compete for scarce resources with other worthy projects. Because

we are acting from a human impulse rather than on the orders of a Supreme Deity, we don't have blueprints for our conduct or, for that matter, the ark we are trying to build. We don't even know the number of potential passengers, although we know that whatever ark we choose to build will be unable to accommodate everything. What will be saved and what will be left behind? There is no automatic answer.

Few individual situations are foreordained. If the nation wants to, it can buy outright the pine barrens and oak savanna needed by the Karner Blue butterfly; or it can build a new hospital to serve the Choctaws who live on the wrong side of the Sans Bois Mountains in Oklahoma; or it can dismantle the dams that block full recovery for the snail darter. It can do any of these things, but not all of them at once. Each of these actions diminishes our capacity to take other worthwhile actions. It is easy to say that society should extract money from developers and give it to black-capped vireos that need protection. But it is not possible to do this and simultaneously ensure that good housing is available and affordable to everyone. Or good health care, for that matter, or a good education. Embracing the goal of saving biodiversity and the goals of providing housing, health care, and education, as well as the many other goals we have taken up during the past two hundred years, makes our choices difficult.

The decisions we face over the next several decades encompass what Guido Calabresi, a legal scholar at Yale, has called "tragic choices." Such choices involve an unavoidable clash among society's fundamental values, he wrote in 1978, "a prospect of insuperable moral difficulty, a nightmare of justice in which the assertion of any right involves a further wrong." No amount of scientific research or careful government planning will make these conflicts go away, because they cannot be resolved merely by making our decisions more knowledgeably or more efficiently or even more democratically. The tragic nature of the choices is due to the identity of the people who must make those choices—us. If we valued only trees and streams, we wouldn't hesitate to save them all, for the economic cost would be irrelevant. If we cherished only cement and steel, any part of nature beyond the minimum necessary to sustain life would become expendable. Only in these extreme circumstances would there be no conflict between reverence for the natural environment and joy in the creations of humanity. Only then would our choices be easy. But humans need some of each and want as much of both as they can get. More of one, less of the other—the trade-off cannot be avoided. Because of this incontrovertible fact, we *must* choose, a nerve-wracking selection among praiseworthy ends that has tragic overtones, and sometimes tragic consequences. It is up to us to make our decisions consciously and thoughtfully. When we pick nature, we must recognize the human losses; when we choose to satisfy human desires, we should shut the door in the ark with as much wisdom and compassion as possible.

Unfortunately, the present system seems unable to do this. In 1973, Congress faced the incoming tide of extinction and, like King Canute, commanded it to stop. But the tide continued to advance, and now the Fish and Wildlife Service is going under. The endangered species list has grown steadily in the past two decades, and that trend shows no sign of stopping. For every species the agency has removed from the list since 1973, it has added more than thirty others. Most of the removals have been for reasons other than the species' recovery, reducing the ratio to less than one successful removal for every *one hundred* additions. More species will achieve some measure of success in the next little while, but each of the successes will be outweighed by the scores joining the list, headed in the opposite direction.

By any measure, efforts to achieve the lofty goals mandated by the Endangered Species Act have failed. The unwillingness to admit this failure—to issue proclamations of victory and extol isolated success stories—should not be confused with a deep moral commitment to biodiversity. "In empirical fact," as the American philosopher John Dewey noted, "the measure of the value a person attaches to a given end is not what he *says* about its preciousness, but the care he devotes to obtaining and using the *means* without which it cannot be attained." If that is the case, Congress has never given much value at all to our natural heritage, for it has never provided the necessary means to reach the goal.

The proper response, however, is not to condemn members of Congress for failing to understand the obligation they created twenty years ago (they never have); or the Fish and Wildlife Service and other federal agencies for failing to save every species on the list (they never have had the means, and they never will); or even private property owners for seeking to ensure that endangered species are saved on someone else's land (they never have had any reason to do anything else). Instead, the time has come to question the goal that underlies the act: Save every species, no matter what the cost.

The thought of deliberately abandoning the effort to save some biological entities is disagreeable, and scaling back the Endangered Species Act is tantamount to endorsing such an unpleasant prospect. The discomfort is enough to push some into the warmly comforting arms of the Noah Principle. That would be a mistake. Crying "no more extinctions" produces a noble sound, but it does nothing to stop extinction. And it has the potential to worsen the plight of biodiversity, because demanding the perfect can prevent us from obtaining the merely good. To do better, we will have to accept the responsibility that comes with being human at this time in history. That is, we must choose to play Noah, however imperfectly.

WHEN CONGRESS passed the Endangered Species Act in 1973, its members acted reflexively, almost without thinking. Congresswoman Leonor Sullivan, Democrat of Missouri, the chair of the Merchant Marine and Fisheries Committee, summed up what must have been the thinking of most members of Congress:

> When we threaten endangered species, we tinker with our own future. We run risks whose magnitudes we understand dimly. And we do so, for the most part, for reasons that can be described most charitably as trivial.

Sullivan's remarks were couched in the optative mood. The implicit assumption, echoed by many conservationists today, was that we could save endangered species without impeding necessary development, because the harm to biodiversity is for "trivial" reasons. If development harms a species here, we can just move the development or the species somewhere else—an easy thing to do. Thus saving everything is not a burden.

Tellico woke Congress from its dream of stopping extinction at bargain-basement prices. Although the dam itself apparently made little economic sense, it was clear from the day it became an issue that the reasons for harming biodiversity are not always trivial. If efforts to save biodiversity are to improve, we must acknowledge that species are endangered sometimes for good reasons indeed. To say otherwise is to condemn all human endeavor as trivial, an environmental reformulation of the doctrine of original sin.

Sometimes these human endeavors, on balance, inflict more harm than benefit. But stopping the bad means stopping the good as well, imposing moral and economic costs on society. It is these costs that make Sullivan's belief a fantasy; blinding ourselves to them has created the swirl of anger and litigation that now besets all discussion of endangered species. Instead of grounding our actions in a Noah Principle that is both unethical and impracticable, we should learn from the past twenty years and revise our basic assumptions, guided by a set of principles that people are able to follow. Here are four of them:

The system for making choices must be ethical.

An ethical system will encourage balancing among different interests, equities, and values. No single one should be allowed to dominate the others; our society is too complex and humans are too varied to expect that. When conflict arises, as it will, the system should not suppress it but instead work toward its equitable resolution. This resolution can occur in many ways, but all the good ones involve what Hans-Georg Gadamer, the great contemporary German philosopher, has called *conversation*, or the "process of coming to an understanding."

A conversation in Gadamer's sense is what the meetings of the BCCP Executive Committee should have been—a forum in which different people try to reach agreement. Imagine that the committee had been free of the chokehold of the present Endangered Species Act. It would have had more flexibility in exploring ways to save biodiversity in the Hill Country. Combining Craig Pease's ecological computer models with good economic data, Austinites could have considered different options that would give species various levels of protection at various costs. Giving the vireo a 50 percent chance of survival, for instance, might be easily affordable. But Austinites treasure their countryside and would probably be willing to bear the cost of greater protection. On the other hand, paying for a 95 percent chance of survival might compromise too many other goals. The discussion might turn to a figure in the middle—a 90 percent chance, perhaps. Suggesting such a small reduction is not necessarily foolish: the last few percentage points of protection are usually by far the most expensive. Whatever the outcome, such a conversation would provide a means to balance the different values held by Austinites, and everyone else.

In fact, the Executive Committee offered no such means. As the participants paid lip service to the all-encompassing value of biodiversity, each side tried to flatten the other. Conservationists played the trump card of the Endangered Species Act, while developers used the staggering costs of trying to save everything as a way to escape from doing anything. And both made frequent references to the possibility of future litigation. Constantly trying to win, rather than accepting compromises and forging an agreement, is anathema to conversation. The art of successful conversation, Gadamer said, "is not the art of being able to win every argument." It depends, paradoxically, on the likelihood that anyone in it might lose. The scary possibility of this "failure" nudges the participants toward something that could be called the truth. This truth is not necessarily a consensus, or a merging of values; instead, individuals may agree to disagree. Yet merely engaging in a conversation, Gadamer argued, inevitably pushes adversaries closer together, as people learn more about the strengths of others' positions and recognize the weaknesses of their own.

Successful democratic institutions, Gadamer thought, often have the character of conversations. What is remarkable about the

Endangered Species Act is its systematic avoidance of this possibility. Ideally, important laws should emerge after a national conversation; passed in a blind surge of piety, the Endangered Species Act represents no considered judgment on the worth of the nation's natural heritage, nor a debate on the means for achieving its protection. And the law itself, as interpreted by the Supreme Court, effectively outlaws the possibility of losing that is the key to a true conversation. In the first years of the act's administration, former Fish and Wildlife director Lynn Greenwalt told us, "I discovered we had a large-caliber firearm here with virtually no end of ammunition. Tellico confirmed it." If biodiversity is supposed to win every argument, it forecloses the possibility of conversation—a denial of our ability to use moral judgment.

Rather than facilitating discussion among parties with conflicting interests, the present system forces the burden of saving biodiversity on whoever happens to live near endangered species, automatically imposing costs on a few to generate benefits for many. Saving the Karner Blue butterfly in Wilton, New York, will presumably benefit the entire Albany region—in theory, the entire country—but it is the men, women, and children of this one town who must put up with the additional mosquitoes without any opportunity to participate in the fundamental decision to save the butterfly. Similarly, protecting the American burying beetle will benefit all of eastern Oklahoma, and perhaps all of the United States, but it is the members of the Choctaw Nation living north of Highway 82 who must wait additional years for the highway. The examples are legion; we have chronicled some in this book. The disparity between those who bear costs and those who receive benefits is wrong. By allowing them to persist, we treat the people of Wilton and the Choctaws simply as tools useful toward the end of saving biodiversity, a stance recognized as immoral since the days of Kant. *I* get to know the Florida scrub jay still exists; *you* get to pay the costs to keep it alive. An ethical system would give those people a voice in the decision-making process.

At the same time, an ethical system would recognize that biodiversity, like the quality of the environment, has value to most Americans; it commands *some* form of duty. The desire to balance competing interests cannot be used as a cover to return to the days of continuous open seasons on wildlife, or unfettered collecting of plants and insects, or mindless, wasteful clearing of habitat. Just as we cannot impose the costs of saving biodiversity on a few to benefit the many, we should avoid imposing the costs of losing biodiversity on the many to benefit the few. Trading the local population of the black-capped vireo for a subdivision would presumably affect all of central Texas, whereas most of the benefits would flow to the developers of the subdivision and the people who bought the houses. The imbalance between the many who bear losses and the few who gain is wrong here, too. Retaining a core set of duties to biodiversity will help give both sides to the conversation equal standing, encouraging parties with conflicting values to find a balanced resolution within the system rather than choosing to cheat or abandoning it altogether for the Elysian Fields of litigation.

Because values vary widely across a nation as large as the United States, the type of resolution may vary as well. People in Texas and California, for example, place different priorities on private property and expect different levels of government involvement in land-use decisions. What seems ethical in one state may not be in another; in one place, property owners may regard it as their duty to contribute heavily to communal goods, whereas in another this may be regarded as unfair. The system should reflect these differing values by allowing the developers, conservationists, and other parties who participate in biodiversity conversations to come to differing arrangements—as long as these are consistent with (or exceed) the core duties.

The system for making choices must be practicable.

Practicability means that the goals of the system must be attainable and the means to attain those goals must be present. Neither is a hallmark of the present system. Insisting on perfection is always attractive, because it seems to guarantee moral purity. It leaves the extremist, clad in white raiment, safely on the sidelines, decrying sellouts and compromises. But draping ourselves in the

Noah Principle is rarely helpful in a practical sense. If we want truly to improve the lot of endangered species, we should stop shooting for the stars, because the arrows will fall back to our feet. By aiming a little closer, we might shoot farther in the desired direction.

There is a danger in returning practicability to our efforts to save biodiversity, as we readily acknowledge. The Endangered Species Act of 1966 tempered the government's responsibility with that qualification, and little meaningful conservation followed. Yet the lesson we draw from the history of endangered species legislation is not that the legal duties owed biodiversity should be expanded further. Rather, the experience of the last two decades suggests that tough federal regulation alone is not a practicable way to save species. The Endangered Species Act of 1973 adopted that approach and ended up turning landowners into the enemies of species on their land and wildlife biologists into ecological mandarins, deciding the fate of resentful communities. Does this mean the nation is caught in a dilemma? Can we neither bring back practicability to the law, because that would let federal agencies and private property owners do nothing, nor have an impracticable law, because that would lead to ceaseless conflict and equally little conservation? No. We believe that the framers of the 1973 law were right in their desire to avoid the "business-as-usual mentality," but wrong in their attempted solution—forcing conservation down people's throats. Instead, the government should return to depending on the power of persuasion, as it did in the earlier law. But this time Congress should back up that persuasive power with something it has never provided: strong financial support.

Given the scandalous unwillingness of Congress to back this lofty mission with significant budget outlays, the Fish and Wildlife Service has been forced to impose conservation duties on other federal agencies and private property owners. In this way, endangered species are transformed into a liability—a constraint on otherwise-legitimate activity, an entry in the minus column of a profit-and-loss statement or a government budget. This treatment encourages reasonable federal agencies to shun endangered species if possible and otherwise-responsible property owners to reach for their bulldozers at the first sight of them. Who wants to live in a Treatment Exclusion Zone in the middle of bug season? Better to mow the lupine whenever it thrusts its ugly head above the surface! As we said above, an equitable system would impose some level of duty on these parties, so this perverse incentive can never be avoided entirely. But setting those duties beyond practicability almost guarantees misbehavior; the only gain is to the members of Congress who do not have to cast politically difficult votes to boost the endangered species budget.

If biodiversity truly is an important value to this country—and, speaking as private citizens, we believe that it is—the public coffers should bear a significant portion of the cost of saving species. Rather than fighting losing battles against ordinary citizens turned outlaw by legislation requiring the impossible, the system should be geared toward *rewarding* those who choose to go beyond the minimum set of duties. Absolutely banning actions that harm endangered species functions, insofar as it functions at all, to grant those species some clout in an economic system that has historically ignored them. The Endangered Species Act was written to do just that, after the political system showed its inability to stop government agencies and big corporations from approving the slaughter of even such popular beasts as humpback whales. But the goal was accomplished in the wrong way—the cheap way. If moneyed interests imperil biodiversity, as is often charged, the proper counterweight is to award some money to the interests that seek to protect it.

The system for making choices must be knowledgeable.

Biologists complain correctly that we know far too little about the natural world to make the best decisions about its treatment. This is unfortunate, because such knowledge is worthy in its own right; it is doubly unfortunate when we need to make decisions about the fate of the natural world. Missing or mistaken data flaw too many conservation decisions. When Fish and Wildlife added the American burying beetle to the endangered species list in 1989, entomologists thought the insect lived only in two small sites. Surveys between 1992 and 1994 found the beetle in big swathes of three states. Errors will always occur, but similar cases are much too common in the annals of the Endangered Species Act. Species are constantly being listed too early or too late, and protection actions all too often misfire as a result. More important, the necessity of proceeding on inadequate data means that we may be expending scarce funds to clear up problems that we might decide were insignificant if we had more complete information. These failures should be combated. A better system would find a way to devote more resources to gathering information.

The system for making choices must be political.

Political is frequently used as a dirty word, sometimes by politicians themselves. But in a democracy, the to-and-fro of politics is how society reconciles incommensurable goals like protecting endangered species and creating houses for the middle class. Threats to biodiversity have biological, economic, social, demographic, and philosophical dimensions, but solutions to those problems are not the exclusive domain of biologists, economists, sociologists, demographers, and philosophers. Relying solely on experts to determine biodiversity policy is as absurd as using public referenda to decide which species are endangered. Science needs to resume its proper place: providing support for policymakers. But—and this is vital—policymakers cannot be required to follow the dictates of experts, whether they are economists or ecologists. In a democratic system, elected officials must be free to make the decisions they feel represent their constituents' wishes. Those wishes will sometimes make the Ph.D.'s roll their eyes in exasperation, but the increasingly likely alternative—a system that lacks public support because it is out of touch with public values—is worse.

Bringing biodiversity into the political arena will knock it off the pedestal of science, and force us to recognize that practicability must govern its protection. At the same time, thrusting biodiversity into the rough-and-tumble world of politics will elevate it alongside such basic values as health, defense, and education, giving it legitimate claim to a greater share of our public resources. No longer able to foist the hard choices onto blue-ribbon panels of scientists, political decision makers will be forced to educate themselves about biodiversity issues. Budget battles will be routine, and members of Congress will inevitably logroll one another for shares of "green pork." Yet as long as the system uses the touchstone of politics, it will make choices based, however tenuously, in publicly shared values—something absent from the present system.

These principles could be embodied in many ways by many mechanisms; the proverb about skinning and cats applies. But they should not be ignored. The present system does that and has foundered as a result. By abjuring the possibility of negotiating among different values in favor of the utopian goal of perfect science-based protection, our nation has created a system whose hallmark is futility. Species hang on in a kind of permanent invalid ward, sustained by activists and litigation, while the harassed Fish and Wildlife Service runs frantically from bedside to bedside, doling out painkillers. Meanwhile, the injured bodies pile up in the emergency room just outside.

What is astonishing is not that the lack of these principles created a law that even its first users, like Fish and Wildlife head Greenwalt, were scared to use. Nor is it the candid assessment of a high Interior Department official, given to us in 1994, that more than half of the House of Representatives would vote down a law whose goal is supported overwhelmingly in public-opinion polls. Nor is it the snarl of litigation over biodiversity that besets communities from the edge of Maine, where environmentalists have filed innumerable actions about the piping plover, to coastal southern California, scene of a huge legal set-to that may ultimately include more than one hundred species. The only surprising thing is that a law with such a weak record of success would be so ardently defended by those who share its goal. All talk of changing the act today boils down to discussions of whether it should be stronger or weaker. Much more important is whether the law can be *better*. Until it adheres to the principles above, we believe that this possibility is foreclosed.

GIVEN THE INDICTMENT of the Endangered Species Act for failing to satisfy these principles, it is fair to inquire whether the authors of this book have a better system in mind. Recognizing the danger of wandering beyond the realm of the practicable, we nevertheless offer some suggestions below. Here, we ask the forbearance of the politically inclined. Our suggestions in no way constitute a specific package of reform measures intended for the next session of Congress. Indeed, they are politically naïve. Their purpose is less to draw a blueprint for a new political system than to sketch the possibilities for change. More concrete, actualizable proposals can come only from the interested parties themselves, not from outside "experts" like us.

In principle, the Endangered Species Act has two stages for action. First, scientists examine a species to determine whether it should be added to the list. If it is listed, the second stage occurs: government agencies design and enact a program to conserve the species. Because the menu of options for government in the second stage is limited, the two stages are in effect merged into one. Biologists decide to list a species, then a rigid set of duties automatically clicks into place. (This doesn't mean that the duties are fulfilled. Indeed, listed species often languish from a lack of funding. Stasis is also the result when the duties, as enumerated in species' recovery plans, are almost impossible to fulfill.)

This automatic response is largely responsible for the criticisms of the act we have discussed. The narrow limits to action reduce the flexibility of the law, making it less practicable; the duties are set so rigidly high that the law unethically elevates them over all others. Tying the set of duties to the listing decision hides the real policy choices (which in fact have already been made automatically) behind a facade of science; and the impossibility of enforcing the letter of the law turns Fish and Wildlife Service biologists into ecological mandarins, judging when the law may be winked at and when it must be fully enforced.

The heart of our proposal is to separate the two tasks. We would change the import of the list, which affects the first stage. And we would increase the range of possible actions in the second stage, which is inevitably to say that we propose *lowering* what could be called our "minimum duty" to biodiversity. Instead of protecting biodiversity solely with a rigid legal ban, we would provide much of the protection with a trust fund, a different and more flexible mechanism that encourages conversation and facilitates choices.

By separating the endangered species list from its attendant duties, we restore the list to its original purpose: an information device, signaling the identities of species with special conservation needs. Part of the information will be, of course, whether the species is endangered or threatened, using the definitions provided by the current law. But other categories might be added, too. When Buff Bohlen proposed adding the threatened status in 1972, for instance, he sought to lower the threshold of endangerment needed for a species to appear on the list. This would alert conservation officials before the species was on its deathbed. Increasing the number of status categories to include species that are not yet classifiable as threatened but still in some danger would be one way of covering a wider range of biodiversity.

Regardless of the number of included categories, restoring the main function of the list to an information device should be accompanied by an aggressive inventory of the nation's natural heritage, at a species and a regional or ecosystem level. Portions of this task have already been accomplished by the Natural Heritage surveys conducted by the fifty states, in conjunction with The Nature Conservancy; another part has been performed by the Fish and Wildlife Service, each state office of which keeps tabs on its listed species; and still another portion is being put together by a scientific team based in Idaho, which has helped develop the technique known as "gap analysis." Simple in concept but hard to execute, gap analysis consists of employing aerial or satellite photographs to map the contours of ecological communities, usually breaking them down by types of vegetation. These maps are then placed atop maps of landownership to learn who owns what and which type of community is most threatened.

In 1993, private property owners objected to a similar proposal, helping to kill a move in Congress to create a National Biological Inventory. (Interior Secretary Bruce Babbitt created one anyway through an internal reorganization.) Our proposal would, we believe, meet with less resistance. This is because of its second part: reducing the minimum duty owed a species under the law. If this is done, the presence of a species on the list does not automatically create draconian constraints, lessening the incentive to hide its presence.

The most obvious way to accomplish this change is to scale back the definition of *take*. Two examples illustrate the possibilities. Limiting the definition to the *intentional, direct harm of an individual member of a listed species* would reduce our duties to biodiversity to the barest of bare bones. (The ban could also apply to only certain categories of species.) Shooting a whooping crane or collecting a Karner Blue butterfly would be against the law. Clear-cutting the oaks and junipers from Steiner Ranch while vireos were away for the winter would not. Grading an area full of American burying beetles would probably not be illegal, either, because any killing of beetles that occurred would be incidental to the action of grading. A second version of the definition would limit it to the *direct harm of an individual member of a listed species*, a more expansive definition that would surely cover the hypothetical case of grading over beetles. Or one might apply the second version to the most endangered species and the first to species that faced less peril.

Exactly how far to scale back the definition of *take* is not something we feel comfortable specifying, because it needs to be determined by a serious national conversation about the value of biodiversity. We can say, however, that the definition must be scaled *back* if the impracticability of the present law is to be addressed; it cannot be increased. Making the law more practicable will inevitably put more biodiversity at risk. By changing the definition of *take* to reduce the minimum duty, we explicitly condone that risk.

A second group of reduced duties would be assigned to federal agencies. Again, we provide two examples of what such duties might entail. One simple plan would be to prohibit only direct, intended harm to endangered species on both public and private property—a kind of glorified anti-poaching law. This would leave biodiversity with much less legal protection, but would still raise the duty of government and private citizens above the level of business-as-usual. A second, more complex scheme would be to have federal agencies keep their current mission to conserve biodiversity on federal land and prevent harm from federally funded projects, but to require those agencies to balance their actions for biodiversity against their other goals. Private property owners, for their part, would only be asked to avoid direct, intentional harm. This more expansive proposal would still be a retreat from the current law—a move, we believe, in the right direction.

If we scale back duties toward endangered species, we create room for meritorious behavior; and by not imposing uniform, perfect, impossible duties, we create room for flexibility. Add a group of dedicated scientists and a large pot of money and there are numerous opportunities to encourage meritorious behavior that is also biologically sensible. This is a description of a national biodiversity trust, essentially a glorified land trust with some special features. Land trusts, legally speaking, are covenants between landowners and communities to maintain something valuable about a piece of property that might not otherwise be maintained. Sometimes the trust owns the land outright; sometimes it compensates the landholder for an economic loss; sometimes it has negotiated legal constraints on the land but has not paid anything—the varieties are endless. The Nature Conservancy is the largest land trust in North America, involved in all fifty states with so little fanfare that most of the people in those states have never heard of it. Such measures, which depend on the consent and compensation of property owners and communities, are evidently popular with Americans. According to the Land Trust Alliance, an organization that coordinates information about them, the number of trusts has ballooned from fewer than fifty in 1950 to about eleven hundred today—all without any formal program to encourage them. Land trusts now cover almost 15 million acres. They are a wonderful American institution, and our proposal will add one more.

Like its brethren, the national biodiversity trust would talk with local people about protecting the ecological communities on their land. In many cases, meritorious behavior needs no financial reward. The state of Wisconsin, for example, has a program to contact landowners and encourage them to conserve two federally listed plant species. The landowner's only reward for agreeing to a nonbinding protection plan is a picture of the plants and a certificate of appreciation. Most landowners happily go along. They may ultimately flatten the plants, but at least they are not *encouraged* to do so by the threat of onerous prohibitions. The program has recently expanded to cover the Karner Blue butterfly and the massasauga rattlesnake, which is on the state endangered list.

Not all exhortative programs can be successful. In that case, the trust can encourage conservation with a potent weapon: money. The money could be used for many purposes, from ecological research to advertising. But a major portion would most likely go to compensating landowners who feel that protecting endangered species imposes too many costs on them. In some cases, the trust could buy out property holders, but this would not have to be a major focus. The Nature Conservancy has come up with a huge number of different local solutions to protecting small parts of the landscape; the national biodiversity trust could copy them, modifying when necessary, with the goal of protecting much larger parts. If adequately funded—a huge, vitally important *if*—a national trust could end many of the disputes over biodiversity once and for all.

The national trust would operate under two constraints. First, participation must be voluntary. Landowners must be able to reject its overtures without penalty, though mechanisms like tax incentives could encourage them to adopt conservation measures short of giving up their property. If the landowner chooses to reject those overtures, the trust will have no power over the use of that land. (Endangered species on the property could still be protected by a prohibition on "take.")

Second, the trust's budget will be established by Congress, a normal event in the life of any federal agency. Without the illusory boundless ark of the Endangered Species Act, however, Congress must honestly face the question of how much biodiversity to save, which in turn is linked to how much the American people think it is worth. Here questions about unpleasant subjects like taxes must be answered. It is time to stop pretending that the country's natural endowment can be protected for free, without hurting anyone. If providing absolute protection to a butterfly like the Karner Blue will cost hundreds of millions or billions of dollars, a biodiversity trust for the whole nation must have a budget of similar scope.

How big would that budget be? The answer must come out of the political process. Here, an adjunct to the trust fund—a biodiversity advisory board—plays an integral part. In our scheme, the board would consist of two halves. One half would consist of a panel of eminent biologists. As a suggestion, its membership could be drawn from the recently formed Club of Earth, whose members include Jared Diamond, Paul Ehrlich, Thomas Eisner, Ernst Mayr, Peter Raven, and Edward Wilson. They would be asked to create a system for establishing priorities. What part of our biological heritage, they might ask themselves, is the most important? What criteria should we use to determine this? The economic value of a species? (How do we measure it? Better ask the economists.) Our society's reverence for it? (Do we dare ask the public?) Its contribution to an ecosystem? (How do we measure *that*? We've no one to ask but ourselves.) The advisory board would have to decide. They might focus on ecosystems, saving the most diverse first. Or they might recommend one of each major ecosystem type, or the ones that are the most endangered. Unsurprisingly, biologists love all living things, and this kind of thinking as a rule makes them profoundly uncomfortable. But the ark is not big enough, and no one is better equipped to decide which species, communities, and ecosystems are more necessary than others and how best to protect them. Importantly, they could work without regard to economic or social considerations, if they so choose; if creepy-crawlies are more biologically important than fuzzy-wuzzies, scientists can tout their value. Here, but only here, biology rules the day.

Working in the next room, so to speak, would be the other half of the advisory board: a panel of social scientists, economists, philosophers, and political scientists among them. They would match the system for establishing biological priorities with one for recognizing and weighing economic, moral, and social values. Getting the most biodiversity for the buck would be part of their task; ensuring that other, nonmaterial human endeavors did not get trampled in the process would be another; touting the economic and social values of biodiversity would be yet another; and making certain that the process was equitable would be still another. Just as the biologists may find occasion to consult the other sciences, so would this team find reason to ask questions of the biologists. What is the most efficient way of reducing the probability of extinction for this species? What is the effect on the productivity of this wetland ecosystem if you cut its area by one-third? How closely are these two species genetically related? The most important aspect of this work and that of the other team would be to confront one of our central precepts head-on: biodiversity has a value to people in and of itself, but the goal of protecting it must be weighed against other values.

The trust would then use the advisory board to draw up its budget. Any budget is composed of individual programs, and these would be pushed by proponents within the advisory board and attacked by the backers of competing programs. But each would need to justify its existence. Why should we give the Florida Scrub Jay Habitat Protection Program more money than the Oak Savanna Restoration Project? Or why give either more money than the Defense Department for its new tanks? Or the Education Department for its teacher-training program? The objections are easy to imagine: how can one possibly compare Florida scrub jays to Karner Blues, or either species to tanks and teachers? Yet this is the lifeblood of our political process: to compare the incommensurable, to calculate the incalculable.

Once the budget was presented on Capitol Hill, Congress would take its turn to ask questions. Things are tight this year—what can we get if we appropriate only $1 billion? How about $100 million? What do we lose by dropping that $900 million? The biologists would scream for more money; the economists would wring their hands over inflationary tendencies; the sociologists would demand that social bonds be protected at all costs—but Congress would eventually make the decision. Rather than making itself subservient to a panel of ecological and economic mandarins, Congress, the representation of the collective national will, would need to make the overall choice.

The protection of biodiversity at the federal level would be the product of a new Endangered Species Act and the biodiversity trust. A strong law would obviate the need for a large trust, of course, and vice versa. Yet an ethical system would find a balance, we believe, different from the one today, with a law so strong that it is routinely opposed and a budget so small that worthy actions go begging for money. It is important to note that this balance—like the threats to biodiversity—may vary across states and localities. If the people of Texas, for example, reject any but the minimum level of protection, a privately funded Texas biodiversity trust or an Austin-funded city trust could supplement the resources of the national trust. If Californians, by contrast, are more comfortable with government restrictions on private property, a stronger local law could back up the federal law. A new Endangered Species Act can define a minimum national duty toward biodiversity, yet still allow local values and conditions to have a voice.

Why should supporters of the Endangered Species Act join in a conversation that contemplates these kinds of change? For them, our proposal will seem biased in one direction, because it lessens the protection for endangered species. The advantages of our suggestions lie in the fictional character of the present system's protective abilities. The law reaches too high, and usually gets little. But in several years of traveling around the country, we have seen how private parties and government workers regard the current system as onerous. By reforming it, supporters may gain something real and valuable: cooperation by property owners in saving biodiversity, either voluntarily or through the use of the trust.

Why *shouldn't* the opponents of the Endangered Species Act join in a conversation that contemplates these kinds of change? For them, the advantages of our system appear to be overwhelming, because it lessens the protection for endangered species. But there are drawbacks. To participate in our system, property owners will have to concede that biodiversity has a place at the table. When environmentalists call for higher taxes or cuts in other programs to fund the biodiversity trust, opponents of the current system must acknowledge the legitimacy of such requests. If creating a useful trust involves a multibillion-dollar budget, developers and their lobbyists must swallow their distaste and not strangle it in Congress.

Both sides may argue that our suggestions seem quixotic, because big new government programs are impossible in today's climate. Yet that argument may tell us more about our society's true values than about the authors' level of political sophistication. Declaring that our government will never spend billions on biodiversity in the face of budget deficits and resistance to new taxes reveals, as John Dewey would point out, our true preferences. To make that claim is to accept tacitly that our nation values its biodiversity less than the space station, or agricultural subsidies, or any of a hundred other federal programs. It suggests that the people of the United States would prefer to have local governments, businesses, and activists snarled in perpetual dispute over the nation's biological heritage. The notion may be true, but it is profoundly discouraging.

In subjecting biodiversity to this kind of conversation, the most difficult pill for either side to swallow would be the possibility of losing. Yet that possibility is also the key to a better program. Rather than reflecting the views of a tiny group of congressional aides, as does the Endangered Species Act, our system would approach the priority awarded by society at large to the preservation of biodiversity. (*Approach* the priority—a perfect match is too much to hope for.) For too long have members of Congress been free to wax rhetorical about the value of the environment while refusing to back necessary increases in the budget for protection. For too long has the Fish and Wildlife Service been saddled with the impossible task of saving everything on a tiny budget. If the Congress really thinks that our natural heritage is worth less than $100 million a year, it falls to senators and representatives to state this unequivocally to the legions of the conservation-minded. Similarly, it is necessary for those most concerned with the fate of biodiversity to make their case clear, without recourse to misleading predictions of impending doom or bogus claims about the vast potential storehouse of medications locked up in every bug and plant. They should not be opposed by their usual foes, because a bigger trust budget would represent greater opportunity to buy out landowners at a profit. The end may resemble something that has never existed: a countrywide debate on the value of biodiversity, and a democratic vote on the means of its protection.

A GRANDIOSE SCHEME like this needs a reality check—what would it do for the whooping crane, the Karner Blue, the Austin Hill Country, the American burying beetle? Such questions are not easy to answer, partly because we have avoided making our illustrative proposal into something inappropriately specific (we are not mandarins). But we can say that the answer would be different for each species, because every situation is different, and because legitimizing trade-offs would of necessity afford different species different levels of protection.

An example is revising the definition of *take* to exclude harm caused by habitat transformation. Adopting either of our suggested definitions would not have much effect on the whooping crane, which already lives on land managed for its care; nor would it have much impact on any of the other species confined to wildlife preserves. The difference would appear outside land dedicated to wildlife, as indicated by the plight of the Karner Blue butterfly, increasingly a target of butterfly aficionados.

Historically, the butterfly lived in northeast Illinois. It was thought to have disappeared in the first decades of the twentieth century—until 1993, when three collectors at a state park on Illinois Beach spotted five of them. They snatched up all five, dropped them in killing jars, and mounted them in collections. After hearing lepidopterological scuttlebutt, Amelia Orton-Palmer of the Fish and Wildlife office in Chicago tracked down the malefactors. She was appalled, she told us, to discover that they were "fully aware" that the butterflies were the first Karner Blues seen there for decades. Two of the leppers, who worked together, agreed to turn over their specimens when they died; the third was unrepentant, even after the Chicago *Tribune* put the story on its front page.

In our scheme, collecting the Karner Blue would still be punished. The difference would be in what happens to the park. If the specimens had been part of a healthy population, the present system would have forced the state to manage the park in a way that would prevent harm to the butterfly and the lupine. This would mean changing the way it clears brush and mows lawns, banning the popular use of all-terrain vehicles in certain sections, and, possibly, a host of other measures. The park would suddenly be faced with an entire new set of responsibilities. Under our system, many or all of those actions would be voluntary. (As of the summer of 1994, however, no more butterflies had been spotted, leaving the park unencumbered for the time being.)

If federal agencies retain an affirmative duty to consider biodiversity, species on public land will probably not be left unprotected by the redefinition of *take*. Thus the National Guard in Camp Gruber would probably still have to adjust its tank-training exercises to avoid habitat for the American burying beetle—it's not that much of an inconvenience. But if Camp Gruber suddenly became an air force base and needed to lay out runways in a particular arrangement, the protection might be reduced. Similarly, the Environmental Protection Agency would probably keep the piece of its pesticide studies that examines the effect of their use on raptors, again because it is not much of an inconvenience. And federal agencies directly concerned with natural resources, such as the Forest Service and the Bureau of Land Management, would integrate biodiversity more tightly into their purposes. Thus the

Forest Service might very well end up deciding to stop logging on some national forests to protect spotted owls.

Counterbalancing any loosening of restrictions would be the trust. The trust could buy more land for the whooping crane, especially in Nebraska, where two dams on the Platte River have drained many of the marshy rest stops it uses while migrating from Texas to Canada. The dams are owned by utilities; the trust could pay them to release more water during the migration, temporarily making the land somewhat more whooper-friendly. Or—another tack—it might fund a campaign to persuade water users to be more attentive to the whooper's needs. The trust might consider funds spent on television advertising to be money well spent to help biodiversity.

Personally speaking, we would hope that the trust would buy and restore big tracts of former oak savanna or pine barrens for the Karner Blue—probably the latter, because land in upstate New York is often cheaper than prime farmland in the Midwest. On the other hand, it could use that money to buy a piece of the Texas Hill Country for the black-capped vireo. Probably not, though. An intelligently run trust would likely make the swap forbidden to the BCCP and snap up the enormous spread of cheap vireo habitat by the Rio Grande. If Austinites want to preserve the Hill Country as a vireo park, they are probably going to have to pay for most of it themselves. A species the trust may well ignore is the American burying beetle. Scattered thinly through three states, it might need land purchases of huge size to feel much protection. One is hard-pressed to imagine anyone doing that. As a result, the beetle would be left mostly to its own resources.

The trust would be unlikely to be able to do everything supporters of the present law want, though. Noah would have a budget and a bottom line, reflecting indirectly the priorities of people with differing aspirations. Because priorities are multiple, the budget would not be infinite; its allocations would reflect the tragic choices faced by the larger society.

These choices will not make everyone happy. Some "needless" losses of biodiversity will occur, if only because mistakes are inevitable. Some "foolish" losses of economic potential will occur, for the same reason. Those who embrace the Noah Principle and those who resist all calls for new government spending will find these suggestions equally objectionable. But in the world of the practicable, the question is not whether a proposal is free from flaws but whether it has the potential to improve our lot and that of the natural world. A system like this has that potential; it is hard to see much improvement coming from what we have now. Whether new institutions take the specific forms we suggest matters less than our acceptance of a primal duty. We must choose to choose.

IN AUGUST 1992, Karl Stephan, the insect collector who discovered American burying beetles in Oklahoma, went beetle hunting with a friend, Ramon Jackson, a zoologist at Eastern Oklahoma State College. Having invented a new, improved beetle trap—the insects fell onto a floatable screen, so they wouldn't drown on the bottom if it rained—the two collectors wanted to test it. After obtaining a permit from the Fish and Wildlife Service to work with *Nicrophorus americanus*, they set out for the Ouachita National Forest, about twenty miles east of Stephan's home. "We sure enough did catch some beetles," Stephan said—four of them.

"And *that*," he said, "put the flat on anything that happened in Le Flore County. Any project that affected over five acres, the Fish and Wildlife Service put a stop to it. The ones that were affected right off were the coal strip-mining companies." The service closed the mines. To reopen them, their owners had to certify to the agency that they were doing everything feasible to protect burying beetles. Obtaining the go-ahead required hiring consultants to survey the land for beetles. In September and October, four companies paid Stephan and Jackson to do just that.

As the two men drove to the first mine, owned by the Heatherly Mining Company, of Henryetta, Oklahoma, they saw everything that people detest about strip mining. They saw huge ugly piles of tailings, huge ugly heaps of torn trees, and huge ugly pieces of machinery. They saw a moonscape of devastated, almost-lifeless earth that would never be the same again. They also saw a crowd of unhappy miners. The foreman approached the two visitors. In Stephan's recollection, the foreman said to them, "If you find one of those beetles, please show it to me."

Stephan and Jackson dug holes and put their new bug traps in the ground. The next morning, some of them contained hungry specimens of *N. americanus*. Stephan put them in a peanut-butter jar with some canned cat food, which he had discovered that burying beetles like to eat, and carried the jar to the foreman. The foreman looked at the bugs for what seemed like a long time. Then he called to his crew. "Fellows!" he shouted. "Come over here! This is the thing that's going to give us all the pink slip!"

Strictly speaking, his fears were groundless. Nobody was fired, because Ken Frazier, the Fish and Wildlife agent in charge, gave Heatherly the green light, allowing operations to continue. On another level, though, the foreman's intuition was on the mark. Nobody had consulted the beetle's human neighbors about its protection, and as a result they had not given their informed consent. Nor would they have been likely to grant it. If anyone was going to pay for protecting the beetle, it was going to be the employees of the mining company, most of whom come from poor families. Because jobs have been scarce in eastern Oklahoma for a long time, they have nowhere else to go; the Fish and Wildlife Service has no resources to compensate the miners, even if it were allowed to. Their livelihoods were spared less from any virtues of the system than from the discovery that the beetle's range was much larger than originally thought. Unsurprisingly, they were less than enthusiastic about the continued existence of the insect. "One of the men told me," Stephan said, "that if he ever saw one of those things crawling around, he would step on it immediately."

Stephan himself would never be so thoughtless. But he could see the man's point. Although the Endangered Species Act had given him a nice sideline as a beetle surveyer, he was troubled by what he had seen of the present system for conserving biodiversity. His discovery of the beetle in Latimer County, Oklahoma, had helped the beetle's chance for survival, and he was glad about that. But he worried about its effect on his neighbors, who might be asked to give up things for a goal they had never agreed to support.

We met Karl Stephan on a warm, moonless night. His living room, made of cinder blocks, was cool. The beetle room to the side was visible as a patch of shadow. He sat in an armchair and told us about the insects he loved. He didn't want to see them go away—they're too interesting. On his lap was a collecting box, specimens of *Nicrophorus americanus* securely inside. A crunching of gravel outside announced the arrival of his wife. He stood up, politely preparing to see his visitors to the door. In a few minutes, we would be watching him pluck insects from the screen.

"If I had known then how they go about things," he said, "I wouldn't have been in favor of listing the beetle at all."

The Endangered Species Act After Twenty Years

Does the Endangered Species Act work? Does the current system, whatever its other defects, actually protect the nation's biodiversity? For more than a decade supporters and opponents of the law have provided mutually contradictory answers to these questions. Some environmentalists extol the Endangered Species Act as a vital and effective watchdog; others concede limitations, but argue that they can be addressed by increasing funding and enforcement. Meanwhile its detractors in the world of affairs regard the act as an onerous impediment to economic growth, ineffective at anything but soaking up money. Barrier to extinction or costly failure—which is correct?

One way of resolving this debate is to inquire into the fortunes of some of the species protected by the act, as we have done in this book. This approach can uncover the reasons for the law's successes and failures, suggest whether the law is likely to achieve its lofty goal of stopping extinction, and point the way toward meaningful reform. But it cannot gauge the act's overall record. That can be accomplished only by examining *all* the species on the endangered and threatened list—a daunting task.

In the twenty years between the end of 1973, when President Nixon signed the Endangered Species Act into law, and the end of 1993, the last full year for which data are available, the U.S. Fish and Wildlife Service added 721 species to the list* (not including the 134 carried over from the pre-1973 list). According to the act, the goal of listing a species is recovery—the point, to quote the law, "at which the measures provided pursuant to this Act are no longer necessary." When a species attains recovery, Fish and Wildlife is supposed to remove it from the list. By this standard, how many species have fully recovered in the past two decades?

Sadly, the number is small. In those years, the agency removed twenty-one species, which is to say that additions to the list outpaced recoveries by a rate of thirty-four to one. Worse, these figures actually overestimate the success rate, because not all of these delistings were due to recovery. Seven species—four fish, two birds, and a pearly mussel—left the list when Fish and Wildlife declared them extinct. (To be fair, only one of these, the dusky seaside sparrow, disappeared on the agency's watch; after listing, the others were discovered to have already been extinct.) And another nine were struck from the list because they should not have been on it to begin with—the data that formed the basis for the agency's decision to list them turned out to be in error. The Pine Barrens treefrog is one example. Listed in 1977, it was initially thought to exist only in seven small areas of a single Florida county. Later surveys found 165 other populations spread across several counties in Florida and Alabama. Acting on this new information, Fish and Wildlife delisted the frog in 1983.

Of the twenty-one delistings, then, only five occurred because the species had actually gained enough ground to warrant removal of the act's protections. This happy result, as Fish and Wildlife has acknowledged, is not always attributable to the Endangered Species Act. In fact, the connection between the law and the species' progress is tenuous in all but one of these cases.

- Three of the recovered species are birds found only in Palau, an island nation under U.S. trusteeship in the Western Pacific. The birds were listed in 1970 on the basis of biological surveys con-

---

*A listed "species" may actually be a full species, subspecies, or a distinct population of a vertebrate species.

ducted just after these small islands had been invaded by U.S. soldiers in the Second World War. After hostilities ended, the wildlife recovered, including the three birds—long before they were listed. (They were delisted in 1985.)

- The southeastern population of the brown pelican, struck from the list in 1985, principally owed its parlous condition to the indiscriminate use of the insecticide DDT. As a result, its recovery was due mostly to the banning of this chemical in 1972, rather than the passage of the Endangered Species Act a year later.

- On the other hand, the American alligator, pronounced fully recovered in 1987, was protected from hunting and other forms of exploitation by the law. This gives it the distinction of being the only member of the list to be removed because of actions taken since 1973.* But even this solitary success has been questioned. Some scientists believe that the species, imperiled by overhunting in the 1950s, was already recovering by the time the act was passed, chiefly because southern states took steps in the 1960s to control the alligator harvest.

If the first twenty years of the act produced only one full recovery, does that mean it is ineffective? Not necessarily. It may only mean that full recovery is an unrealistically strict standard by which to judge the law. Short of removing species from the list entirely, a lesser measure of success is reclassification—changing a species' classification from endangered to threatened, a sign of significant progress toward full recovery. Between 1973 and 1993, Fish and Wildlife reclassified eleven species. As before, few of these actions can be attributed unambiguously to the protection of the Endangered Species Act:

- The Tinian monarch, a Pacific bird, was a victim of war, much like the Palau birds. It had mostly recovered by 1970, when it appeared on the endangered list. But instead of delisting it completely, Fish and Wildlife concluded in 1987 that the monarch still faced enough problems that it should remain on the list as a threatened species.

---

*Technically, Fish and Wildlife did not actually delist the alligator. It resembles the endangered American crocodile, and the agency fears that hunters will accidentally kill crocodiles if they are allowed to shoot alligators. For this reason, the alligator still receives most of the law's protections.

- The snail darter was reclassified in 1984 when scientists discovered it was more prevalent than they had thought.

- The Arctic peregrine falcon and the bald eagle's populations in five states were reclassified in 1984 and 1978, respectively. Like the brown pelican, the falcon owed its decline to DDT; much of its improvement, to the near-complete ban on the insecticide in 1972. The bald eagle's reclassification came when Fish and Wildlife decided to change its official taxonomy (for purposes of listing the bird). Prior to 1978, the agency divided the species into a northern subspecies, which was unlisted, and a southern subspecies, which was listed as endangered. In that year, it jettisoned the division and amended the listing in the following way: endangered in all lower states except Michigan, Minnesota, Wisconsin, Washington, and Oregon; threatened in those five states; and unlisted in Alaska. Most of the eagle's improvement, however, is mainly for the same reason as the brown pelican's and peregrine falcon's: the banning of DDT in 1972. (In July 1994, after our twenty-year period, the agency proposed reclassifying the bald eagle in all states where it is now listed as endangered; and in October 1994, the agency delisted the falcon.)

- Four species of trout were reclassified—three in 1975 and one in 1978—to allow use of the law's provision for taking a threatened species in special cases. The fish had been subject to conservation efforts before the act and were on the road to recovery when the new law was passed. Its strict prohibition against taking an endangered species outraged local fishermen, who had supported the earlier protection efforts. Reclassification allowed a limited fishing season for the trout; indeed, when the agency proposed the first batch of reclassifications, the states of California and Nevada asked it to make a final decision in time for the summer trout season.

- The Minnesota population of the gray wolf was reclassified in 1978 for similar reasons. This large predator used to be common in the state, which is why its residents killed most of them. Fish and Wildlife did not want to help increase their number without giving local people the right to protect themselves and their property.

- The Utah prairie dog, reclassified in 1984, regained ground quickly after the power of the act stopped pest-control programs from poisoning the creature. Because local ranchers still regarded the animal as a pest, though, Fish and Wildlife reclassified it to permit a limited amount of legal killing, which would avoid a substantially greater amount of illegal killing.

- The Aleutian Canada goose, reclassified in 1990, was once widespread throughout the Aleutians. It suffered after nineteenth-century settlers used the islands as fox farms. By 1967, when it was placed on the endangered list, the foxes, now feral, had driven the goose to the edge; fewer than 300 survived. A Fish and Wildlife program to eradicate the foxes and hunting restrictions in the goose's wintering grounds allowed the goose population to increase, triggering the decision to reclassify it. By the end of 1993, the bird's population stood at 7,500.

By this measure, the unambiguous success stories are still rare. Only the reclassifications of the Utah prairie dog and the Aleutian Canada goose are related to actions undertaken through the act. And the partial recovery of the prairie dog may quickly stall, because the conflict with private landowners has never been resolved. Still, official reclassification may be too stringent a standard.

A final, still less stringent, gauge of accomplishment is the number of species that are doing well, even if they have not recovered enough to be delisted or reclassified. The agency provides a rough estimate of this number in its biennial report to Congress, *Endangered and Threatened Species Recovery Program*; the latest edition, containing data from fiscal year 1992, was released in mid-1994. It presented a mixed picture of the act's success. Only 69 of the 711 species listed by September 30, 1992—not quite 10 percent of the tally—had populations described by the agency as "improving," indicating active progress toward full recovery. Twenty-eight percent had "stable" populations, a sign that their declines had been halted. But a full 33 percent were "declining"; the population status of 27 percent of the listed species was unknown; and 2 percent—14 species—were thought to be extinct. Fewer than 60 percent of the listed species had a recovery plan, without which progress is difficult. And of those with recovery plans, more than 80 percent had not achieved half the objectives listed in their plan.

Even the few "improving" species were not always being helped in the way envisioned by the framers of the Endangered Species Act, let alone the aficionados of untrammeled wilderness who support it.

- The Socorro isopod, an aquatic cousin of the potato bug, is a case of recovery being in the eye of the beholder. The isopod once inhabited a few springs near the town of Socorro, New Mexico. The town's use of the springs for its water supply threatened to wipe out the isopod. Today, it has almost achieved complete recovery, because in 1989 the Fish and Wildlife Service dug eight bathtublike concrete tanks into an acre of land, surrounded the land by a chain-link fence, and transplanted the whole species into the tanks. Eight populations now thrive, one in each tank; they will probably never leave.

- The Loch Lomond coyote-thistle has a similar story. The plant lives only in a single wetland near Yountville, California, which is now owned by the state. Enclosed by a fence, the wetland has become a de facto coyote-thistle zoo; it is bounded by a mini–storage facility, two still-to-be-developed parcels of land, and a state highway with a right-of-way that extends into the pool. The protection afforded by this arrangement has encouraged Fish and Wildlife to propose reclassifying the species from endangered to threatened—an ambition not universally shared by the employees of the California Fish and Game Department.

- The Pahrump poolfish, a small desert fish sometimes known as the Pahrump killifish, was extirpated in the wild in 1975 when people emptied its sole habitat, a spring. Fortunately, scientists had captured some poolfish beforehand. The Fish and Wildlife Service transplanted the fish to two springs in Nevada, preparing them by poisoning many of the indigenous fish. It also placed the fish in an artificial tank fed by an artesian well. According to biologist James Deacon, the poolfish is really an "exotic reintroduction"—exactly the kind of unnatural intrusion the agency is otherwise fighting.

Not all the success stories are questionable. Some of the hundreds of listed species are making real progress, as evidenced by the agency's intention to delist or reclassify them in the future. A few examples:

- The Columbian white-tailed deer saw its population jump from less than 1,000 in the 1970s to more than 7,000 in 1994. The species gained ground in large part because of the establishment of the Julia Butler Hanson National Wildlife Refuge, near Kathlamet, Washington; the Bureau of Land Management has recently completed a land exchange in Oregon that will provide similar opportunities for the species to recover. Although buying land for wildlife refuges can take place without the authorization of the act, the attention paid the deer has been encouraged by its status as an endangered species. The agency is putting together a proposal to reclassify the deer from endangered to threatened.

- The Kendall Warm Springs dace, a fish, exists only in the channel, a few hundred feet long, between a group of warm springs and a waterfall that pours into Wyoming's Green River. Beset by fishers, who used it for bait, and ranchers, who drove their cattle through the stream, the fish was one of the original members of the 1973 list. After consulting with Fish and Wildlife, the Forest Service, which owns the land around the stream, put a fence around the spring and stream, forcing the ranchers to detour around the area and discouraging the fishers as well. Other efforts to secure the fish's habitat and start refugia populations at a nearby hatchery have encouraged Fish and Wildlife to consider reclassifying it to threatened status.

- The Magazine Mountain shagreen, a snail, lives in a rocky slope on land owned by the Forest Service near the top of Magazine Mountain in Arkansas. Although the species' habitat is not significantly degraded, plans to increase public access to the mountaintop led Fish and Wildlife to list the snail in 1989. Since then, Fish and Wildlife has eliminated most of the potential threats. If it can reach a long-term agreement with the Forest Service on managing the mountaintop with the species' interests in mind, the agency will consider delisting the snail.

One could, in principle, continue through the endangered species list in this way, scrutinizing each success story for flaws or each tale of woe for silver linings. The exercise would do little to change the inescapable conclusion, however. The Endangered Species Act has failed to help the overwhelming majority of species under its care to reach "the point at which the measures provided pursuant to this Act are no longer necessary."

Does this mean that the Endangered Species Act is an unqualified failure? Not necessarily. Because many species are rare or limited to small territories, they may be so extinction-prone as to be virtually unrecoverable, at least by Fish and Wildlife. After all, emergency-room doctors are not expected to save as many patients as their colleagues in less harried medical practices. Moreover, the agency cannot prevent endangerment; it can only step in when the situation has become critical. Finally, Fish and Wildlife has had only twenty years to reverse the effects of more than three centuries of habitat transformation.

Does this mean that the future of the Endangered Species Act may still be bright? Undoubtedly not. In recent years, the annual additions to the list have grown in number. At the end of the 1980s, the tally of U.S. species on the list stood at 563; in the first four years of this decade, that figure increased by almost half to 836. In the first six months of 1994 alone, Fish and Wildlife officially added 72 species to the list, proposed adding another 27 species, reclassified one from threatened to endangered, and concluded that 3 more may warrant listing. Meanwhile, on the other side of the ledger, the agency delisted one species (the eastern north Pacific population of the gray whale), rejected petitions to delist another three, and withdrew one proposed listing because of erroneous data.

The next few years will see more of the same. At the end of 1992, Fish and Wildlife settled a lawsuit from several environmental groups by agreeing to consider listing more than 400 species by October 1996. It is widely expected that most or all of those species, which are now in Category 1, will make it onto the list. None of this addresses the thousands of species lingering in Category 2, with some evidence of endangerment but not enough to support immediate action. Many of these, too, will make it onto the list. Meanwhile, the largest group of potential delistings consists of the 14 species the agency believes are extinct.

Species are appearing on the endangered list at an ever-increasing rate, which means that the nation's biodiversity is increasingly menaced. There are many reasons why, but the overwhelming fact remains that the current system for protecting biodiversity has not fulfilled the hopes expressed two decades ago when Congress passed the Endangered Species Act. The best that can be said about the act is that in many cases it has apparently slowed the fall to extinction. But in the long run it will not stave off disaster. Reforming the law and strengthening our efforts to save biodiversity must begin with the acceptance of that fact.

Notes

I. SEVENTEEN BEETLES

3–6 Stephan's life and discovery of *Nicrophorous americanus*: Interview, Karl Stephan; H. V. Weems, foreword, in K. Stephan, "The Bothrideridae and Colydiidae of America North of Mexico (Coleoptera: Clavicornia and Heteromera)," *Occasional Papers of the Florida State Collection of Arthropods* (Gainesville: Florida Department of Agriculture and Consumer Services, 1989).

3–4 Latimer County, Choctaws, Wilburton: M. Singer, "A Reporter at Large," *The New Yorker*, 2 April 1979, 25–27; R. S. Cotterill, *The Southern Indians* (Norman: University of Oklahoma Press, 1954); *Adventure Guide to Oklahoma's Kiamichi Country* (Oklahoma City: Oklahoma Department of Tourism & Recreation, n.d.); other information from Office of County Clerk, Wilburton, Okla.

6 Date of find: Letter, S. W. Forsythe to G. E. Larsen, 14 February 1992, Ken Frazier's files, U.S. Fish and Wildlife Service (USFWS), Tulsa, Okla. (hereafter cited as Frazier's files).

7–8 Burying beetle species: Interview, Stewart Peck; S. B. Peck and M. M. Kaulbars, "Synopsis of the Distribution and Bionomics of the Carrion Beetles (Coleoptera: Silphidae) of the Conterminous United States," *Proceedings of the Entomological Society of Ontario* 118 (1987): 47–80; R. H. Arnett, Jr., *American Insects* (New York: Van Nostrand Reinhold, 1985), 299–300; R. H. Arnett, Jr., *Beetles of the United States* (New York: Van Nostrand Reinhold, 1963). Opinions differ on whether there are fifteen (Peck) or seventeen (Arnett) North American members of *Nicrophorus*. There are either forty-four or forty-six members of the Silphidae.

8 Twelve million beetles: T. L. Erwin, "Tropical Forests: Their Richness in Coleoptera and Other Arthropod Species," *The Coleopterists Bulletin* 36 (1982): 74–75.

"inordinate fondness": Quoted in S. J. Gould, "A Special Fondness for Beetles," *Natural History* 102 (January 1993): 4–12, at 4.

Number of species: E. O. Wilson, *The Diversity of Life* (Cambridge, Mass.: Belknap Press, 1992), 132–141.

8–9 Behavior of burying beetle: Interviews, Michael Amaral (USFWS), Curtis Creighton, Andrea Kozol; A. J. Kozol et al., "The American Burying Beetle, *Nicrophorus americanus:* Studies on the Natural History of a Declining Species," *Psyche* 95 (1988): 167–176; C. Raithel, *American Burying Beetle (Nicrophorus americanus) Recovery Plan* (Washington, D.C.: USFWS, 1991).

9 Earliest-known insect image: Peck and Kaulbars, "Synopsis of the Distribution."

10 Fabre's work: J. H. Fabre, "Experiments with Burying-Beetles and The Burying Beetle," in *The Insect World of J. Henri Fabre*, ed. E. W. Teale (Boston: Beacon Press, 1991), 232–258 ("This hoarder," 234).

11 Thirty-five states, three provinces: Letter, M. J. Amaral to B. Strohm, 3 April 1992, M. J. Amaral's files, USFWS, Concord, N.H. (hereafter cited as Amaral's files).

11–12 Davis article: Interview, Lloyd R. Davis, Jr.; L. R. Davis, Jr., "Notes of Beetle Distributions, with a Discussion of *Nicrophorus americanus* Olivier and Its Abundance in Collections (Coleoptera: Scarabaeidae, Lampyridae, and Silphidae)," *The Coleopterists Bulletin* 34 (1980): 245–251 ("never met," 249; "this species," 250).

11 Endangerment theories (footnote): Interviews, Amaral, Kozol (pigeon theory); D. F. Schweitzer and L. L. Master, *"Nicrophorus americanus*, American Burying Beetle: Results of a Global Status Survey," Eastern Heritage Task Force, The Nature Conservancy, unpublished report to USFWS, 17 April 1987, Amaral's files (DDT theory); letter, K. Stephan to A. Hecht, 2 September 1989, Frazier's files (lights theory).

12 "We are rapidly": T. L. Erwin, "The Tropical Forest Canopy: The Heart of Biotic Diversity," in *Biodiversity*, ed. E. O. Wilson (Washington, D.C.: National Academy Press, 1988), 123–129, at 129.

13 Shoshone pupfish: F. Taylor et al., "Rediscovery of the Shoshone Pupfish at Shoshone Springs, Inyo County, California," *Bulletin of the Southern California Academy of Sciences* 87 (1988): 67–73.

Black-footed ferret: D. Weinberg, "Decline and Fall of the Black-Footed Ferret," *Natural History* 95 (February 1986): 62–69.

Palos Verdes Blue butterfly: Interview, Richard Arnold; "An 'Extinct' Butterfly Flutters Back to Life," *New York Times*, 5 April 1994; R. Tobin, *The Expendable Future: U.S. Politics and the Protection of Biological Diversity* (Durham, N.C.: Duke University Press, 1990), 252–253.

14 Most species are extinct: D. Raup, "Biological Extinction in Earth History," *Science* 231 (28 March 1986): 1528–1533.

Normal and current worldwide extinction rates: Wilson, *The Diversity of Life*, 280.

U.S. extinction rate: Interview, Peter Hoch.

Counties with endangered species: U.S. Environmental Protection Agency, Endangered Species Protection Program database (Washington, D.C., 1993). We thank Margery Exton of the E.P.A.'s Environmental Fate and Effects Division for providing us with the data.

15–23 Hospital, State Highway 82, and beetle: Interviews, Donald Crain, Neal McCaleb, Kyle McKinley, Jack Pate (U.S. Bureau of Indian Affairs), Eugene Stipe (Oklahoma legislature), Brian Schmitt; Oklahoma Department of Transportation (ODOT), Summary of Consultation, Endangered Species (American Burying Beetle) Involvement, SH 82 Red Oak to Lequire Project, n.d., Kyle McKinley's files, ODOT, Oklahoma City, Okla.

17 "harass, harm": *U.S. Code,* vol. 16, sec. 1532(19).

Ninety-six species: USFWS, "Endangered and Threatened Wildlife and Plants," *Code of Federal Regulations,* title 50, parts 17.11 and 17.12 (Washington, D.C., 1991).

So many mollusks (footnote): "Wildlife Champion Reluctantly Departs," Washington *Post,* 2 April 1978.

Milne's letter: Interview, Margery Milne; letter, L. J. Milne to M. Bentzien, 10 April 1980, Frazier's files.

18–21 Story of beetle listing: Interviews, Robert Allen, Amaral, Michael Bentzien, Anne Hecht, Lawrence Master, Patricia Mehlhop, Paul Nickerson, Dale Schweitzer.

18 Perkins's report: P. D. Perkins, "North American Insect Status Review," Final Report to Office of Endangered Species, USFWS, 1983, Amaral's files.

"Category 2" status: *Federal Register* (hereafter cited as *FR*) 49 (22 May 1984): 21670.

19 Block Island: Interviews, Charles Remington, Schweitzer.

Schweitzer-Master survey: Schweitzer and Master, *"Nicrophorus americanus."*

Decline of beetle: *FR* 53 (11 October 1988): 39617–39621.

Form letter: Letter, USFWS to ODOT, 5 May 1988, cited in Letter, Forsythe to Larsen (1992).

21 1989 survey: Noted in Letter, Forsythe to Larsen (1992).

Listing of beetle: *FR* 54 (13 July 1989): 29652–29655.

21–22 Highway surveys: P. Mehlhop, "Survey for *Nicrophorus americanus,* American Burying Beetle, Along Proposed Highway Routes Between the Towns of Red Oak and Lequire in East-Central Oklahoma," unpublished report to ODOT, 22 June 1990, Frazier's files; Letter, Forsythe to Larsen (1992).

22 ODOT's position and meetings: Interviews, McCaleb, Frazier; letter, S. Forsythe to Division Administrator, Federal Highway Administration, U.S. Department of Transportation, 17 September 1990, Frazier's files.

Page-one headline: "Flesh-Eating Beetle Blocking Highway," Tulsa *World,* 7 October 1990.

Collapse of negotiations: Letter, S. Forsythe to G. Larsen, 21 December 1990, Frazier's files.

22–23 De facto cancellation of highway: Biological opinion, M. Spear to G. Larsen, 11 February 1991, Frazier's files ("The proposed highway," 10). Immediately afterward, ODOT tentatively set out a third new route and asked the Heritage Inventory to survey it. Five beetles were found. ODOT gave up (Interview, Carl McCall [ODOT]; letter, S. Forsythe to G. Larsen, 27 September 1991, Frazier's files).

24 "foremost argument" and "that our fellow": P. Ehrlich and A. Ehrlich, *Extinction* (New York: Ballantine Books, 1981), 57, 58.

25 The Noah Principle: D. W. Ehrenfeld, "The Conservation of Non-Resources," *American Scientist* 64 (1976): 648–656 ("because they exist," 654–655).

26 208 beetles: Interview, Creighton; memorandum, M. Spear to Assistant Regional Director–AFF, Region 2, 18 February 1992, Frazier's files.

Reversal of opinion: Letter, Forsythe to Larsen (1992).

26–27 Outcome of the highway: Interviews, Frazier, McKinley, Ramon Jackson (beetle preserve).

27 Pipeline, coal companies, and Camp Gruber: Interviews, Stipe (local counsel), Creighton, Frazier; "Insect Job on in Arkoma," Dallas *Morning News*, 2 May 1990; " 'Beetlemania' " Alters Pipeline Plan," Tulsa *World*, 4 February 1990.

Hundreds of beetles: K. Frazier, Current Status of the American Burying Beetle within the Midwest Geographic Recovery Area, 20 January 1993, Frazier's files.

Frazier's beetle hours: Interview, Frazier.

2. KINDS OF

30 Problems with the Ark: J. Browne, *The Secular Ark: Studies in the History of Biogeography* (New Haven: Yale University Press, 1983), 1–31; D. C. Allen, *The Legend of Noah: Renaissance Rationalism in Art, Science, and Letters* (Urbana: Illinois University Press, 1949), 182–191 (Kircher's Ark).

31 Early taxonomic systems: E. Mayr, *The Growth of Biological Thought: Diversity, Evolution, and Inheritance* (Cambridge, Mass.: Belknap Press, 1982), 147–155; L. N. Magner, *A History of the Life Sciences* (New York: Marcel Dekker, 1979), 342–348.

31–33 Linnaeus and history of species concept: Mayr, *Growth*, 171–180, 258–259 (*"Natura,"* 259); Browne, *The Secular Ark*, 16–27; J. L. Larson, *Reason and Experience: The Representation of Natural Order in the Work of Carl von Linné* (Los Angeles: University of California Press, 1971); S. Atran, "Origin of the Species and Genus Concepts: An Anthropological Perspective," *Journal of the History of Biology* (hereafter cited as *JHB*) 21 (1987): 195–279 ("second Adam," 261).

32 Taxonomy for *N. americanus:* S. P. Parker, ed., *Synopsis and Classification of Living Organisms*, vol. 2 (New York: McGraw-Hill, 1982), 495.

33–35 Darwin and species: Mayr, *Growth*, 265–269, 400–417; G. DeBeer, "Charles Darwin," in *Dictionary of Scientific Biography,* eds. C. C. Gillispie et al. (New York: Scribner's, 1974), vol. 3, 571 ("How extremely stupid"); C. Darwin, *The Origin of Species* (New York: Mentor, 1958), 61–67, 434–447 ("The endless disputes" and "undiscovered and undiscoverable," 447); J. Beatty, "What's in a Word? Coming to Terms in the Darwinian Revolution," *JHB* 15 (1982): 215–239.

33–35 Darwin and finches: F. Sulloway, "Darwin and His Finches: The Evolution of a Legend," *JHB* 15 (1982): 1–15; F. Sulloway, "Darwin's Conversion: The *Beagle* Voyage and Its Aftermath," *JHB* 15 (1982): 325–396; P. R. Grant, *Ecology and Evolution of Darwin's Finches* (Princeton, N.J.: Princeton University Press, 1986) ("perfect gradation" and "most curious fact," 6). See also the excellent J. Wiener, *The Beak of the Finch* (New York: Alfred A. Knopf, 1994).

35–36 Naturalists and geneticists: Mayr, *Growth*, 540–550. The basic laws of genetics were discovered almost simultaneously by three botanists, each of whom paid tribute to the then-unknown work of Gregor Mendel, a learned Austrian monk who decades before had performed groundbreaking genetic experiments on pea plants. As a consequence, the beginning of genetics in 1900 is often described as the "rediscovery" of Mendel's laws.

36 Jordan's work: E. Mayr, "Species Concepts and Definitions," in *The Species Problem*, ed. E. Mayr, American Association for the Advancement of Science Symposium, no. 50 (Washington, D.C.: AAAS, 1957), 1–22 ("begins with," 4–5).

"have no actual existence": C. E. Bessey, "The Taxonomic Aspect of the Species Question," *The American Naturalist* 42 (1908): 218–224, at 218.

Mayr's species definition: Mayr, *Growth*, 273 (emphasis in original).

37 "Quasispecies": R. M. May, "How Many Species?" *Philosophical Transactions of the Royal Society B* 330 (29 November 1990): 293–304.

Owens pupfish: Interview, Phil Pister; E. P. Pister, "Species in a Bucket," *Natural History* 102 (January 1993): 14–19.

38 Ligers and tiglons: E. O. Wilson, *The Diversity of Life* (Cambridge, Mass.: Belknap Press, 1992), 38–39.

A species' *occupation:* Elton's work and this term are described in D. Worster, *Nature's Economy* (Garden City, N.Y.: Anchor Books, 1979), 295–300.

38–39 Ecological niches for burying beetles: S. Trumbo, "Reproductive Success, Phenology, and Biogeography of Burying Beetles (Silphidae, *Nicrophorus*)," *The American Midland Naturalist* 124 (1990): 1–11; S. Trumbo, "Interference Competition Among Burying Beetles (Silphidae, *Nicrophorus*)," *Ecological Entomology* 15 (1990): 347–355; R. J. Putnam, *Carrion and Dung: the Decomposition of Animal Wastes* (London: E. Arnold, 1983), 38–42.

39 Beetles and mites: D. S. Wilson, "The Effect of Population Structure on the Evolution of Mutualism: A Field Test Involving Burying Beetles and Their Phoretic Mites," *The American Naturalist* 121 (1983): 851–874.

"impossible" and "Should a large": P. R. Ehrlich, "Some Axioms of Taxonomy," *Systematic Zoology* 13 (1964): 109–123, at 110.

"national biological inventories": P. R. Ehrlich and E. O. Wilson, "Biodiversity Studies: Science and Policy," *Science* 253 (16 August 1991): 758–761, at 761.

1.8 million discovered species: N. E. Stork, "Insect Diversity: Facts, Fiction, and Speculation," *Biological Journal of the Linnaean Society* 35 (1988): 321–337.

40 Number of undiscovered species: J. Terborgh, *Diversity and the Tropical Forest* (New York: W. H. Freeman, 1992), 1.

Hammond's estimate: World Conservation Monitoring Centre (WCMC), *Global Biodiversity* (New York: Chapman & Hall, 1992), 24–26. See also N. E. Stork, "How Many Species Are There?" *Biodiversity and Conservation* 2 (1993): 215–232.

41 Erwin's estimates: T. L. Erwin and J. C. Scott, "Seasonal and Size Patterns, Trophic Structure, and Richness of Coleoptera in the Tropical Arboreal Ecosystem: The Fauna of the Tree *Leuhea seemannii* Triana and Planch in the Canal Zone of Panama," *The Coleopterists Bulletin* 34 (1980): 305–322 (1,200 species); T. L. Erwin, "Tropical Forests: Their Richness in Coleoptera and Other Arthropod Species," *The Coleopterists Bulletin* 36 (1982): 74–75 (30 million insect species). Erwin later suggested that the real figure might be 50 million (T. L. Erwin, "The Tropical Forest Canopy: The Heart of Biotic Diversity," in *Biodiversity*, ed. E. O. Wilson [Washington, D.C.: National Academy Press, 1988], 123–129).

Fungi and nematode species: R. M. May, "How Many Species Inhabit the Earth?" *Scientific American* 267 (October 1992): 44–45.

10 million in the oceans: J. F. Grassle, "Deep-Sea Benthic Diversity," *BioScience* 41 (1991): 464–469.

42 7 million to 80 million insects: Interview, Nigel Stork; Stork, "How Many Species Are There?"

British Museum: Stork, "Insect Diversity."

"still an underestimate": Wilson, *The Diversity of Life*, 162.

43 Definition of biodiversity: Wilson, *The Diversity of Life*, 393 ("the variety").

43–44 Annan's discovery: R. Annan, "Account of a Skeleton of a Large Animal, found near Hudson's River," *Memoirs of the American Academy of Arts and Sciences* 3 (1793): 160–164 (all quotes; we have modernized the orthography).

44 History of attitudes toward fossils: M. J. S. Rudwick, *The Meaning of Fossils: Episodes in the History of Paleontology*, 2d ed. (New York: Neale Watson Academic Publications, 1976); Mayr, *Growth*, 319.

44–45 Alternative extinction explanations: Mayr, *Growth*, 347–350.

45 Darwin on extinction: Darwin, *The Origin of Species*, 316–320 ("seiz[ing] on" and "have caused," 319).

45–46 Catastrophic extinctions: C. C. Swisher et al., "Coeval ^{40}Ar/^{39}Ar Ages of 65.0 Million Years Ago from Chicxulub Crater Melt Rock and Cretaceous-Tertiary Boundary Tektites," *Science* 257 (14 August 1992): 954–958 (Yucatán asteroid); N. Eldredge, *The Miner's Canary* (New York: Prentice-Hall, 1991), 106–170 (dissenting views).

46 Lyell's parable: C. Lyell, *Principles of Geology*, 11th ed., vol. 2 (New York: D. Appleton and Co., 1892), 453 ("a great number").

47 North American wildlife in the Pleistocene: T. L. Kimball and R. E. Johnson, "The Richness of American Wildlife," in *Wildlife and America*, ed. H. P. Brokaw (Washington, D.C.: Council on Environmental Quality, 1978), 3–17; E. Anderson, "Who's Who in the Pleistocene: A Mammalian Bestiary," in Martin and Klein, *Quaternary Extinctions*, 40–90; D. W. Steadman

and P. S. Martin, "Extinction of Birds in the Late Pleistocene of North America," in ibid., 466–477.

47 Paleo-Indian extinctions: P. S. Martin, "Prehistoric Overkill: The Global Model," in Martin and Klein, *Quaternary Extinctions,* 354–403 (mammals that avoided extinction, 368); R. S. Miller and D. B. Botkin, "Endangered Species, Models and Predictions," *American Scientist* 62 (1974): 172–181 ("a zoologically impoverished," 172).

48 New Zealand wildlife: C. King, *Immigrant Killers* (Auckland: Oxford University Press, 1984), 15–40 (Polynesians and moas); L. Molloy, *The Ancient Islands* (Wellington, N.Z.: Port Nicholson Press, 1982), 11 (frogs and weta); C. H. Daugherty et al., "Neglected Taxonomy and Continuing Extinctions of Tuatara (*Sphenodon*)," *Nature* 347 (1990): 177–179 (tuatara).

Steadman's work: Interview, David Steadman; D. W. Steadman, "Prehistoric Extinctions in Polynesia," paper presented at annual meeting of the American Association for the Advancement of Science, 23 February 1994.

48–49 Rats and cats: I. Atkinson, "Introduced Animals and Extinctions," in *Conservation for the Twenty-first Century,* eds. D. Western and M. C. Pearl (New York: Oxford University Press, 1989), 54–75; G. Foster, *A Voyage Round the World* (London, 1777), 128 ("had no sooner").

49–50 Stephens Island wren: Interview, Ian Atkinson; P. R. Millener, "The Only Flightless Passerine: The Stephens Island Wren," *Notornis* 36 (1989): 280–284; E. Fuller, *Extinct Birds* (New York: Viking/Rainbird, 1987), 192–196; W. L. Buller, "On a New Species of *Xenicus* from an Island off the Coast of New Zealand," *Ibis,* 7th series, 1 (1895): 236–237; R. A. Falla, *New Zealand Bird Life Past and Present,* Cawthron Lecture Series, no. 29 (Nelson, N.Z.: R. W. Stiles, 1955), 14–16.

50–51 WCMC and its lists: Interview, Jo Taylor.

50 Black list: Interview, Taylor (increase in listed birds); F. D. M. Smith et al., "Estimating Extinction Rates," *Nature* 364 (5 August 1993): 494–496. Their figures, except those citing dates of admittance to the black list, are taken from WCMC, *Global Biodiversity.*

51 One species every twenty minutes: Wilson, *The Diversity of Life,* 280.

Raven's prediction: P. H. Raven, "Our Diminishing Tropical Forests," in Wilson, *Biodiversity,* 119–122. Raven argued in 1986 that the current extinction rate was five species a day and would rise to ten species a day after the turn of the century. If there are about 250,000 higher plants (all the estimates here involve higher plants), then at these rates a quarter of them will vanish by 2010.

3 · THE CRISIS

53–54 Preston's life: Interviews, Jane Preston, Richard Root, Daniel Simberloff; R. Root, "Resolution of Respect," *Bulletin of the American Ecological Society* 70 (1990): 244–247.

Pattern of birds on Preston's grounds: F. W. Preston, "The Commonness and Rarity of Species," *Ecology* 29 (1948): 254–283.

55 Preston's publications: F. W. Preston, "The Canonical Distribution of Commonness and Rarity: Part I," *Ecology* 43 (1962): 185–215, and "The Canonical Distribution of Commonness and Rarity: Part II," *Ecology* 43 (1962): 410–432. Preston first examined the species-area curve in "Time and Space and the Variation of Species," *Ecology* 41 (1960): 611–627.

Bird species in Quaker Run Valley: Preston, "Commonness and Rarity," 257.

55–58 Preston's species-area analysis: Preston, "Canonical Distribution, Part II," 425–426 ("some strange accident," 425; "impulse toward," 426).

58–59 MacArthur-Wilson paper and book: Interview, Edward O. Wilson; R. H. MacArthur and E. O. Wilson, "An Equilibrium Theory of Insular Zoogeography," *Evolution* 17 (1963): 373–387; R. H. MacArthur and E. O. Wilson, *The Theory of Island Biogeography* (Princeton, N.J.: Princeton University Press, 1967). Unlike Preston, Wilson and MacArthur did not claim to know the exact form of the species-area equation, but they adopted $S = cA^z$ as a good approximation.

59–60 Island biogeography experiment: Interviews, Simberloff, Wilson; E. O. Wilson, *Naturalist* (Washington, D.C.: Island Press, 1994), 260–281.

61 Simberloff's second set of experiments: D. S. Simberloff, "Experimental Zoogeography of Islands: Effects of Island Size," *Ecology* 57 (1976): 629–642 ("Species number," 629).

Papers on island biogeography: See the list in C. L. Shafer, *Nature Reserves: Island Theory and Conservation Practice* (Washington, D.C.: Smithsonian Press, 1990), table 1, 14–15.

61–62 Limitations of wildlife preserves: Preston, "Canonical Distribution, Part II," 427 (all quotes).

62–63 Surveys by Terborgh and Diamond: J. Terborgh, "Preservation of Natural Diversity: The Problem of Extinction Prone Species," *BioScience* 24 (1974): 715–722; J. Terborgh, "Faunal Equilibria and the Design of Wildlife Preserves," in *Tropical Ecological Systems*, eds. F. B. Golley and E. Medina (New York: Springer-Verlag, 1975), 369–380; J. M. Diamond, "Distributional Ecology of New Guinea Birds," *Science* 179 (23 February 1973): 759–769.

Diamond extends argument: J. M. Diamond, "Biogeographic Kinetics: Estimation of Relaxation Times for Avifaunas of Southwest Pacific Islands," *Proceedings of the National Academy of Sciences USA* 69 (1972): 3199–3203, at 3203 ("many rain forest species").

Local and global extinction: D. S. Simberloff, "Species Turnover and Equilibrium Island Biogeography," *Science* 194 (5 November 1976): 572–578.

63 Early concern over Amazon: G. Kolata, "Theoretical Ecology: Beginnings of a Predictive Science," *Science* 183 (1 February 1974): 400–401, 450.

64 "a nearly clean": R. A. Foresta, *Amazon Conservation in the Age of Development* (Gainesville: University of Florida Press, 1991), 33.

A million species: C. Holden, "Scientists Talk of the Need for Conservation and an Ethic of Biotic Diversity to Slow Species Extinction," *Science* 184 (10 May 1974): 646–647.

One species per hour: N. Myers, *The Sinking Ark* (New York: Pergamon Press, 1979), 17.

64 Lovejoy's calculation: T. E. Lovejoy, "A Projection of Species Extinctions," in *Global 2000 Report to the President: Entering the Twenty-first Century* (Washington, D.C.: U.S. Council on Environmental Quality, 1980), vol. 2, 328–331.

Ehrlichs' projection: P. Ehrlich and A. Ehrlich, *Extinction* (New York: Ballantine Books, 1981), 193–195, 347–348 ("Someone had better," 300).

Extinction claims: L. R. Brown et al., *Saving the Planet: How to Shape an Environmentally Sustainable Global Economy* (New York: W. W. Norton, 1991), 28 (20 percent by 2011, citing unnamed "leading biologists"); I. Deshmukh, *Ecology and Tropical Biology* (Boston: Blackwell Scientific Publications, 1986), 322 (forty thousand per year, citing "informed guesses"); P. Eastman and T. Bodde, "Endangered Species Act," *BioScience* 32 (1982): 246 (1 million by end of century, citing unpublished "estimate" by Thomas Eisner); E. Eckholm, "The Age of Extinction," *The Futurist*, October 1978, 289 (half a million by end of century, no source given); letter, Donald Davis to Norman Myers, 23 June 1977, cited in Myers, *The Sinking Ark*, 20 (3 million by end of century, no source given); E. C. Wolf, *On the Brink of Extinction: Conserving the Diversity of Life* (Washington, D.C.: Worldwatch Institute, 1987), 6 (several hundred species a day, no source given); D. H. Meadows et al., *Beyond the Limits: Confronting Global Collapse, Envisioning a Sustainable Future* (Post Mills, Vt.: Chelsea Green, 1992), 64 (increasing exponentially, no source given); K. Miller and L. Tangley, *Trees of Life: Saving Tropical Forests and Their Biological Wealth* (Boston: Beacon Press, 1991), 17 (25 percent by 2041, citing agreement among "most scientists"); N. Myers, *A Wealth of Wild Species: Storehouse for Human Welfare* (Boulder, Colo.: Westview Press, 1983), 9 (10 to 20 percent by 2000, no source given) and 214 (one an hour, no source given); P. H. Raven, "Our Diminishing Tropical Forests," in *Biodiversity*, ed. E. O. Wilson (Washington, D.C.: National Academy Press, 1988), 121 (five species a day, no source given); W. Mansfield, cited in "World Conservation Meeting Warns of Greed," *New York Times*, 29 November 1990 (six species per hour, no source given); "Gone, but Not Forgotten," *Times Union* (Albany, N.Y.), 6 May 1992 (between half a species an hour and twelve, citing "varying estimates").

65 "Let us suppose": Myers, *A Wealth of Wild Species*, 214.

Lovejoy's species-area curve: Lovejoy, "A Projection of Species Extinctions" ("underestimate[d] the impact," 330).

"the diversity of species": Ehrlich and Ehrlich, *Extinction*, 347.

65–66 Simberloff's projection: D. S. Simberloff, "Mass Extinction and the Destruction of Moist Tropical Forests," *Zhurnal Obschei Biologii* 45 (25 March 1984): 767–778; D. S. Simberloff, "Are We on the Verge of a Mass Extinction in Tropical Rain Forests?" in *Dynamics of Extinction*, ed. D. K. Elliott (New York: John Wiley & Sons, 1986), 165–180.

66 Simberloff's calculations repeated: See the list in W. V. Reid, "How Many Species Will There Be?" in *Tropical Deforestation and Species Extinction*, eds. T. C. Whitmore and J. A. Sayer (New York: Chapman & Hall, 1992), 55–73.

Simberloff revisits data: Simberloff, "Species Turnover."

66 Robins: We have adopted the metaphor in F. E. Smith, "Ecosystems and Evolution," *Bulletin of the Ecological Society of America* 56 (1975): 2–6.

Shortcomings of experiments: D. S. Simberloff, "Equilibrium Theory of Island Biogeography and Ecology," *Annual Review of Ecology and Systematics* 5 (1974): 161–182; Simberloff, "Species Turnover."

66–67 Connor and McCoy: Interviews, Edward F. Connor, Earl D. McCoy; E. F. Connor and E. D. McCoy, "The Statistics and Biology of the Species-Area Relationship," *The American Naturalist* 113 (1979): 791–833.

68 Boecklen and Gotelli: Interviews, William J. Boecklen, Nicholas J. Gotelli; W. J. Boecklen and N. J. Gotelli, "Island Biogeographic Theory and Conservation Practice: Species-Area or Specious-Area Relationships?" *Biological Conservation* 29 (1984): 63–80 ("not impressive," 73). The margin of error discussed in the text is what statisticians call a "95 percent confidence interval." This interval is the range in which—if scientists repeated their measurements again and again in the same way—the true value would lie 95 percent of the time.

Study of nature reserves in East Africa: M. E. Soulé, B. A. Wilcox, and C. Holtby, "Benign Neglect: A Model of Faunal Collapse in the Game Reserves of East Africa," *Biological Conservation* 15 (1979): 259–272.

69 Criticism of extension of species-area curve from islands to continents: Simberloff, "Species Turnover."

Simberloff's ambivalence: Interview, Simberloff; Simberloff, "Equilibrium Theory" ("best single predictor," 171); Simberloff, "Are We on the Verge" ("very crude predictor," 169).

69–70 Brown and Brown: K. S. Brown and G. G. Brown, "Habitat Alteration and Species Loss in Brazilian Forests," in Whitmore and Sayer, *Tropical Deforestation*, 119–142 ("should represent" and "Thus the group," 127). Similar findings have been observed in Puerto Rico, which was almost stripped of forest at the turn of the century and is now mostly reforested, without many extinctions (A. E. Lugo, "Estimating Reductions in the Diversity of Tropical Forest Species," in Wilson, *Biodiversity*, 58–70).

70 Heywood and Stuart: V. H. Heywood and S. N. Stuart, "Species Extinctions in Tropical Forests," in Whitmore and Sayer, *Tropical Deforestation*, 91–117 ("extensive inquiries" and "unable to obtain," 96).

71 Relaxation time: Diamond, "Biogeographic Kinetics."

Time before extinctions: Interview, Connor; Diamond, "Biogeographic Kinetics"; Shafer, *Nature Reserves*, 18–19, 67, 103.

72–73 Ivory-billed woodpecker: Interviews, Jerome Jackson, Fran James; P. R. Ehrlich, D. S. Dobkin, and D. Wheye, *Birds in Jeopardy* (Stanford, Calif.: Stanford University Press, 1992), 30–31; J. Fisher, N. Simon, and J. Vincent, *Wildlife in Danger* (New York: Viking, 1969), 266–268; E. H. Forbush, *Natural History of the Birds of Eastern and Central North America*, revised and abridged by John R. May (Boston: Houghton Mifflin Co., 1925), 307 ("They are shot").

73–74 Clearing of the eastern forest: Senate, *Timber Depletion, Lumber Prices, Lumber Exports, and Concentration of Timber Ownership*, Report on Senate Resolution 311, 66th Congress, 2nd Session, 1920 (*The Caper Report*) (pre-European forest); M. Williams, *Americans and Their Forests: A Historical Geography* (New York: Cambridge University Press, 1989), 13, 60–67, 112–117, 119, 120, 358–360 (U.S. land clearing; "improved," 13); Food and Agricultural Organization of the United Nations, *Forest Resources Assessment 1990: Tropical Countries*, FAO Forestry Paper 118 (Rome: FAO, 1993), Table 4-C (Amazon clearing). The "eastern" region of the United States covers all states east of the Mississippi plus Minnesota, Iowa, Missouri, Arkansas, and Louisiana. Some authors put the clearing for New England even higher. See, e.g., D. R. Foster, "Land-Use History (1730–1990) and Vegetation Dynamics in Central New England, U.S.A.," *Journal of Ecology* 80 (1992): 753–772.

74 Puritan attitudes toward forest: R. Nash, *Wilderness and the American Mind*, rev. ed. (New Haven, Conn.: Yale University Press, 1973), pp. 23–43; W. Bradford, *Of Plymouth Plantation*, ed. S. E. Morison (New York: Alfred A. Knopf, 1952), 62 ("a hideous").

Forest fires: S. Pyne, *Fire in America: A Cultural History of Wildland and Rural Fire* (Princeton, N.J.: Princeton University Press, 1982), 56–57.

Amazon edge effect: D. Skole and C. Tucker, "Tropical Deforestation and Habitat Fragmentation," *Science* 260 (25 June 1993): 1905–1911.

74–75 99 percent disturbed: J. C. Greenway, Jr., *Extinct and Vanishing Birds*, Special Publication no. 13 (Washington, D.C.: American Committee for International Wild Life Protection, 1958), 37.

75 160 eastern forest birds: Interview, Stuart Pimm.

75–76 Black list of eastern forest birds: J. D. Williams and R. M. Nowak, "Vanishing Species in Our Own Backyard: Extinct Fish and Wildlife of the United States and Canada," in *The Last Extinction*, eds. L. Kaufman and K. Mallory (Cambridge, Mass.: MIT Press, 1986), 107–139; A. W. Schorger, *The Passenger Pigeon* (Madison: University of Wisconsin Press, 1955); G. Laycock, "The Last Parakeet," *Audubon* 71 (March 1969): 21–25; A. O. Gross, "The Heath Hen," *Memoirs of the Boston Society of Natural History* 6 (1928): 509–531; J. Terborgh, *Where Have All the Birds Gone?* (Princeton, N.J.: Princeton University Press, 1989), 60–62 (Bachman's warbler).

76 Accuracy of species-area curve: The reader may wonder, *does* the species-area curve successfully predict eastern forest extinctions? Using a typical z-value of 0.3, halving the eastern forest would reduce the number of species there by about 20 percent. A more conservative z-value (customary in calculating larger areas) of 0.15 would give a reduction of about 10 percent. Thus the standard species-area curve would predict that the eastern forest would have lost between 10 and 20 percent of its original 160 bird species— between 16 and 32 species. In fact, it lost 5.

The disparity attracted enough attention that in December 1993 a *U.S. News & World Report* cover article used it as evidence that the extinction crisis was nothing but a "doomsday myth." Spurred by the article, Stuart Pimm, the Tennessee biologist, and Robert Askins, a biologist at Connecticut College, in New London, studied old collecting records to learn how many eastern forest birds resided wholly or principally in the eastern deciduous and coastal pine forest, making them candidates for global extinction. The answer: 28. Next, they amended the usual black list, striking off the heath hen (another subspecies of the same species survives in the West) and adding the red-cockaded woodpecker (kept from extinction only by human effort, Pimm said). The number of extinctions remained at 5. Using Askins's research, they produced a careful estimate of peak deforestation: 50 percent. Combining this with a z-value of 0.25, Pimm and Askins predicted that 15 percent of the bird species in the eastern forest should have become extinct.

The two men compared their prediction with their data in two ways, conservative and liberal. Picking the smallest number of extinctions (4, excluding the red-cockaded woodpecker) and the greatest number of eastern forest birds (28, including the birds that lived partly outside the forest) produced a conservative estimate of extinction: 4 out of 28, or 14 percent. Picking the largest number of extinctions (5, including the woodpecker) and the smallest number of forest birds (13 of the 28 lived *only* in the eastern forest) produced a liberal estimate: 5 out of 13, or 38 percent. Because the predicted percentage, 15 percent, lies within this range, Pimm and Askins argued that the history of the eastern forest in fact demonstrates the accuracy of the species-area curve.

Have Pimm and Askins rescued $S = cA^z$? They don't account for disturbance from factors like fire or the edge effect, which other ecologists claim has more than doubled the impact of current deforestation in Amazonia. Nor were all the species on their black list lost entirely from habitat transformation. The ivory-bill, pigeon, and parakeet were hunted, and the warbler, which lived in low canebrakes, may have benefited from logging. Finally, red-cockaded woodpeckers are hardly extinct: as many as 10,000 may exist. All these factors will keep the pot of controversy bubbling—but none of them will address the fact that we need much more detailed knowledge about what's on the ground before we can construct a sensible biodiversity policy.

76–77 Preston's assumption: Interviews, Connor, McCoy; Preston, "Canonical Distribution, Part I," 190 (assumption).

78 Seven Amazon regions: G. T. Prance, "The Phytogeographic Subdivisions of Amazonia and Their Influence on the Selection of Biological Reserves," in *Extinction Is Forever,* eds. G. T. Prance and T. S. Elias (New York: New York Botanical Garden, 1977), 195–213.

79 Thirty-five animals and fifty-nine plants: California Department of Fish and Game, "Descriptions of Habitat Types for Species Associated with Coastal Sage Scrub in the Natural Community Conservation Planning Regions of Southern California," Natural Diversity Data Base, unpub. ms., 3 May 1993, Sacramento, Calif.

Utah species: J. Woolf, "All Creatures Great and Small: Are They Worth Saving?" Salt Lake *Tribune,* 14 June 1992.

'Alala: "A Caw for Action on the 'Alala," *Science* 256 (22 May 1992): 1136.

Gopher tortoises: Interview, Russell Burke.

TVA and mollusks: U.S. Environmental Protection Agency, Endangered Species Protection Program database (Washington, D.C., 1993).

Mussels: J. D. Williams et al., "Conservation Status of Freshwater Mussels of the United States and Canada," *Fisheries* 18 (1993): 6–22.

4. UNCOOKING THE FROG

82–84 Karner Blue population in Albany: The band of lupine stretched from what is today the intersection of Washington and Manning avenues, looped down to the southeast corner of the state office campus, crossed the campus, and remet Washington by the state police academy, proceeded west along Washington to Fuller Avenue, north along Fuller to the Penn Central line, and then east through the southern substation back to Manning. Its approximate outlines (and the description of its abundance) are from R. Dirig, "Historical Notes on Wild Lupine and the Karner Blue Butterfly at the Albany Pine Bush, New York," in *The Karner Blue Butterfly,* Minnesota Agricultural Experiment Station, Miscellaneous Publication 84-1994 (St. Paul, 1994), 21–34, esp. fig. 5. See also R. Dirig and J. F. Cryan, "Pine Bush Lepidoptera: The Fragile Ecology of the Karner Blue and Buck Moth," unpub. ms., rev. ed., April 1975, Robert Dirig's files, L. H. Bailey Hortorium, Cornell University, Ithaca, N.Y. (hereafter cited as Dirig's files) R. Dirig and J. F. Cryan, "Obituary: Laurence Remington Rupert," *Journal of the Lepidopterists' Society* 40 (1986): 242–245. The history of the area is drawn from W. Kennedy, *O Albany! Improbable City of Political Wizards, Fearless Ethnics, Spectacular Aristocrats, Splendid Nobodies, and Underrated Scoundrels* (New York: Viking, 1983), and D. Rittner, "Man's Activities in the Pine Bush," in *Pine Bush: Albany's Last Frontier,* ed. D. Rittner (Albany, N.Y.: Pine Bush Historic Preservation Project, 1976), 217–226. Because the evidence consists mainly of scattered references and imperfect oral recollections, it is likely that this account is inaccurate in some details, but its outline is surely correct.

87 Listing of Karner Blue: *Federal Register* (hereafter cited as *FR*) 57 (14 December 1992): 59236–59244.

87–89 Description of Karner Blue life cycle: D. Schweitzer, "Fact Sheet for the Karner Blue Butterfly with Special Reference to New York," in *Karner Blue Butterfly, Population and Habitat Viability Assessment (PHVA) Workshop, Briefing Book* (Zanesville, Ohio: The WILDS and IUCN/SSC Captive Breeding Specialist Group, 1992); Karner Blue Element Stewardship Abstract, The Nature Conservancy, in *Karner Blue Butterfly, Briefing Book,* section 3 (nectar sources and "windowpane," 12); D. Savignano, "Field Investigations of a Facultative Mutualism Between *Lycaeides melissa samuelis* Nabokov (Lycaenidae), the Karner Blue Butterfly, and Attendant Ants" (Ph.D. thesis, University of Texas at Austin, 1990) (ants and caterpillars).

88 "mud-puddle clubs": J. A. Shuey, "Dancing with Fire: Ecosystem Dynamics, Management, and the Karner Blue (*Lycaeides melissa samuelis* Nabokov)" unpub. ms., The Nature Conservancy, Indianapolis, 1993, 8.

Karner Blue's historic range: Interview, Robert Dirig; *FR* 57 (14 December 1992): 59236–59244.

Saunders, Nabokov, Scudder, and Karner Blue (footnote): B. Boyd, *Vladimir Nabokov: The American Years* (Princeton, N.J.: Princeton University Press, 1991), 37–38, 58–59, 107, 113–114, 168, 226–227; R. Dirig, "Karner's Famous Blue Butterfly," in Rittner, *Pine Bush,* 197–210; V. Nabokov, "The Nearctic Forms of *Lycaeides* Hüb. (Lycaenidae, Lepidoptera)," *Psyche* 50

(September–December 1943): 87–99 (creation of *L. m. samuelis*); S. Scudder, "My First Namesake," *Ottawa Naturalist* 15 (1901): 121–122; F. M. Brown, "The Types of Lycaenid Butterflies Named by William Henry Edwards, Part III: Plebejinae," *Transactions of the American Entomological Society* 96 (September 1970): 353–433, at 365–367.

89 Butterfly-lupine dependence: Interview, Ryk Peter Spoor; R. Dirig, "Historical Notes."

Savannas and barrens as perfect compromise: Interview, Michelle Grigore.

89–90 Nature not in lockstep: D. B. Botkin, *Discordant Harmonies* (New York: Oxford University Press, 1990); S. T. A. Pickett and John N. Thompson, "Patch Dynamics and the Design of Nature Reserves," *Biological Conservation* 13 (1978): 27–37.

90 Ecological role of fire: H. E. Wright, Jr., and M. L. Heinselman, "Ecological Role of Fire: Introduction," *Quaternary Research* 3 (1973): 319–328; E. V. Komarek, "Fire Ecology Review," *Proceedings, Tall Timbers Fire Ecology Conference* 14 (1974): 201–216 ("The earth," 204).

Fire and lupine: V. A. Nuzzo, "Extent and Status of Midwest Oak Savanna: Presettlement and 1985," *Natural Areas Journal* 6 (1986): 6-36.

91–92 Fire and Karner Blue: Interview, Dirig; T. J. Givnish, E. S. Menges, and D. F. Schweitzer, *Minimum Area Requirements for Long-Term Conservation of the Albany Pine Bush and Karner Blue Butterfly: An Assessment*, vol. 4, Appendix T, *Rapp Road Sanitary Landfill Expansion* (Albany, N.Y.: Malcolm Pirnie, August 1988), 14; Shuey, "Dancing with Fire."

91 Native American use of fire: Our brief treatment of this vast, fascinating topic draws on W. Cronon, *Changes in the Land: Indians, Colonists, and the Ecology of New England* (New York: Hill and Wang, 1983), esp. 49–52; G. M. Day, "The Indian as an Ecological Factor in the Northeastern Forest," *Ecology* 34 (1953): 329–346; S. Pyne, *Fire in America: A Cultural History of Wildland and Rural Fire* (Princeton, N.J.: Princeton University Press, 1982), esp. 71–81 (fire hunting, 74–75; "by firing the leaves," 75; Lewis and Clark, 71–72); M. Williams, *Americans and Their Forests: A Historical Geography* (New York: Cambridge University Press, 1989), 32–49, 60–62.

"Such a fire": A. Van der Donck, *A Description of the New Netherlands* (1656), trans. C. Gehring, unpub. ms., State Museum of New York, Albany, 1993.

91–92 Impact of Native American burning: Pyne, *Fire in America*, 75–81; Day, "The Indian"; D. A. Axelrod, "Rise of the Grassland Biome, Central North America," *The Botanical Review* 51 (1985): 164–201 (Great Plains); A. Steuter, "Human Impacts on Biodiversity in America: Thoughts from the Grassland Biome," *Conservation Biology* 5 (1991): 136–137 (Great Plains); Williams, *Americans and Their Forests*, 42–49 (bison range, 46).

92 Spread of Karner Blue by fire: A. M. Shapiro, "New Distributional Data on Three Northeastern United States Butterflies," *Journal of the Lepidopterists' Society* 23 (1974): 265–269.

92–93 Native American decline: H. F. Dobyns, *Their Number Became Thinned: Native American Population Dynamics in Eastern North America* (Knoxville: University of Tennessee Press, 1983); R. Thornton, *American Indian Holocaust and Survival* (Norman: University of Oklahoma Press, 1987); D. R. Snow and K. M. Lanphear, "European Contact and Indian Depopulation in the Northeast: The Timing of the First Epidemics," *Ethnohistory* 35 (1985): 15–33, table 1 (1634 smallpox epidemic); A. W. Crosby, "Virgin Soil Epidemics as a Factor in the Aboriginal Depopulation in America," *William and Mary Quarterly* 33 (1976): 289–299 (Huron and Iroquois losses); F. Fenner et al., *Smallpox and Its Eradication* (Geneva: World Health Organization, 1988), 238–240 (eighteenth-century outbreaks); Cronon, *Changes in the Land,* 87–91 (settlements in clearings).

93–94 European expansion: Williams, *Americans and Their Forests,* 60–72, 112–117, 361–368 ("in the center," 362).

94 Settlers' views of fire and New York code: Pyne, *Fire in America,* 51–59, 239–241.

Loss of oak savanna and pine barrens: Interviews, John Cryan, Steve Packard, Thomas Givnish; Nuzzo, "Extent and Status of Midwest Oak Savanna"; J. F. Cryan, "Retreat in the Barrens," *Defenders,* January/February 1985, 18–29.

95 Remaining Karner Blue populations: *FR* 57 (14 December 1992): 59236–59244.

95–97 Wilton: Interviews, Roy J. McDonald, Larry Gordon (county government); J. H. Kunstler, *The Geography of Nowhere* (New York: Simon & Schuster, 1993), 147–173; "Ban on Aerial Spraying Changes Adirondacks' Black Fly Strategy," *Times-Union* (Albany, N.Y.), 25 June 1990 (blackflies).

96 Letter and maps, and McDonald's reaction: Letter, P. E. Nye to S. Porto, 11 March 1993, Lee Coleman's files, *The Gazette* (Schenectady, N.Y.), Saratoga bureau (hereafter cited as Coleman's files); "McDonald Rips Spraying Rules," *The Gazette,* 19 March 1993.

DEC rationale: Letter, R. L. Bendick to R. McDonald, 29 April 1993, Coleman's files.

Threats to dig up lupine and rumors: Interviews, John Cannone, numerous residents of Saratoga County.

97 Mosquitoes and meeting: Interviews, Laura Sommers, Lee Coleman; "Ouch! Mosquitoes Feast at Wilton Meeting on Aerial Spraying," *The Saratogan* (Saratoga Springs, N.Y.), 3 June 1993.

97–98 Geology of Hudson Valley and pine barrens: R. Dineen, *Geology and Land Uses in the Pine Bush, Albany County, New York,* New York State Museum and Science Service, circular 47 (Albany, 1975), 11–14; R. G. LaFleur, "Glacial Lake Albany," in *Pine Bush,* 1–10; J. Donahue, "Origins and Topography of the Pine Bush," in ibid., 17–22; J. F. Cryan, "Retreat in the Barrens," *Defenders,* January/February 1985, 18–29 (twenty-two barrens).

98–99 History of Pine Bush forest: Interview, Paul Huey; P. Huey, "History of the Albany Pine Bush from 1624 to 1815, Albany County, New York," in Dineen, *Geology and Land Uses,* 7–8.

98 Smallpox and Mohawks: Interview, Dean Snow; Snow and Lanphear, "European Contact and Indian Depopulation."

Pine Bush and Karner Blue in nineteenth century: R. Dirig, "Historical

Notes" ("abounded in flocks"); D. Rittner, "An Early History of Pine Bush Entomology," *Skenecteda,* May 1979, 3–7.

99 Cane's letter and Dirig's talk, memorandum, and visit: Interviews, Cryan, Dirig, James Cane; letter, J. Cane to Xerces Society, 9 January 1973, Dirig's files; R. Dirig and J. F. Cryan, "The Karner Blue Project: January 1973 to December 1976," *Atala* 4 (1976): 22–26.

Name of Xerces Society: Interview, Claire Kremen (Xerces Society).

99–100 Dirig fights rezoning: Interviews, Cryan, Dirig, Cane.

100–101 "The miminum-area question" and Cryan's species-area curve: J. F. Cryan, affidavit, *In the Matter of the Application of Save the Pine Bush, et al., Against the Common Council of the City of Albany and the City of Albany* [Pine Bush III], RJI-01-91-ST3183, 10 October 1991, 2; and J. F. Cryan, affidavit, *In the Matter of the Application of Save the Pine Bush, et al., Against the City of Albany* [Pine Bush I], 8 September 1986, both from John F. Cryan's files, New York State Department of Environmental Conservation, New York (hereafter cited as Cryan's files).

101 Loss of tax revenue: Albany Pine Bush Preserve Commission, *Management Plan and Final Environmental Impact Statement for the Albany Pine Bush Preserve* (Syracuse, N.Y.: Environmental Design & Research, 1993), 92.

Lawsuits: *Save the Pine Bush v. City of Albany* [Pine Bush I], 530 NYS2d 295 (1986), 536 NYS2d 60 (1987); *Save the Pine Bush v. Planning Board* [Pine Bush II], 518 NYS2d 466 (1986), 522 NYS2d 111 (1987); *Save the Pine Bush v. Common Council,* 591 NYS2d 897 (1992).

City agrees to address minimum-area question: T. J. Givnish, *Guidelines for the Preliminary Research Program, Albany Pine Bush Preserve* (Albany, N.Y.: Malcolm Pirnie, 24 November 1989), 1; Givnish, Menges, and Schweitzer, *Minimum Area Requirements.*

101–102 Pine Bush Commission and Pine Bush Preserve: Interview, Stephanie Gebauer; Albany Pine Bush Preserve Commission, *Management Plan.*

102 Five burns since 1991 and two outcrops: Interviews, Gebauer, Peter Nye, Sommers.

Populations in Saratoga Sand Belt: D. Savignano, "Karner Blue Butterfly Research and Management Plan for Saratoga County," report to the Audubon Society of New York State et al., January 1992, Laura Sommers's files, New York Department of Environmental Conservation, Albany.

102–103 Saratoga County airport: Interview, Tom Miller (airport manager), Cryan, Gordon.

103 Queensbury: Interview, Sommers; "Karner Blue to Be Protected," *Post-Star* (Glens Falls, N.Y.), 20 October 1991.

Clifton Park: Interview, Donald MacElroy; " 'Critical Habitat' Determines the Effect on Projects," *Capital District Business Review* (Albany, N.Y.), 16 March 1992.

103–104 Encore Electronics, Johnson's Auto Crushers, and reduced complaints: Interviews, Cannone, Marcel Zucchino; "Blue Meets Green," *The Saratogan* (Saratoga Springs, N.Y.), 15 July 1993; Savignano, "Karner Blue Butterfly Research," 50–53; authors' visit to area.

104–105 New Hampshire population: Interviews, Krista Helmboldt, David Van Luven (The Nature Conservancy, N.H.); "Butterfly, Project to Coexist," *Concord Monitor,* 14 January 1992.

105 Indiana population: Interview, Ralph Grundel (Midwest Steel program); D. F. Schweitzer, "The Status of the Karner Blue Butterfly (*Lycaeides melissa samuelis* Nabokov) at Indiana Dunes National Lakeshore," report prepared for Indiana Dunes National Lakeshore, Porter, Ind., 1 September 1992 ("most natural setting," 16); *FR* 57 (14 December 1992): 59237; "Butterfly Gets to Dictate Policy to Steel Mill," *Post-Tribune* (Gary, Ind.), 16 March 1993; "Endangered Species Success Story Told," Chesterton (Ind.) *Tribune,* 16 May 1994.

105–106 Wisconsin population: Interviews, Givnish, Marv Clark (Fort McCoy); C. A. Bleser, "Karner Blue Butterfly, Management and Monitoring Activities in Wisconsin, 1990–Spring 1992," unpub. ms., Bureau of Endangered Resources, Department of Natural Resources, Madison, Wis., 1992.

105 Fish and Wildlife Service consultations (footnote): D. Barry, L. Harroun, and C. Halvorson, *For Conserving Endangered Species, Talk Is Cheaper Than We Think* (Washington, D.C.: World Wildlife Fund, February 1992), 1–10 (consultation record); O. A. Houck, "The Endangered Species Act and Its Implementation by the U.S. Departments of Interior and Commerce," *University of Colorado Law Review* 64 (1993): 277–370 (criticism of record, 319).

106 Michigan and Illinois populations: Interviews, John Lerg (Michigan), Amelia Orton-Palmer (Illinois).

107 Crossgates Mall preserve: Interviews, Cryan, Sommers, Spoor; J. F. Cryan, "The Karner Blue Butterfly (*Lycaeides melissa samuelis* Nabokov) in the Hudson Valley Sand Belt of New York State, Part II: An Annotated List of Hudson Valley Sand Belt Populations and Their Status," unpub. ms., 25 May 1980, Cryan's files, 10–12; authors' visit to site.

108–110 Preserve requirements: Interviews, Givnish, Alan Haney.

110 Kanab ambersnail: Interviews, Brandt Child, Paul Seby, James Woolf; "All Creatures Great and Small: Are They Worth Protecting?" Salt Lake City *Tribune,* 14 June 1992; *FR* 56 (15 November 1991): 58020–58025; Complaint for Declaratory and Injunctive Relief, *Brandt and Venice Child v. U.S.A.,* U.S. Dist. Ct., District of Utah, Central Division, Salt Lake City, 93-C-839W, 21 September 1993.

111 Florida scrub jay: Interviews, Tom Hill, Glen Woolfenden, John Fitzpatrick; G. E. Woolfenden and J. W. Fitzpatrick, "Florida Scrub Jays: A Synopsis After 18 Years of Study," in *Cooperative Breeding in Birds,* eds. P. B. Stacey and W. D. Koenig (London: Cambridge University Press, 1990), 241–266; U.S. Fish and Wildlife Service, *Recovery Plan for the Florida Scrub Jay* (Atlanta, 1990).

111–112 King salmon: B. Lane, "Identity, Treaty Status, and Fisheries of the Lower Elwha Tribe," unpub. ms. prepared for *United States et al. v. State of Washington et al.,* 384 F. Supp. 312 (1974), 25 July 1975, authors' files, Seattle (S'Klallam Nation and legends); U.S. General Accounting Office, *Costs and Alternatives for Restoring Fisheries in the Elwha River,* GAO/RCED-91-104 (Washington, D.C.: Government Printing Office, March 1991); U.S. General

Accounting Office, *Interior Favors Removing Elwha River Dams, but Who Should Pay Is Undecided,* GAO/RCED-92-168 (Washington, D.C.: Government Printing Office, June 1992).

113 California gnatcatcher: Interviews, Jonathan Atwood, Larry Eng, Monica Florian.

5. REASONS PECULIARLY OUR OWN

115–118 Whooping crane description: R. P. Allen, *The Whooping Crane,* National Audubon Society, Research Report No. 3, Washington, D.C., June 1952 (range, 50–67; Catesby and "they make," 8; Preston and "with pitiable," 183); P. A. Johnsgard, *Crane Music: A Natural History of American Cranes* (Washington: Smithsonian Institution Press, 1991), 75–94 (life cycle); R. P. Allen, *On the Trail of Vanishing Birds* (New York: McGraw-Hill, 1957), 29–134, 212–233; R. Doughty, *Return of the Whooping Crane* (Austin: University of Texas Press, 1989); F. McNulty, *The Whooping Crane: The Bird That Defies Extinction* (New York: Dutton, 1966).

116–118 Florida reintroduction: Interview, Stephen Nesbitt.

117–118 Creation of Aransas and whooper population in 1938, 1949, and 1954: Doughty, *Return of the Whooping Crane,* 22–23.

118 Rearing birds at Patuxent: Doughty, *Return of the Whooping Crane,* 84–93; R. C. Erickson, "Propagation Studies of Endangered Wildlife at the Patuxent Center," *International Zoo Yearbook* 20 (1980): 40–47.

Whooping crane population in 1994: Interview, James Lewis (USFWS). Of those birds, 168 were wild, in Aransas, Florida, Calgary, and the Rocky Mountains; 120 others were captive at zoos (Rio Grande, San Antonio) and laboratories (Patuxent, International Crane Foundation).

119–120 Hornaday: M. C. DeSormo, *John Bird Burnham—Klondiker, Adirondacker, and Eminent Conservationist* (Saranac Lake, N.Y.: Adirondack Yesteryears, 1987), 190–197 ("I am no," 190); S. Fox, *The American Conservation Movement: John Muir and His Legacy* (Madison: University of Wisconsin Press, 1981), 148–151, 163–171; W. T. Hornaday, *Thirty Years War for Wildlife* (New York: Scribner's, 1931); W. T. Hornaday, *Our Vanishing Wild Life, Its Extermination and Preservation* (New York: Scribner's, 1913) ("Today the thing," 8); W. T. Hornaday, "The Extermination of the American Bison, with a Sketch of Its Discovery and Life History," in *Annual Report of the Board of Regents of the Smithsonian Institution,* Part II (1887) (Washington, D.C.: Government Printing Office, 1889) (Hornaday and bison); T. R. Dunlap, *Saving America's Wildlife: Ecology and the American Mind, 1850–1950* (Princeton, N.J.: Princeton University Press, 1988), 6–7 (bison refuge); P. Mathiessen, *Wildlife in America* (New York: Viking, 1987), 180–181.

120 Deer market: Hornaday, *Our Vanishing Wild Life,* 236–243 ("an immense volume," 238); W. T. Hornaday, *Wild Life Conservation in Theory and Practice* (New Haven, Conn.: Yale University Press, 1914), 103–110. The $20 million figure is misleading—it does not include the cost of obtaining the meat.

120–122 Direct uses of species: N. Myers, *A Wealth of Wild Species: Storehouse for Human Welfare* (Boulder, Colo.: Westview Press, 1983), provides a wealth of examples.

120–121 Drugs from natural world: Interviews, Laurie Ostroff (Bristol-Myers, ursodiol), Jan Winer (Merck, ivermectin); C. Mann and M. Plummer, *The Aspirin Wars: Money, Medicine, and 100 Years of Rampant Competition* (New York: Alfred A. Knopf, 1991), 21–22 (salicin); N. R. Farnsworth, "Screening Plants for New Medicines," in *Biodiversity*, ed. E. O. Wilson (Washington, D.C.: National Academy Press, 1988), 83–97 (119 drugs, digoxin, atropine, L-dopa).

121 "The honeybee": E. O. Wilson, U.S. Senate, *Endangered Species Act Oversight*, Hearings before the Subcommittee on Environmental Pollution, Committee on the Environment and Public Works, 97th Congress, 1st Session, 10 December 1981, 288.

Mouse DNA: E. O. Wilson, "The Current State of Biodiversity," in Wilson, *Biodiversity*, 3–18.

121–122 "Even species": T. Eisner, "The Hidden Value of Species Diversity," *Bioscience* 42 (1992): 578.

122 Hornaday, birds, and insects: Hornaday, *Our Vanishing Wild Life*, 221–222 ("devoured 145," 222).

Ten to thirty other species: P. H. Raven, "Ethics and Attitudes," in *Conservation of Threatened Plants*, eds. J. Simmons et al. (New York: Plenum Publishing, 1976), 155–179, at 155.

122–123 Tambalacocque and dodo: S. A. Temple, "Plant-animal Mutualism: Co-evolution with Dodo Leads to Near Extinction of Plant," *Science* 197 (26 August 1977): 885–886.

123 Ecosystem services: P. Ehrlich and A. Ehrlich, *Extinction* (New York: Ballantine Books, 1981), 102–113.

"If the [living world]": A. Leopold, *Round River* (New York: Oxford University Press, 1953), 146–147.

123–124 Rivet poppers: Ehrlich and Ehrlich, *Extinction*, xi–xiv ("Any sane person" and "And frighteningly," xii).

125 Whooper's insignificant value: Doughty, *Return of the Whooping Crane*, 15 (hunters); Allen, *The Whooping Crane*, 13–14 (commercial value of skin and eggs); McNulty, *The Whooping Crane*, 31–32 (flutes); J. Ingold et al., "Phylogeny of Cranes (Aves: Gruidae) Deducted from DNA-DNA Hybridization and Albumin Micro-complement Fixation Analyses," *Auk* 106 (1989): 595–602 (genetic relatives); C. Krajewski, "Phylogenetic Relationships Among Cranes (Gruiformes: Gruidae) Based on DNA Hybridization," *Auk* 106 (1989): 603–618. The value would be higher if people were willing to pay premiums for the last few whoopers. Hunters and collectors often made no distinction between sandhill cranes and whoopers, though, suggesting that the former would make a good substitute.

Visitors to Aransas: Interview, Beverly Fletcher (Aransas National Wildlife Refuge) ("tower pair").

125–126 Captain Ted's: Interview, Bobbi Appell; *Captain Ted's Whooping Crane Tours*, brochure, n.d., Rockport, Tex.

126 $5 million: "Rare Whooping Cranes to Call Florida Home," St. Petersburg *Times*, 27 February 1992.

Aransas's other attractions: S. Halpern, "Losing Ground," *Audubon*, July/August 1992, 71–79.

Oil and gas exploration around Aransas: Allen, *The Whooping Crane*, 208–209.

127 NCI first program: Interviews, Michael Grever, Saul Schepartz, Ken Snader (one-quarter of cancer drugs), Elaine Blume.

127–128 Second NCI program: Interviews, Gordon Cragg, Schepartz; D. C. Daly, "The National Cancer Institute's Plant Collections Program: Update and Implications for Tropical Forests," in *Sustainable Harvest and Marketing of Rain Forest Products*, eds. M. Plotkin and L. Famolare (Washington, D.C.: Island Press, 1992), 224–229; National Cancer Institute, *Annual Report of the Natural Products Branch, Developmental Therapeutics Program, Division of Cancer Treatment, October 1, 1993–September 30, 1994*, n.d. (initial results); C. Joyce, *Earthly Goods: Medicine-Hunting in the Rain Forest* (Boston: Little, Brown, 1994), 226–234, 251–268 (three AIDS compounds).

129 Food sources and "most have been sampled": World Conservation Monitoring Centre, *Global Biodiversity* (New York: Chapman & Hall, 1992), 331, 361 (500 insects).

Whooping crane numbers: Allen, *The Whooping Crane*, 3; Doughty, *Return of the Whooping Crane*, 21–22 (later calculations).

No major impacts from reintroduction: USFWS and Florida Game and Fresh Water Fish Commission, "Environmental Assessment, A Proposal to Establish a Nonmigratory Flock of Whooping Cranes on Kissimmee Prairie, Osceola County, Florida," unpub. ms., Jacksonville, Fla., 27 November 1992.

130 Ecological inutility of other species: G. Orians and W. E. Kunin, "Ecological Uniqueness and Loss of Species," in *The Preservation and Valuation of Biological Resources*, eds. G. H. Orians et al. (Seattle: University of Washington Press, 1990), 146–184, esp. 147–148, 157–158 (fungibility of photosynthetic plants and small plant-eating herbivores); H. Rolston, *Environmental Ethics: Duties to and Values in the Natural World* (Philadelphia: Temple University Press, 1988), 130 (Raven's manzanita).

"everything is connected": B. Commoner, *The Closing Circle: Nature, Man, and Technology* (New York: Columbia University Press, 1974), 5.

Ecosystems don't exist as such: K. Shrader-Frechette and E. D. McCoy, *Method in Ecology: Strategies for Conservation* (New York: Cambridge University Press, 1993), 11–69.

130–131 Dodo: Interview, Mark Witmer; M. C. Witmer and A. S. Cheke, "The Dodo and the Tambalacoque Tree: An Obligate Mutualism Reconsidered," *Oikos* 61 (1991): 133–137.

131 "Keystone" species: Interview, J. Terborgh; L. S. Mills, M. E. Soulé, and D. F. Doak, "The Keystone-Species Concept in Ecology and Conservation,"

BioScience 43 (1993): 219–224; D. Ehrenfeld, "Why Put a Value on Biodiversity?" in Wilson, *Biodiversity*, 212–216 ("If the California condor," 215).

131 Changes in communities: S. L. Pimm, *The Balance of Nature? Ecological Issues in the Conservation of Species and Communities* (Chicago: University of Chicago Press, 1991), 277–356.

131–132 American chestnut and its loss: C. Keever, "Present Composition of Some Stands of the Former Oak-Chestnut Forest in the Southern Blue Ridge Mountains," *Ecology* 34 (1953): 44–53; J. F. McCormick and R. B. Platt, "Recovery of an Appalachian Forest Following the Chestnut Blight, or Catherine Keever—You Were Right!" *American Midland Naturalist* 104 (1980): 264–273; Pimm, *The Balance of Nature?*, 347–348.

132 "The fact that": E. Sober, "Philosophical Problems for Environmentalism," in *The Preservation of Species*, ed. B. Norton (Princeton, N.J.: Princeton University Press, 1986), 175–176 (emphasis added).

"apparently originated": M. Sagoff, "On the Uses of Biodiversity," unpub. ms., University of Maryland, College Park, September 1993, 2.

133 "My Aunt Tillie": M. Sagoff, "Fact and Value in Ecological Science," *Environmental Ethics* 7 (1985): 99–116, at 112.

The value of biodiversity as a whole: Rolston, *Environmental Ethics*, 126–159; M. Sagoff, "Ethics, Ecology, and the Environment: Integrating Science and Law," *Tennessee Law Review* 56 (1988): 78–229, esp. 179.

134 Most efficient use of Aransas: The ideas and some of the language in this paragraph come from Sagoff, "Ethics, Ecology," 196–197.

135 "prudential" arguments: I. Kant, *Groundwork of the Metaphysic of Morals* (1785), trans. H. J. Paton (New York: Harper & Row, 1964), 42–49.

"Value is an intrinsic": D. Ehrenfeld, *Beginning Again* (Oxford: Oxford University Press, 1993), 199.

135–136 Noah Principle: D. Ehrenfeld, *The Arrogance of Humanism* (Oxford: Oxford University Press, 1978), 207–208 ("Long-standing existence"); D. Ehrenfeld, "The Conservation of Non-Resources," *American Scientist* 64 (1976): 648–656.

136 "ultimate example": Ehrenfeld, *The Arrogance of Humanism*, 208.

136–137 Smallpox and debate over fate: B. Dixon, "Smallpox—Imminent Extinction, and an Unresolved Dilemma," *New Scientist* 69 (1976): 430–432; "A Captive Virus," New York *Newsday*, 2 August 1988; "Destruction of Last Vials of Virus Set," Atlanta *Journal*, 26 March 1991; "Time to Die for Killer Virus," Los Angeles *Times*, 18 May 1993; "Another Reprieve for Smallpox Virus," *The Lancet* 342 (28 August 1993): 505–506; F. Fenner et al., *Smallpox and Its Eradication* (Geneva: World Health Organization, 1988); B. Mahy, J. Esposito, and J. C. Venter, "Sequencing the Smallpox Virus Genome," *ASM News* 57 (1991): 577–580; B. Mahy et al., "The Remaining Stocks of Smallpox Virus Should Be Destroyed," *Science* 262 (19 November 1993): 1223–1224; W. K. Joklik et al., "Why the Smallpox Virus Stocks Should Not Be Destroyed," *Science* 262 (19 November 1993): 1225–1226; "WHO Sets Execution Date for Remaining Smallpox Virus," Seattle *Times*, 1 November 1994.

137   "there is simply": Ehrenfeld, *The Arrogance of Humanism,* 208.

138–141   Allen and breeding ground of cranes: Allen, *On the Trail,* 29–118, 212–233 ("the biggest, rarest," 56; "who is headquartering," 66; headline, 76); R. P. Allen, *A Report on the Whooping Crane's Northern Breeding Grounds* (New York: National Audubon Society, 1956); "Whooping Cranes' Nests Discovered," New York *Herald Tribune,* 13 July 1955; "Habitat Reached After a Month's Failure," New York *Herald Tribune,* 14 July 1955; "Four Whooping Crane Offspring Are Sighted," New York *Herald Tribune,* 15 June 1955 (Allen yelling); "Whooping Cranes Safe," New York *Herald Tribune,* 16 July 1955; L. Martin, "Can the Whooping Crane Be Saved?" *Natural History* 55 (November 1946): 426–428, 436–437 (photos, call for midwesterners to help Allen).

141   "have singled out": Allen, *The Whooping Crane,* 204.

142   "Whatever has *value*": F. Nietzsche, *The Gay Science,* trans. W. Kaufmann (New York: Vintage Books, 1974), 242.

If every person on Earth: We have borrowed language from J. B. Callicott, "On the Intrinsic Value of Non-Human Species," in Norton, *The Preservation of Species,* 138–172, esp. 142–143.

Leopold and passenger pigeon: A. Leopold, "On a Monument to a Pigeon," in *A Sand County Almanac* (New York: Oxford University Press, 1968), 108–112.

"it is the useless": Sagoff, "On the Uses of Biodiversity," 7.

143–144   "perfect" duties and their extent: Kant, *Groundwork of the Metaphysic of Morals,* 53–57; M. Sagoff, *The Economy of the Earth* (Cambridge: Cambridge University Press, 1988), 218 ("does not admit"), 219–220 ("is meritorious").

144   "To balance the ethical": Sagoff, "Ethics, Ecology," 204.

6. "THE AWFUL BEAST IS BACK"

147–148   Bell and fish: Interviews, Griffin Bell, Donald Cohen; D. S. Cohen, "Judicial Predictability in United States Supreme Court Advocacy: An Analysis of the Oral Argument in *Tennessee Valley Authority v. Hill,*" *University of Puget Sound Law Review* 2 (1978): 89–136 ("I have in" and "Mr. Attorney General," 94); G. B. Bell and R. J. Ostrow, *Taking Care of the Law,* rev. ed. (Macon, Ga.: Mercer University Press, 1986), 42–44.

148   TVA and Tellico: *Environmental Defense Fund v. Tennessee Valley Authority,* 339 F. Supp. 806 (1972); *Hiram G. Hill, Jr. et al. v. Tennessee Valley Authority,* 419 F. Supp. 753 (1976); *Tennessee Valley Authority v. Hiram G. Hill, Jr. et al.,* 437 US 153 (1977); Cohen, "Judicial Predictability"; Z. Plater, "In the Wake of the Snail Darter: An Environmental Law Paradigm and Its Consequences," *University of Michigan Journal of Law Reform* 19 (1986): 805–862; G. Bennett, *Dilemmas: Coping with Environmental Problems* (London: Earthscan Publications, 1992), 13–53; W. B. Wheeler and M. J. McDonald, *TVA and the Tellico Dam, 1936–1979* (Knoxville: University of Tennessee Press, 1986), 23–49.

148–149   Flabbergasting members of Congress: Interview, Donald Barry. Then a staff attorney at the Department of the Interior solicitor's office, Barry said the decision had "a bombshell impact" on Capitol Hill.

149–150 Whooping crane meeting, Erickson's plan, and his reasoning (footnote): Interviews, Ray C. Erickson, Jack H. Berryman, John S. Gottschalk; R. Doughty, *Return of the Whooping Crane* (Austin: University of Texas Press, 1989), 85–88; F. McNulty, *The Whooping Crane: The Bird That Defies Extinction* (New York: Dutton, 1966), 134–138, 156–157, 177–179. Between 1957 and 1970, the branch of the Interior Department charged with wildlife management was called the Bureau of Sport Fisheries and Wildlife. Before and after, it was called the Fish and Wildlife Service. To simplify matters, we refer to it throughout the text as Fish and Wildlife.

150–151 Mundt and Patuxent program: Interview, Erickson.

151 CREWS and first endangered species lists: Interviews, Erickson, Berryman; U.S. Department of the Interior, CREWS, *Rare and Endangered Fish and Wildlife of the United States*, unpub. ms., August 1964, Ray Erickson's files, Salem, Oregon ("preliminary draft"); U.S. Department of the Interior, CREWS, *Rare and Endangered Fish and Wildlife of the United States*, Resource Publication 34 (Washington, D.C., December 1968); U.S. Department of the Interior, Office of Endangered Species and International Activities, *Threatened Wildlife of the United States*, Resource Publication 114 (Washington, D.C., March 1973).

Udall's prescience and Janzen's memo: Interviews, Erickson, Gottschalk.

152 Land and Water Conservation Fund and its restrictions: M. Bean, *The Evolution of National Wildlife Law* (New York: Praeger, 1983), 230–231.

Habitat-purchase plan and legal difficulties: Interview, Gottschalk; U.S. Department of the Interior, "Legislative Authority for Endangered Species Program," *Interior Decisions* 72 (13 January 1965): 13–21.

152–153 Gottschalk and Denton: House, *Department of the Interior and Related Agencies Appropriations for 1966*, Hearings before a Subcommittee of the Committee on Appropriations, 89th Congress, 1st Session, 2 February 1965, 1520–1533 ("According to," 1520–1521; "the prevention," 1521).

153 Rejection of Gottschalk's plan: House, *Department of the Interior and Related Agencies Appropriations for 1966*, H. Report 205, 89th Congress, 1st Session, 25 March 1965, 14.

Udall's testimony: S. Udall, testimony, in House, *Miscellaneous Fisheries and Wildlife Legislation—1965*, Hearings before the Subcommittee on Fisheries and Wildlife Conservation, Committee on Merchant Marine and Fisheries, 89th Congress, 1st Session, 15 July 1965, 150–157 ("a clear policy," 153).

"It would be most": Senate, *Conservation of Certain Species of Fish and Wildlife*, S. Report 1463, 89th Congress, 2d Session, 17 August 1966, 5.

153–154 Endangered Species Act of 1966: Bean, *The Evolution of National Wildlife Law*, 319–320.

154 "insofar . . . their authorities": *U.S. Statutes at Large* 80 (1966): 926.

Modification of pest control programs and Udall's hopes: Udall, testimony (15 July 1965), 153.

Lip service: The law was amended by the 1969 Endangered Species Conservation Act, which blocked the importation of endangered species into the United States; extended the Lacey Act's ban on interstate commerce in unlawfully taken wildlife to reptiles, amphibians, mollusks, and crustaceans; added invertebrates to the species covered by the law; increased spending from the Land and Water Conservation Fund; and spelled out the procedure for adding species to the official U.S. endangered species list. But these amendments did not explicitly prohibit killing or harming listed species (S. Yaffee, *Prohibitive Policy: Implementing the Federal Endangered Species Act* [Cambridge, Mass.: MIT Press, 1982], 42).

154 USFWS acquires Key deer habitat: USFWS, Division of Real Estate, *Land and Water Conservation Fund, Summary of Land Obligations*, Washington, D.C., n.d.

155–156 Whale imbroglio: Interviews, E. U. Curtis Bohlen, Berryman, Gottschalk; R. Tobin, *The Expendable Future: U.S. Politics and the Protection of Biodiversity* (Durham, N.C.: Duke University Press, 1990), 205–206; *Federal Register* (hereafter cited as *FR*) 35 (30 July 1970): 12222 (proposal).

155 Gottschalk's conclusion: Interview, Gottschalk; memorandum, J. S. Gottschalk to W. Hickel, 28 September 1970, John S. Gottschalk's files, Arlington, Va. (hereafter cited as Gottschalk's files).

Hickel intends to list whales: U.S. Department of the Interior, "Secretary Hickel Bans Imports of Products from Eight Endangered Species of Whales," press release, 24 November 1970, Gottschalk's files.

155–156 Hickel is fired and rule is published: "Hickel Dismissed by Nixon," *New York Times*, 26 November 1970; *FR* 35 (2 December 1970): 18319–18322.

156 Bohlen's background and rewriting law: Interview, Bohlen.

"simply [did] not provide": R. M. Nixon, "Environmental Message of 8 February 1972," quoted in N. P. Reed, testimony, in Senate, *Endangered Species Conservation Act of 1972*, Hearings before the Subcommittee on the Environment, Committee on Commerce, 92d Congress, 2d Session, 4 August 1972, 67.

157 House and Senate bills: House, *Predatory Mammals and Endangered Species*, Hearings before the Subcommittee on Fisheries and Wildlife Conservation, Committee on Merchant Marine and Fisheries, 92d Congress, 2d Session, 20 and 21 March and 10 and 11 April 1972, 3–46; Senate, *Endangered Species Conservation Act of 1972*, 4 and 10 August 1972, 3–53.

Congressional proclamations: *Congressional Record* (hereafter cited as *CR*), 93d Congress, 1st Session, 24 July 1973 ("the extinction," 25668; "for too long," 25693); *CR*, 93d Congress, 1st Session, 18 September 1973 ("protect man," 30165).

158 "*shall* utilize, where practicable": H.R. 13081 (administration's bill), Section 3(d), in House, *Predatory Mammals*, 23 (emphasis added).

158–159 Talbot's background: Interview, Lee M. Talbot.

159–160 Evolution of the Endangered Species Act of 1973: Interviews, Bohlen, John Ehrlichman, Paul Lenzini, Frank Potter, Jr., Talbot, and John Whittaker; H.R. 13081, in House, *Predatory Mammals*, 22–27; S. 3199 and S. 3818, in Senate, *Endangered Species Conservation Act of 1972*, 9–53; H.R. 37 and H.R. 4758, in House, *Endangered Species*, Hearings before the Subcommittee on Fisheries and Wildlife Conservation and the Environment, Committee on Merchant Marine and Fisheries, 93d Congress, 1st Session, 15, 26, and

27 March 1973, 87–113, 165–185; S. 1592 and S. 1983, in Senate, *Endangered Species Act of 1973,* Hearings before the Subcommittee on the Environment, Committee on Commerce, 93d Congress, 1st Session, 18 and 21 June 1973, 3–49; S. 1983, in *CR,* 93d Congress, 1st Session, 24 July 1973, 25662–25668; H.R. 37, in *CR,* 93d Congress, 1st Session, 18 September 1973, 30157–30175; and S. 1983 (conference version), in *CR,* 93d Congress, 1st Session, 19 December 1973, 42621–42629.

160 Floor votes: *CR,* 93d Congress, 1st Session, 19 December 1973, 42535 (Senate unanimously agrees to conference version), and 20 December 1973, 42915–42916 (House vote).

161 List of federal projects: G. C. Coggins and I. S. Russell, "Beyond Shooting Snail Darters in Pork Barrels: Endangered Species and Land Use in America," *Georgetown Law Journal* 70 (1982): 1421–1525.

Law was "prescient": M. O'Connell, "Six Biological Reasons Why the Endangered Species Act Doesn't Work—And What to Do About It: Response," *Conservation Biology* 6 (1992): 140–143, at 140.

162 Smithsonian's plant list: Tobin, *The Expendable Future,* 95–96.

Seven professionals for five centuries: This is based on figures given in K. Schreiner, testimony, in House, *Endangered Species Oversight,* Hearings before the Subcommittee on Fisheries and Wildlife Conservation and the Environment, Committee on Merchant Marine and Fisheries, 94th Congress, 1st Session, 1 October 1975, 14–15.

Budget figures and Greenwalt's request: Tobin, *The Expendable Future,* 57, 182 (actual appropriations); L. Greenwalt, testimony, in House, *Endangered Species Oversight* (1 October 1975), 20–22 (needs).

162–163 Greenwalt and Yates, and actual appropriations (footnote): L. Greenwalt, testimony, in House, *Department of the Interior and Related Agencies Appropriations for 1977,* Hearings before a Subcommittee of the Committee on Appropriations, 94th Congress, 2d Session, 23 February 1976, 356–357 ("Can't we" and "Not very," 357); Tobin, *The Expendable Future,* 57, 182 (actual appropriations [footnote]).

163 First additions to list: U.S. Fish and Wildlife Service, "Endangered and Threatened Wildlife and Plants," *Code of Federal Regulations,* title 50, parts 17.11 and 17.12, Washington, D.C., 1991 (kangaroos, madtom, crocodile, darter, Hawaiian birds); Tobin, *The Expendable Future,* 88 (grizzly bear).

164–169 Story of TVA v. Hill: Interviews, Bell, Cohen, Zygmunt Plater; *Environmental Defense Fund v. Tennessee Valley Authority; Hiram G. Hill, Jr. et al. v. Tennessee Valley Authority; Tennessee Valley Authority v. Hiram G. Hill, Jr. et al.;* Plater, "In the Wake"; Bennett, *Dilemmas: Coping with Environmental Problems,* 13–53; Wheeler and McDonald, *TVA and the Tellico Dam,* 134–213.

164–165 Discovery of snail darter: Interview, David Etnier; E. Kinkead, "Tennessee Small Fry," *The New Yorker,* 8 January 1979, 52–55.

165–166 Campaign of Hill, Etnier, and Plater: Interviews, Etnier, Plater, Cohen (T-shirt).

166 Listing and habitat designation: *FR* 40 (9 October 1975): 47505–47506 (list-

ing; "would result in," 47505); *FR* 41 (1 April 1976): 13926–13928 (critical habitat).

167 "required federal agencies": A. Wagner, statement, in Senate, *Endangered Species Act Oversight*, Hearings before a Subcommittee on Resource Protection, Committee on Environment and Public Works, 95th Congress, 1st Session, 22 July 1977, 493 (emphasis added).

168 Infighting over snail darter suit (footnote): Interview, Bell; Bell and Ostrow, *Taking Care of the Law*, 42–44.

169 Supreme Court decision: *TVA v. Hill* ("shows clearly," 187; "plain intent" and "to halt," 184, emphasis added).

Lawsuits and lousewort dispute: *Sierra Club v. Froehlke*, 534 F.2d 1289 (1976) (Indiana bat); *National Wildlife Federation v. Coleman*, 529 F.2d 359 (1976) (Mississippi sandhill crane); House, *Endangered Species Act Amendments of 1978*, H. Report 1625, 95th Congress, 2d Session, 25 September 1978, 12 (lousewort).

170 Baker-Culver bill: S. 2899, in Senate, *Amending the Endangered Species Act of 1973*, Hearings before the Subcommittee on Resource Protection, Committee on Environment and Public Works, U.S. Senate, 95th Congress, 2d Session, 13 and 14 April 1978, 3–15.

Senate approves Culver-Baker bill: *CR*, 95th Congress, 2d Session, 19 July 1978, 21603.

Duncan's amendment: *CR*, 95th Congress, 2d Session, 14 October 1978, 38148.

Endangered Species Committee: *U.S. Code*, vol. 16, sec. 1536(e).

171 Endangered Species Committee ruling: *Endangered Species Technical Bulletin* (hereafter cited as *ESTB*) 4 (January 1979): 1.

Andrus's reaction: M. L. Corn and P. Baldwin, *Endangered Species Act: The Listing and Exemption Processes*, Report 90-242, Congressional Research Service, Washington, D.C., 1990, 25 ("Frankly").

Grayrocks Dam (footnote): *CR*, 95th Congress, 2d Session, 14 October 1978, 38140–38147 (Roncalio's amendment); *ESTB* 3 (December 1978): 1 (settlement); *ESTB* 4 (January 1979): 1 (committee's exemption).

Baker tries to abolish committee: *CR*, 96th Congress, 1st Session, 29 January 1979, 1277 (S. 242 and S. 243); *CR*, 96th Congress, 1st Session, 13 June 1979, 14572–14576 (Amendment no. 249, S. 1143).

171–172 Duncan's second amendment and Senate rejection: *CR*, 96th Congress, 1st Session, 18 June 1979, 15301 (amendment); *CR*, 96th Congress, 1st Session, 17 July 1979, 18934–18939 (rejection); Wheeler and McDonald, *TVA and the Tellico Dam*, 212–213.

172–173 Conference bill and final votes: *CR*, 96th Congress, 1st Session, 1 August 1979, 21987–22002 (conference bill and House vote); *CR*, 96th Congress, 1st Session, 10 September 1979, 23863–23872 (Senate vote; "Mr. President, the awful beast" and "If you want," 23867).

173 Tellico gates close: "Gates Fall and Waters Rise as Tellico Dam Is Finished," *New York Times*, 30 November 1979.

173 Rediscovery of snail darter: Interview, Etnier (delisting); *FR* 49 (5 July 1984): 27510–27514 (change in status).

174 Outcome of Tellico: Interview, Mark Hughes (University of Tennessee); Tellico Reservoir Development Agency, *A Decade of Progress* (brochure), September 1992.

"As a society": *CR*, 95th Congress, 2d Session, 19 July 1978, 21572–21573.

Congress balks: Garn withdrew his amendment rather than force a vote (*CR*, 95th Congress, 2d Session, 19 July 1978, 21574).

175 God Committee since Tellico: *FR* 57 (3 June 1992): 23405–23408 (owl meeting); Corn and Baldwin, *Endangered Species Act*, 27–29 (three other applications).

7. THE "IS" AND THE "OUGHT"

176–177 Details of Babbitt's visit: "Austin Ecological Effort Praised," Austin *American-Statesman* (hereafter cited as *A-S*), 14 March 1993 ("You're at the ten-yard line"). Because of the extensive coverage given this issue by the Austin *American-Statesman*, we hereafter give shortened versions of article titles from that newspaper.

178–179 Austin growth: U.S. Department of Commerce, *State and Metropolitan Area Data Book 1991*, Washington, D.C., 1991, table 2, xx (resident population, percent change, 1980–1990).

179–180 Vireo description: Interview, Joe Grzybowski; U.S. Fish and Wildlife Service (USFWS), *Black-capped Vireo (Vireo atricapillus) Recovery Plan*, Austin, Tex., 1991; letter, S. Hamilton to B. Todd, in "Minutes of Work Session," Executive Committee, Balcones Canyonlands Conservation Plan (BCCP), 15 January 1992, City of Austin files, Environmental and Conservation Services Department, Austin, Tex. (hereafter cited as City of Austin files).

179 Indians and vireo: J. W. Graber, "Distribution, Habitat Requirements, and Life History of the Black-Capped Vireo (*Vireo atricapillus*)," *Ecological Monographs* 31 (1961): 311–336.

180 Cowbirds and vireo: Interview, Grzybowski; J. Terborgh, *Where Have All the Birds Gone? Essays on the Biology and Conservation of Birds That Migrate to the American Tropics* (Princeton, N.J.: Princeton University Press, 1991), 52–58.

Current status of vireo: Interviews, Grzybowski, Carol Beardmore (fewer than one hundred pairs).

180–181 Vireo's progress toward listing: *Federal Register* (hereafter cited as *FR*) 52 (6 October 1987): 37420.

181–183 Development of and fight over Steiner Ranch: Interviews, Don Bosse, Ralph K. M. Haurwitz (*A-S*), Thomas Steiner, Christi Stevens, Kim Tyson (*A-S*); "Refuges for Bugs, Birds, and Human Beings," Austin *Chronicle*, 1 March 1991; "Austin Negotiators Struggle . . . ," *A-S*, 3 June 1990.

183 Parke background: Interviews, Fred Purcell, James Reddell; letter, P. Hartigan to J. Stegman, 8 February 1985, USFWS, Austin, Tex. (petition to list six cave invertebrates).

184 Cave invertebrates: USFWS, *Draft Recovery Plan for Endangered Karst Invertebrates in Travis and Williamson Counties, Texas,* Albuquerque, N.M., 1993.

184–185 Fire ants: Interviews, Reddell, Walter Tschinkel (Florida State University), Edward O. Wilson; C. Mann, "Fire Ants Parlay Their Queens into a Threat to Biodiversity," *Science* 263 (18 March 1994): 1560–1561.

185 Proposed listing of cave invertebrates: *FR* 50 (18 July 1985): 29238 (petition and Category 1 status); *FR* 53 (19 April 1988): 12787 (proposed listing).

185–186 Purcell's threat and Earth First! "cave-in": Interviews, William Bunch, Purcell, Stevens; "Refuges for Bugs, Birds, and Human Beings."

186 Listing of cave invertebrates: *FR* 53 (16 September 1988): 36030.

187 Thou shalt not take: Some exceptions have always existed. A little-used provision in the earlier law allowed otherwise-prohibited acts if they enhanced the survival prospects of the species (M. Bean, *The Evolution of National Wildlife Law* [New York: Praeger, 1983], 354, n. 176).

San Diego mesa mint: K. Rosenberry, "The Effect of the Endangered Species Act on Housing Construction," *The Hastings Law Journal* 33 (1982): 551–582, at 576–577.

187–188 1982 amendments: House, *Endangered Species Act Amendments of 1982,* Conference Report 835, 97th Congress, 2d Session, 17 September 1982 ("unique partnership," 31); M. Bean, S. G. Fitzgerald, and M. O'Connell, *Reconciling Conflicts Under the Endangered Species Act* (Washington, D.C.: World Wildlife Fund, 1991), 7–10; Bean, *The Evolution of National Wildlife Law,* 354.

188–189 Early habitat-conservation plans: Interview, Lindell Marsh (North Key Largo); Bean, Fitzgerald, and O'Connell, *Reconciling Conflicts,* 7–10 (little early use), 52–65 (San Bruno plan), 66–80 (Coachella Valley).

189 City and county officials meet with USFWS: Interviews, David Pimentel, David Tilton; "List of early Austin HCP meetings," n.d., City of Austin files.

Effects of fragmentation: L. D. Harris and G. Silva-Lopez, "Forest Fragmentation and the Conservation of Biological Diversity," in *Conservation Biology,* eds. P. L. Fiedler and S. K. Jain (New York: Chapman & Hall, 1992), 198–237.

190 Warbler description: USFWS, *Golden-Cheeked Warbler (Dendroica chrysoparia) Recovery Plan,* Albuquerque, N.M., 1992; letter, Hamilton to Todd.

Department of Agriculture clearing program: *FR* 55 (4 May 1990): 18347.

191 Meeting with The Nature Conservancy: "List of early Austin HCP meetings."

List of parties: "Agenda, Austin Regional Habitat-Conservation Plan Organizational Meeting," 7 October 1988, City of Austin files.

First full meeting: C. Sexton, "Notes on Habitat-Conservation Plan Organizational Meeting (7 October 1988)," 11 October 1988, City of Austin files.

Housing figures: U.S. Department of Commerce, *Housing Units Authorized by Building Permits,* Washington, D.C., 1983, 1987.

El Paso failure: Interview, Bosse.

191–192 Executive Committee and plan of action: Executive Committee, BCCP, "Minutes of Regular Meeting" (hereafter cited as BCCP Minutes), 9 December 1988, City of Austin files.

192 Biological Advisory Team: Biological Advisory Team (BAT), BCCP, "Minutes of the Biological Advisory Team Meeting," 18 October 1988, City of Austin files.

192–193 PVA process: Interviews, Kent Butler, Grzybowski, Craig Pease, Mark Shaffer, Michael Soulé; M. E. Soulé, *Viable Populations for Conservation* (Cambridge: Cambridge University Press, 1987).

193 October 1989 BAT meeting: BCCP Minutes, 29 September 1989; Executive Committee, BCCP, *Newsletter*, October–November 1989, City of Austin files.

193–195 Pease's results: C. Pease and L. G. Gingerich, "The Habitat Requirements of the Black-Capped Vireo and Golden-Cheeked Warbler Populations Near Austin, Texas," ms., Department of Zoology, University of Texas, Austin, 1989.

193 Territory sizes: USFWS, *Black-Capped Vireo*, 17; Pease and Gingerich, "The Habitat Requirements," 30 (warbler).

194 Blue jay: T. M. Engels and C. W. Sexton, "Negative Correlation of Blue Jays and Golden-Cheeked Warblers Near an Urbanizing Area," *Conservation Biology* 8 (March 1994): 286–290.

194–195 Warbler and vireo preserves: Pease and Gingerich, "The Habitat Requirements," 30 (warbler), 27 (vireo).

195 Pease presents results to Executive Committee: BCCP Minutes, 26 January 1990.

195–196 Committee expectations: Interviews, Butler ($30 million, views of other counties), Bryan Hale (twenty thousand acres).

196 Intent to list warbler: "Concern for Birds Halts Perot Project," Dallas *Times Herald*, 9 February 1990.

Listing within one year: BCCP Minutes, 23 February 1990.

Earth First! charges: Interviews, Bunch, Stevens.

197–198 Perot and illegal clearing: "Concern for Birds Halts Perot Project"; "Workers to Stop . . . ," *A-S*, 17 February 1990; D. Wright, "Death to Tweety," *The New Republic* 207 (6 July 1992): 910; *FR* 55 (4 May 1990): 18844–18845 (further clearing).

197 Listing of warbler and reaction: "Protected Bird Halts . . . ," *A-S*, 3 May 1990; "Warblers Throw RR2222 . . . ," *A-S*, 5 May 1990; "County Studies Building . . . ," *A-S*, 10 May 1990. Emergency listing avoided the drawn-out formal listing process but protected the bird for only 240 days. The agency granted the warbler normal protection 237 days later (*FR* 55 [27 December 1990]: 53160).

Public hearing: "Hundreds Flock to . . . ," *A-S*, 12 May 1990 ("Can I just" and "We can't generalize").

198 Butler's background: Interview, Butler ("turnkey plan"); BCCP Minutes, 30 June 1989 (Butler wins job).

199 Butler's rough outline: BCCP Minutes, 15 and 29 June 1990.

200 Butler's team tries to hold coalition together: Interviews, Robert Brandes, Butler; BAT, "Biological Advisory Team Comments," Question 3, Answer f, in BCCP Minutes, 22 February 1991, City of Austin files; BCCP Minutes, 8 March 1991; Executive Committee, BCCP, "Minutes of Work Session," 11 January 1991, City of Austin files.

Wildlife refuge: Interview, Butler; "Habitat's Plan's Price . . . ," *A-S,* 12 January 1991 (effect on plan's cost). The value of land within the refuge's proposed boundaries was about one-fourth the average value of land in the BCCP area near Austin.

201 Butler's final draft and new committee: Interview, Butler.

Austin approves bond issue and starts buying land: Interviews, Butler, Junie Plummer.

Committee submits proposed preserve design: "Council Vote Starts . . . ," *A-S,* 26 February 1993.

201–202 Bird letter: Interviews, J. B. Ruhl (premium for letter), Harry Savio.

202 Individual habitat-conservation plans: "Developers Tired of . . . ," *A-S,* 27 June 1993.

Real-estate boom: "West Lake Building . . . ," *A-S,* 29 July 1993; "Residential Development Activity Continues Upward Trend," *Growth Watch,* City of Austin, Department of Planning and Development, July 1993, 1 (number one real-estate market, citing *Ernst and Young's National Real Estate Advisor*).

$130 million: Interview, Butler; "Aleshire Pushes BCCP . . . ," *A-S,* 7 May 1993.

202–203 Travis County bond issue: "Balcones Plan May . . . ," *A-S,* 29 July 1993 (bond issue plans); "Voters Will Weigh . . . ," *A-S,* 24 October 1993 ("there is no certainty," "near impossible to proceed," and political action committee [exceptions included the Texas Capital Area Home Builders Association and Earth First!]); "Environmental, Business Groups . . . ," *A-S,* 14 October 1993; "BCCP Plan Called . . . ," *A-S,* 18 October 1993; "Opposites Attract, Unite . . . ," *A-S,* 24 October 1993; "Balcones Plan Follows . . . ," *A-S,* 31 October 1993.

202 Travis County and state legislature: BCCP Minutes, 14 June 1991 (first attempt); "Backers Search for . . . ," *A-S,* 29 May 1993 (second attempt).

203 Babbitt's visit: "Babbitt Urges Voters . . . ," *A-S,* 25 October 1993 ("flagship" and "is the most").

Bond issue defeat: Interview, Butler; "BCCP Bonds Dealt . . . ," *A-S,* 3 November 1993; "BCCP's Life Was . . . ," *A-S,* 6 November 1993 ("originally envisioned").

203–204 Aftermath of bond issue defeat: Interviews, Bosse, Butler ("litigation hell"), Plummer (land acquisition), Purcell (his lawsuit); Complaint, *Williamson County Commissioners Court v. Bruce Babbitt,* U.S. District Ct., Western Dist. of Texas, Austin Division, No. A94-CA-219-SS, 29 March 1994 (Williamson County lawsuit).

204–205 Babbitt's view: Interview, Bruce Babbitt.

205 "The plan was supposed": Quoted in "Opposites Attract, Unite . . ."

205 Listing based solely on biology: *U.S. Code*, vol. 16, sec. 1533(b)(i)(A); House, *Endangered Species Act Amendments of 1982*, Merchant Marine and Fisheries Committee, H. Report No. 97-567, 17 May 1982, 12.

206 "Is" and "ought": D. Hume, *A Treatise of Human Nature*, vol. 3 (Oxford: Clarendon Press, 1888), 469–470.

207–208 95 percent chance: Pease and Gingerich, "The Habitat Requirements," figure 4. This figure presents three plots of the relation between an area's carrying capacity (which the population is assumed to have attained) and the probability of extinction over a century. The plots vary by the coefficient of variation of survivorship and fecundity; the 95 percent figure is from the middle plot.

208 Ecological mandarins: We have taken this phrase from A. D. Tarlock, "Earth and Other Ethics: The Institutional Issues," *Tennessee Law Review* 56 (1988): 43–76, at 75–76.

208–209 Land-swap proposal: Interviews, Butler, Joey Crumley, Johnston.

209 "to cast social": M. Sagoff, *The Economy of the Earth* (Cambridge: Cambridge University Press, 1988), 200.

210 Well-managed ranch and vireos: Interview, Tim Taylor.

8. NOAH'S CHOICE

213 "Tragic choices": G. Calabresi and P. Bobbitt, *Tragic Choices* (New York: W. W. Norton, 1978) ("a prospect," 18).

214 Species removed from and added to list: The Appendix discusses the history of delistings and listings in greater detail.

"In empirical fact": J. Dewey, *Theory of Valuation* (Chicago: University of Chicago Press, 1939), 27.

215 Crying "no more extinctions": Our argument parallels the pollution-control example in M. Sagoff, *The Economy of the Earth* (Cambridge: Cambridge University Press, 1988), 216.

"When we threaten": *Congressional Record*, 93rd Congress, 1st Session, 18 September 1973, 30162.

216–217 Gadamer: H. Gadamer, *Truth and Method*, 2d rev. ed., trans. J. Weinsheimer and D. Marshall (New York: Continuum Publishing Co., 1988), 362–379, 383–389 ("process of coming," 385; "is not the art," 367).

222 1992–1994 beetle surveys: Interview, Ken Frazier; K. Frazier, "1993 Status of the American Burying Beetle," n.d., USFWS, Tulsa, Okla.

224 Two stages merged into one: If a species is listed as threatened, the secretary of the Interior has the discretion to adopt regulations that can allow taking and other acts normally prohibited by the law. Of the 201 species listed as threatened, 50 are covered by such regulations.

225–226 Scientific team in Idaho: J. Michael Scott et al., "Species Richness," *BioScience* 37 (December 1987): 782–788.

226 National Biological Inventory: Interview, Bruce Babbitt.

227 National biodiversity trust: The idea for a biodiversity trust fund has been explored by others, most notably John Baden of the Foundation for Research

on Economics and the Environment in Seattle. See, e.g., J. Baden, "Species Preservation Without Tears," *Wall Street Journal,* 2 June 1992.

228 Number of trusts: Interview, Laura Deans (Land Trust Alliance); Land Trust Alliance, "1994 Land Trust Survey," mimeograph, Washington, D.C., November 1994.

Wisconsin program: Interview, Dave Kopitzke.

233–234 Illinois Karner Blue population: Interview, Amelia Orton-Palmer; "Field & Street," *Chicago Reader,* 28 May 1993.

APPENDIX

239–240 Number of species listed since 1973: Our counts of listed endangered species are derived mainly from the list itself, provided in computer database form by George Drewry (USFWS). When the Endangered Species Act was passed in 1973, the list included 134 species found in the U.S. and its territories; 21 species were removed from the list between 1973 and 1993; and at the end of 1993, the list included 836 species (not including separate populations of the same species). Two of the delisted species remained on the list in some other form. Thus, the number of new listings between 1973 and 1993 totals 721.

240 Definition of recovery: *U.S. Code,* Title 16, Section 1532(3) ("at which the measures").

Species removed from the list: Our count of delistings comes from U.S. Fish and Wildlife Service, *Endangered and Threatened Wildlife and Plants* (Washington, D.C., 15 July 1991) for the period through July 15, 1991; and individual accounts in the *Federal Register* for the period since then. The first source gives the reason for each delisting; for the more recent cases, we discerned the reason for delisting from the *Federal Register* notice. The one exception to this method is the Rydberg milk-vetch, a plant in Utah, which we count as a data error but which is listed in the USFWS source as recovered. The plant was identified as a separate species in 1964 on the basis of samples collected in 1905. Because no botanist could find more milk-vetches, the species was thought to be extinct. In 1976 more were discovered; the species was listed as threatened two years later. In the 1980s, plants previously thought to belong to another species were reclassified as Rydberg milk-vetch, which led to the discovery that more of the plants existed than originally believed. The official notice of delisting states that "the discovery of 11 additional populations" led to the conclusion that the "original classification as threatened was in error." *Federal Register* (hereafter cited as *FR*) 54 (14 September 1989): 37941–37943, quotes from 37941–37942.

Pine Barrens treefrog: *FR* 48 (22 November 1983): 52740–52743

Five recoveries: *FR* 50 (12 September 1985): 37192–37194 (Palau birds); *FR* 50 (4 February 1985): 4945–4948 (brown pelican); *FR* 52 (4 June 1987): 21059–21064 (American alligator).

241 Questions about alligator's recovery: The most important alligator populations are in Louisiana, where state efforts to protect the creature have been in existence since 1964, when state law banned commercial alligator hunting. In 1970 the Lacy Act was amended to block interstate transport of illegally

hunted wildlife, including the alligator. As a result of these actions, alligator populations in Louisiana exploded; the state, which wanted to reopen commercial harvesting, recommended in 1971 that the species be removed from the early federal endangered list. It wasn't. The exasperated state authorities petitioned for a delisting under the Endangered Species Act, which was granted in September 1975. T. Joanen and L. McNease, "Recent History of the Alligator Management Program in Louisiana," unpub. ms. (Grand Chenier: Louisiana Department of Wildlife and Fisheries, 26 January 1981). We are grateful to Brian Seasholes for sending us a copy of this report, along with others like it. See also G. Laycock, "Searching for Truth in Alligator Country," *National Wildlife*, October/November 1987, 13–18.

241–243 Reclassifications: *FR* 52 (6 April 1987): 10890–10892 (Tinian monarch); *FR* 49 (5 July 1984): 27510–27514 (snail darter); *FR* 49 (20 March 1984): 10520–10526 and *FR* 59 (5 October 1994): 50796–50808 (Arctic peregrine falcon); *FR* 59 (12 July 1994): 35584–35594 (bald eagle); P. Ehrlich, D. S. Dobkin, and D. Wheye, *Birds in Jeopardy* (Stanford, Calif.: Stanford University Press, 1992), 25–27 (falcon and eagle); *FR* 40 (16 July 1975): 29863–29865 (Lahontan cutthroat trout, Paiute cutthroat trout, Apache trout); *FR* 43 (18 April 1978): 16343–16345 (greenback cutthroat trout); J. A. Yuskavitch, "A Tale of Two Trouts," *Trout*, Winter 1993, 26–47 (trout species); T. R. Dunlap, *Saving America's Wildlife* (Princeton, N.J.: Princeton University Press, 1988), 166–70, and *FR* 43 (9 March 1978): 9612–9620 (gray wolf); *FR* 49 (29 May 1984): 22330–22334 (Utah prairie dog); *FR* 55 (12 December 1990): 51106–51114 (Aleutian Canada goose); and U.S. Fish and Wildlife Service, *Endangered Species Act Success Stories*, mimeograph (Washington, D.C., December 1993), 2 (1993 goose population).

243 Number of species doing well: U.S. Department of the Interior, *Endangered and Threatened Species Recovery Program* (Washington, D.C., December 1992), 17–20.

244 Socorro isopod: Interviews, Gerald Burton, Charles Painter, Rick Sanchez, Mike Hatch; *FR* 43 (27 March 1978): 12690–12691.

Loch Lomond coyote-thistle: Interview, Ann Howald (California Department of Fish and Game); *FR* 58 (29 November 1993): 62629–62633 (proposal for reclassification).

Pahrump poolfish: Interviews, Donna Withers (USFWS), Brian Seasholes (quoting James Deacon).

244–245 Columbian white-tailed deer: Interview, Gary Miller (USFWS); *Endangered and Threatened Species Recovery Program*, 199, 243.

245 Kendall Warm Springs dace: Interview, Larry Shanks (USFWS); U.S. Department of the Interior, *Threatened Wildlife of the United States*, Bureau of Sport Fisheries and Wildlife, Resource Publication 114 (Washington, D.C., March 1973), 36.

Magazine Mountain shagreen: Interview, Paul Hartfield (USFWS).

246 USFWS actions in first six months of 1994: These actions have been compiled by perusing the *Federal Register*, January–June 1994.

Next few years: Interviews, Jasper Carlton (Biodiversity Legal Foundation; listing lawsuit), Georgia Parham (USFWS); *Endangered and Threatened Species Recovery Program*, 19 (fourteen extinct species).

Acknowledgments

Many people on all sides of the contentious issue of endangered species helped us to write this book, almost always treating us with courtesy, even when they understood our conclusions might differ from theirs. It is a pleasure to thank them now. *Noah's Choice* is also the title of an article in the July/August 1993 *Earthwatch* by Norman Myers, who has sounded the alarm over the world's vanishing species for more than a decade. Although we settled on our title before encountering his piece, we happily acknowledge the numerous articles and books he has written, as well as the opportunities he gave us to talk with him. One of the treats in writing *Noah's Choice* was the chance to speak often with Edward O. Wilson and Daniel S. Simberloff; we have also benefited from many conversations with (and faxes from) Ike Sugg of the Competitive Enterprise Institute. All three read early drafts of part of the manuscript, as did Gwenda Blair, Robert P. Crease, Robert Dirig, Ken Frazier, Stephen S. Hall, Stephen and Donald Mann, John Miller, Cassie Phillips, Stuart Pimm, Mark Sagoff, Mark Walters, John West, and Ed Zuckerman. We checked direct quotations with the speaker, although inevitably this was not always possible. In all cases, we are delighted to acknowledge their help.

For our trip to Oklahoma, we are grateful for the hospitality of Zev Trachtenberg, and the patience of Curt Creighton, Karl Stephan, and especially Ken Frazier, who put up with our unending requests for more information. In Florida, Stephen Nesbitt kindly allowed us to see the whooping crane, a creature that gives new life to tired words like *magnificent*. On an earlier trip to see the Florida scrub jay, we were given time and material by many people, especially John W. Fitzpatrick, Tom Hill, Glen Woolfenden, and the staff at Archbold Biological Station; we thank Margo Hammond for hospitality in Tampa. This last group is the most prominent example of an unhappy phenomenon most journalists come to know—the people who devote much time to helping you, only to see their contributions seemingly slighted in the actual text. A second example is Michael Amaral and Andrea Kozol, who allowed us to accompany them on a burying beetle transplanting expedition to an island off the coast of Rhode Island. A third telephonic example is the help we received from Louis Campbell, Tom Carr, Michelle Grigore, Harold Mayfield, John Shuey, and Doris Stifel, all of whom told us the story of the Karner Blue butterfly's demise in Ohio—a story that, alas, ended up on the cutting-room floors of our computers. Almost every species or incident to which we devote more than passing mention is another instance; we apologize to all who helped us and assure them that their contributions are imprinted, palimpsest-style, just beneath the pages.

A small army of people helped us in Austin. Kent Butler introduced us to the labyrinthine tale of the Balcones Canyonlands Conservation Plan and kept us informed of the developments there; one of our worst experiences in writing this book was hearing his discouraged voice the day after the county bond election. Joe Grzybowski and Craig Pease gave us invaluable assistance in coming to terms with the biology; Clif Ladd and James Reddell gave us ground-level (and below-ground-level) tours of the Hill Country; William Bunch and Christi Stevens put up with intrusive visits and phone calls; Robert Brandes introduced us to the splendid city he lives in. We are grateful to them all.

On issues of ethics and philosophy, we received instruction from Holmes Rolston III, Mark Sagoff, and, briefly but illuminatingly, Kristin Shrader-Frechette. One of the great pleasures in writing this book was to listen to these fine thinkers slicing our confusion into its component parts and reassembling them into new intellectual designs. A special thank-you is owed to four friends and colleagues: Gardner Brown, Jr., who shared with us his years of thinking about the economics of endangered species; Bob Crease, who guided us to and through Hans-Georg Gadamer; Kai Lee, who helped us through the thicket of tragic choices and the opposition of planning and negotiation; and John Miller, a former member of Congress who pointed out the advantages of bringing biodiversity into the political arena. For the past three years George Drewry and Jay Sheppard of the U.S. Fish and Wildlife Service in Washington, D.C., have patiently taken our calls and provided us with megabytes of data covering the species listed under the Endangered Species Act. We thank Bruce Babbitt for taking the time to speak with us.

Here one author (MLP) notes that his wife, Cassie Phillips, works for the Weyerhaeuser Company, a timber corporation with land in the Pacific Northwest and the Southeast. For some years, Weyerhaeuser has been actively involved in the controversy over the Endangered Species Act, especially, though not exclusively, with the northern spotted owl in the Pacific Northwest. The shimmer of a potential conflict of interest is one reason that both authors decided not to discuss the owl in this book. A better reason—one that was probative to the other author—is that the owl is an exceptional case. The ecological, socioeconomic, and political issues surrounding biodiversity are better represented by species like the Karner Blue butterfly, the black-capped vireo, and the American burying beetle.

The recitation of thank-yous and acknowledgments above is far from complete, of course. Around the country are scores of puzzled people, many of them biologists, who received mysterious phone calls from two authors researching a book on endangered species; you know who you are, and we thank each of you for your time, your knowledge, and your willingness to share both with strangers. A tally of formal interviews follows, divided by chapters. For reasons of space, we have named people only once, although many contributed to more than a single chapter.

"Seventeen Beetles": Robert Allen, Michael Amaral, Richard Arnold, Michael Bentzien, Jerry Chambers, Donald Crain, J. Curtis Creighton, Lloyd R. Davis, Jr., Ken Frazier, Anne Hecht, Peter Hoch, Ramon Jackson, Andrea Kozol, Lawrence Maloney, Lawrence Master, Neal McCaleb, Terry McFall, Kyle P. McKinley, Patricia Mehlhop, Margery Milne, Paul Nickerson, Jack Pate, Stewart Peck, Charles Remington, Rebecca Rudman, Brian Schmitt, Dale F. Schweitzer, Karl Stephan, Eugene Stipe.

"Kinds Of": Ian A. E. Atkinson, Terry Erwin, Donald Falk, Harriet Gillett, Chris Magin, Paul Martin, Ernst Mayr, Phil Pister, Martin J. S. Rudwick, David W. Steadman, Nigel Stork, Jo Taylor, Erik Wheaton, Jack Williams.

"The Crisis": Cleber Alho, William J. Boecklen, Russell Burke, Edward F. Connor, Phyllis Croley, Richard M. DeGraaf, Jared Diamond, Frank Egerton, Jackie Fauls, John Fedkiw, John W. Fitzpatrick, David Foster, Alwyn Gentry, Nicholas J. Gotelli, Vernon Heywood, Frank R. Hildreth, Tom Hill, Tim Hurner, Jerome Jackson, Fran James, Patrick Kangas, Susan Koch, Thomas Lacker, J. P. Lanly, Thomas Lovejoy, Jane Lubchenko, Ariel E. Lugo, Douglas MacCleery, Marc Mangel, Michael Mares, Earl D. McCoy, Norman Myers, William Newmark, John O'Keefe, Paul Opler, David Pemberton, Stuart Pimm, Jane Preston, James F. Quinn, Richard Root, Robert Schneider, Paul M. Seby, Craig L. Shafer, Daniel Simberloff, K. D. Singh, Andrew Smith, Michael Soulé, Simon Stuart, Jo Taylor, John Terborgh, Richard Vane-Wright, Dave Wesley, Timothy Whitmore, Edward O. Wilson, Glen E. Woolfenden, Henry Woolsey, Donald E. Wudtke, Dawn Zattau, Barbara Zimmermann.

"Uncooking the Frog": Jonathan Atwood, Karen Becker, Cathy Bleser, Daniel Botkin, Louis W. Campbell, James H. Cane, John Cannone, Cathy Carnes, Tom Carr, Brandt Child, Marv Clark, Ken Cole, Lee Coleman, John Cryan, Robert Dirig, Larry Eng, John Fitzpatrick, Monica Florian, Sue Fox, Stephanie Gebauer, Charles Gehring, Thomas Givnish, Larry Gordon, Michelle Grigore, Ralph Grundel, Paul Hammond, Alan Haney, Phil Hassrick, Krista Hemboldt, Tom Hill, Paul Huey, Charles Kjos, Dave Kopitzke, Claire Kremen, John Lerg, Harold Mayfield, Donald MacElroy, Roy J. McDonald, Tom Miller, William L. Minckley, Gary Nabhum, Peter Nye, Kathy O'Brien, Amelia Orton-Palmer, Steve Packard, Stephen Pyne, Dolores Savignano, Paul Seby, Scott Shaw, John Shuey, Dean R. Snow, Laura

Sommers, Ryk Peter Spoor, Doris Stifel, David Van Luven, Thomas Wharton, James Woolf, Glen Woolfenden, Marcel Zucchino.

"Reasons Peculiarly Our Own": Bobbi Appell, George Archibald, John C. Avise, Nell Baldacchino, Chris Beecher, Elaine Blume, Charles Bolsinger, Gardner Brown, Tom Copmann, Gordon Cragg, Robert P. Crease, M. Dianne DeFuria, Robin Doughty, Rod Drewien, Roger Edwards, David Ehrenfeld, Thomas Emerton, Beverly Fletcher, Michael Grever, Michael Hanemann, Roger Hexem, Paul Heyne, Kai Lee, James Lewis, Curt Meine, Robert Mendelsohn, Stephen Nesbitt, Steve O'Brien, Gordon Orians, Laurie Ostroff, Randy Perry, Holmes Rolston III, Mark Sagoff, Saul Schepartz, Kristin Shrader-Frechette, Ken Snader, Richard Spelt, Jr., Tom Stehn, Stan Temple, Martin Weitzman, Jan Winer, Mark Witmer.

" 'The Awful Beast Is Back' ": John W. Aldrich, Donald Barry, Michael J. Bean, Griffin Bell, Jack H. Berryman, Richard Bishop, E. U. Curtis Bohlen, Donald S. Cohen, John Ehrlichman, Ray C. Erickson, David Etnier, Jon Goldstein, John S. Gottschalk, Brian Greber, Lynn Greenwalt, Mark Hughes, Rudy Lachenmeier, Paul Lenzini, Lynn Llewellyn, Ralph Morganweck, Nathaniel Reed, Robert Nelson, Zygmunt J. B. Plater, Frank M. Potter, Jr., Nathaniel P. Reed, Chandler S. Robbins, Keith Schreiner, Lee M. Talbot, Gary Taylor, John Whittaker.

"The 'Is' and the 'Ought' ": Bruce Babbitt, Carol Beardmore, Don Bosse, Robert Brandes, William Bunch, Kent Butler, Dan Byfield, Robert Carnes, Joseph Crumley, Peter Dwyer, William Elliott, Tom Engles, James Fries, George Gau, Joe Grzybowski, Bryan Hale, Sam Hamilton, Ralph K. M. Haurwitz, Michael Heymann, Deborah Holle, Joseph Johnston, Jim Jones, Terry Jones, Clif Ladd, Joe Lasarde, William Lehman, Jane Lyons, Michael O'Connell, Craig Pease, David Pimentel, Junie Plummer, Sanford Porter, Fred Purcell, James Reddell, Katherine Rosenberry, J. B. Ruhl, Robert Russell, Henry Savio, Charles Sexton, Katherine Stark, Thomas Steiner, Christi Stevens, Ike Sugg, Tim Taylor, David Tilton, Bruce Todd, Walter Tschinkel, Kim Tyson, Brad Vincent, Robert Walker, Dave Williams.

"Noah's Choice": Blair Csuti, Laura Deans, Susan Doran, David Kopitzke, Georgia Parham, J. Michael Scott, Mark Shaffer.

Appendix: Gerald Burton, Jasper Carlton, George Drewry, Larry England, Paul Hartfield, Mike Hatch, Dale Hoffmann, Ann Howald, David Marshall, Gary Miller, Charles Painter, Robert Ruesink, C. Eugene Ruhr, Rick Sanchez, Brian Seasholes, Larry Shanks, Jay Sheppard, Rollin Sparrowe, Donna Withers.

Others: Mark Clough, Dave Foreman, Maurice Hornocker, Deborah Jensen, David John, Herbert Kale, David Klinger, Lynn Maguire, Tom Melius, William L. Minckley, Dennis Murphy, Chris Nagano, Reed Noss, Howard Quigley, David Redmond, Richard Schroeder, Ellen Shell, Roger Swaine, Dewey Youngblood. We also wish to thank the support staff at Fish and Wildlife, INPE, IUCN, The Nature Conservancy, WCMC, and WWF who sent us material that we requested.

In addition to direct interviews, we should acknowledge the contributions of several sources whose modest presence in our notes does not reflect their overarching importance to the development of this book. Thankfully, Edward O. Wilson's *The Diversity of Life* appeared long before our book was finished; we consulted it constantly. We also found numerous occasions to consult *Biodiversity*, edited by Wilson. Stephen Pyne's *Fire in America* opened our eyes to the importance of fire as an ecological force, and concomitantly to the role of humans in shaping nature. Craig L. Shafer's *Nature Reserves* was a valuable sourcebook for our foray into island biogeography, as was Connor and McCoy's article "The Statistics and Biology of the Species-Area Relationship," published in *The American Naturalist*.

Sources we relied upon heavily include the following, without being exhaustive (full citations are in the notes). For background on the Endangered Species Act: Michael Bean, *The Evolution of Wildlife Law*; Michael Bean, Sarah Fitzgerald, and Michael O'Connell, *Reconciling Conflicts Under the Endangered Species Act*; Kathryn Kohm, editor, *Balancing on the Brink of Extinction*; Daniel Rohlf, *The Endangered Species Act*; Ike Sugg, "Caught in the Act," *Cumberland Law Review* (October 1993); Richard Tobin, *The Expendable Future*; and Steven Yaffee, *Prohibitive Policy*. For the history of the American landscape: William Cronon, *Changes in the Land*; Peter Matthiessen, *Wildlife in America*; Michael Williams, *Americans and Their Forests*; and Stephen Fox, *The American Conservation Movement*. For the history of ecology: Donald Worster, *Nature's Economy*. For ecology itself: Stuart Pimm, *The Balance of Nature?*, and Michael Soulé, editor, *Viable Populations for Conservation*. For the current state of biodiversity: The World Conservation Monitoring Center, *Global Biodiversity*. For philosophical, legal, and ethical issues: Lon Fuller, *The Morality of Law*; Hans-Georg Gadamer, *Truth and Method*; Paul Heyne, "Economics, Ethics, and Ecology," in R. E. Meiners and B. Yandel, editors, *Taking the Environment Seriously*; Michael Pollan, *Second Nature: A Gardener's Education*; and numerous articles and books by Holmes Rolston III, Mark Sagoff, and Elliott Sober. We should also salute the editors of *Wild Earth*, for their unflagging belief in returning the majority of this nation to wilderness conditions. Although we do not share all of their attractive vision, we applaud their honesty in decrying the "eat our cake and have it, too" attitude promoted by far too many in the environmental movement. They are more than willing to face hard choices.

Although Flaubert and Nabokov apparently turned in text of such lapidary perfection that intervention in their behalf was unneeded and unwanted, we are made of humbler stuff. One author (MLP) would like to thank Bruce Chapman and the members of the Discovery Institute for their support; the second (CCM) wishes to extend his gratitude, as always, for the editorial counsel of William Whitworth, Corby Kummer, Cullen Murphy, Sue Parilla, and Lowell Weiss at *The Atlantic Monthly* (where this book began), as well as that of Ellis Rubenstein, John Benditt, and Josh Fischman at *Science*. It is a joy to tip our safari hats to Jonathan Segal at Knopf, who bestowed upon us the wonderful gift of his thoughtful enthusiasm. To thank Jonathan is tantamount to thanking Ida Giragossian, so closely do they work together, but we should also express our gratitude for her labors in our behalf. A salute, as ever, to our agent, Rick Balkin, a friend indeed. Finally, each author thanks the other for his company all the way through the fascinating, infuriating process of writing this book.

Index

A NOTE ABOUT THE AUTHORS

Charles C. Mann is a contributing editor for both *Science* and *The Atlantic Monthly*. He also writes for *The New York Times Magazine* and Sunday *Book Review, The Sciences, Smithsonian, Mother Jones*, the Washington *Post*, and the Los Angeles *Times*. The recipient of an Alfred P. Sloan Foundation Science Writing Prize, he has won several awards for his magazine writing. He is co-author of *The Second Creation: Makers of the Revolution in Twentieth-Century Physics* and *The Aspirin Wars: Money, Medicine, and 100 Years of Rampant Competition*.

Mark L. Plummer is Senior Fellow at the Discovery Institute in Seattle, specializing in environmental issues. He holds a doctorate in economics from the University of Washington and was part of a team of scientists that worked for the National Acid Precipitation Assessment Program. He has written for various economic journals, *The Atlantic Monthly*, and *Science*. He is co-author with Charles C. Mann of *The Aspirin Wars*.

A NOTE ON THE TYPE

The text of this book was set in Ehrhardt, a typeface first released by the Monotype Corporation of London in 1937. The design of the face was based on a seventeenth-century type, probably cut by Nicholas Kis, used at the Ehrhardt foundry in Frankfurt. The original cutting was one of the first typefaces bearing the characteristics now referred to as "modern."

Composed by Creative Graphics,
Allentown, Pennsylvania

Printed and bound by The Haddon Craftsmen,
Scranton, Pennsylvania

Designed by Cassandra J. Pappas